Optimizing Power & Reliability in Mobile Computing with DVFS

Dedication

This book is dedicated to
Maa, Soma Dey, and Baba, Sudip Dey
for their unconditional love and faith on me.
Baba passed away on 4th January, 2022,
and was not able to see me get the doctorate,
but his blessings are always with me.

Acknowledgements

I would like to take this opportunity to extend my thanks to many people who directly and indirectly supported me during my PhD journey. First of all, I would like to thank my parents - Sudip Dey and Soma Dey, and Min Zhang, my ex-partner, without whom I might never have found this PhD program. Although we might not be together any more, but I am glad that I came across this funded PhD at the University of Essex under the supervision of Dr. Amit Kumar Singh and Prof. Klaus Dieter McDonald-Maier. Next, it goes without saying that how lucky I have been to be supervised by Dr. Amit Kumar Singh and Prof. Klaus Dieter McDonald-Maier, who have always supported me and have given me the full freedom to pursue my research during my PhD. I couldn't have asked for any better to be my mentor and advisor during my PhD journey than Dr. Amit Kumar Singh and Prof. Klaus Dieter McDonald-Maier.

Many thanks also to everyone in the Embedded and Intelligent Systems Laboratory at the University of Essex for their continued support, advise and friendship. I would also like to thank Dr. Vishwanathan Mohan and Dr. Morteza Varasteh for being my supervisory panel members and for keeping me on track with the PhD program. Further, my sincere thanks to all my colleagues and friends (Dani, Karthik, Albert, Andrea, Gregory, Omi, Raul, Antoine, Masha, Ritesh, Ramesh, Luis) at the Samsung R&D Institute UK, who have provided me with a plethora of knowledge in the commercial edge / mobile computing domain, for being supportive when I needed, great drinking sessions and, of course, amazing muscle aching badminton sessions.

Finally, greatest thanks go to my family members (the big Indian family), who are living thousands of miles away, for understanding why I had to bail on the socials and family gatherings; for understanding that I have been busy with my PhD.

Declaration

This book is based on the doctoral thesis titled, "Novel DVFS Methodologies For Power-Efficient Mobile MPSoC."
Cite: Dey, Somdip (2023) *Novel DVFS Methodologies For Power-Efficient Mobile MPSoC*. Doctoral thesis, University of Essex.

Copyright

While every precaution has been taken in the preparation of this book, the publisher assumes no responsibility for errors or omissions, or for damages resulting from the use of the information contained herein.

OPTIMIZING POWER & RELIABILITY IN MOBILE COMPUTING WITH DVFS

First edition. May 10, 2023.

Copyright © 2023 Somdip Dey.

Written by Somdip Dey.

About the author

Somdip Dey, FRSA

Somdip Dey, FRSA, also professionally known as InteliDey, is an Embedded Artificial Intelligence scientist, engineer, entrepreneur, AI art & music creator and TED speaker. Dey is the CEO of Nosh Technologies, the CTO of Blockway Technologies and a Lecturer at the University of Essex, UK. He is also the Danah Zohar Professor of Quantum Philosophy & Professor of Practice (AI/ML) at Woxsen University, India. He has more than 13 years of industrial experience including working for Microsoft and Samsung in developing numerous technological products that are currently used by billions of people in different ways. For contributions to improving society through applications of embedded machine learning Dey is elected a Life Fellow of the Royal Society of Arts, named an MIT Innovator Under 35, an Outstanding Achiever in Education, Science & Innovation at the 2023 India UK Achievers Honours and a 2022 World IP Review Leader. He is also a member of the Forbes Technology Council and regularly appears in news including Forbes, Entrepreneur, Business Insider, Tech Crunch and many more.

Abstract

Low power mobile computing systems such as smartphones and wearables have become an integral part of our daily lives and are used in various ways to enhance our daily lives. Majority of modern mobile computing systems are powered by multi-processor System-on-a-Chip (MP-SoC), where multiple processing elements are utilized on a single chip. Given the fact that these devices are battery operated most of the times, thus, have limited power supply and the key challenges include catering for performance while reducing the power consumption. Moreover, the reliability in terms of lifespan of these devices are also affected by the peak thermal behaviour on the device, which retrospectively also make such devices vulnerable to temperature side-channel attack. This book is concerned with performing Dynamic Voltage and Frequency Scaling (DVFS) on different processing elements such as CPU & GPU, and memory unit such as RAM to address the aforementioned challenges. Firstly, we design a Computer Vision based machine learning technique to classify applications automatically into different categories of workload such that DVFS could be performed on the CPU to reduce the power consumption of the device while executing the application. Secondly, we develop a reinforcement learning based agent to perform DVFS on CPU and GPU while considering the user's interaction with such devices to optimize power consumption and thermal behaviour. Next, we develop a heuristic based automated agent to perform DVFS on CPU, GPU and RAM to optimize the same while executing an application. Finally, we explored the affect of DVFS on CPUs leading to vulnerabilities against temperature side-channel attack and hence, we also designed a methodology to secure against such attack while improving the reliability in terms of lifespan of such devices.

Contents

List of Figures

Chapter 1

Introduction

Mobile computing systems [B'far, 2004, Satyanarayanan, 2010, Lukow-icz et al., 2004, Singh et al., 2020, Isuwa et al., 2022] such as smartphones and smart wearables utilizing Multi-Processor System-on-a-Chip (MP-SoC) have become an integral part of our daily lives. Given the fact that these devices are easily accessible to us and are mostly battery operated, the key objectives are to optimize performance, power consumption, thermal behaviour and security of such devices. One of the most popular ways to achieve these objectives is to perform Dynamic Voltage and Frequency Scaling (DVFS) on different processing elements such as CPU, GPU (Graphical Processing Unit) and RAM (Random Access Memory). In this chapter, we explore the concept of DVFS and its operational importance in MPSoCs. This chapter offers reflections on some of the key challenges of operating an MPSoC. The major contributions made by this book in an attempt to address these challenges are also highlighted. A snapshot of each chapter is also presented here to illustrate the structure of the book. Finally, the publications that were made during the period of this research are listed at the end of the chapter.

1.1 Motivation

Modern smartphones such as Samsung Galaxy S20, Note20, iPhone and wearable devices such as Samsung Galaxy Watch and Apple Watch devices have become an integral part of most people's daily lives. We heavily rely on these battery operated smart devices to perform a plethora of day-to-day tasks such as controlling our smart home [Jiang et al., 2004, Wang et al., 2013, Kumar and Lee, 2014], watching our favourite TV series, playing your favourite games and keeping track of our social and active lives. With an increase in the performance demand of embedded/mobile applications, which cannot be satisfied by simply increasing the operating frequency of a single-core processor or by customizing the single processor core, we could notice the rise of Multi-Processor System-on-a-chip [Jerraya and Wolf, 2004, Wolf et al., 2008, Singh et al., 2013], where multiple processing cores are utilized on a single chip system.

Moreover, most of these modern battery operated smartphones and wearables now come equipped with heterogeneous Multi-Processor System-on-a-Chip (MPSoC) [Kumar et al., 2005, Dey et al., 2019d], which utilizes different types of processing cores such as CPU, GPU (Graphical Processing Unit), to cater for the performance and power consumption requirement of executing different types of applications on such devices. According to several studies [Singh et al., 2013, Reddy et al., 2017, Dey et al., 2019c], especially by Singh et al. [Singh et al., 2013], applications, consisting of several workloads/tasks, could be classified into three different types: compute intensive, memory intensive, and mixed (compute and memory intensive), based on the number of instructions per cycle or memory accesses. To execute these different types of workloads heterogeneous MPSoCs come equipped with different types of processing elements such as CPU & GPU, and memory units such as RAM (Random Access Memory) [Patterson and Hennessy, 2016].

Given the fact that these embedded/mobile devices operate on battery, one of the key challenges of operating such devices is reducing the power consumption of the device so that these devices could operate longer on battery without the need of charging. According to [Muthukaruppan et al., 2013], there are five popular methods leading to the reduction of power consumption in mobile platforms utilizing MPSoCs, which includes:

1. *Dynamic Power Management* (DPM) allows idle processing elements or other idle components of the system to be suspended if required in order to reduce power consumption [Gupta et al., 2017].

2. *Dynamic Voltage Frequency Scaling* (DVFS) allows processing elements to operate at variable voltage and frequency (V-F) levels [Shin et al., 2000, Khriji et al., 2022] to reduce power consumption. DVFS manages power consumption of the processing elements by balancing the trade-off between performance and power consumption. The main ideology behind DVFS is to vary the operating voltage (V) and frequency (F) of a processing element dynamically, based on the current workload and performance requirements. By adjusting the voltage and frequency, DVFS can achieve optimal performance while minimizing power consumption. More details on DVFS and power consumption are provided in section 2.1 of Chapter 2.

3. Customization of the processing elements to match the processing needed of a workload on an MPSoC [Lin and Fei, 2010].

4. Customizing cache based memory access [Gordon-Ross et al., 2004].

5. Mapping tasks of an application to the processing elements so that workload could be balanced across all processing elements in an MPSoC. This improves utilization of the processing elements effectively and reduces power consumption on the device [Benoit and Robert, 2008].

At the operating system level, we could only use DPM and DVFS based methodologies for power consumption reduction, which could further add to the resource mapping and allocation techniques. Thus, software based profiling systems mostly utilize these two methodologies to profile power consumption for a set of applications on heterogeneous MPSoCs. Moreover, out of the aforementioned methodologies, DVFS is a very popular mechanism used to reduce the power consumption of the MPSoC by the means of reducing the dynamic power consumption ($P \propto V^2 f$) by reducing the operating frequency of the processing elements. Since, the dynamic power consumption in an MPSoC is proportional to the operating frequency of the processing elements, as shown in the equation, executing the application on a reduced operating frequency leads to a reduced power consumption of the device.

In majority of the modern heterogeneous MPSoCs, CPU, GPU and RAM support DVFS, where each of these components affects the total power consumption of the device differently for different types of applications. For example, when we observed the power consumption due to the effects of DVFS in CPU, GPU and RAM (denoted as memory only) in Odroid XU4 [odr, b], utilizing Exynos 5422 MPSoC [exy, a], while idle (when no other application is executing other than background processes of the OS), we observed that big CPUs, LITTLE CPUs, GPU and memory consumes 34%, 8%, 9% and 3% of the average power consumption respectively of the device on an average (as shown in Fig. 1.1.(a)). Here, the Exynos 5422 MPSoC utilizes ARM's big.LITTLE processor technology [Kim et al., 2014], where two different types of CPUs (big and LITTLE) are utilized to cater for performance and power consumption requirements of executing applications. In Fig. 1.1.(a), the average power consumed by the big CPUs, LITTLE CPUs, GPUs, Memory and rest of the components such as the fan (active cooling), hardware storage & on-chip communication network of the Exynos 5422 MPSoC while idle is 3.53 watts (W).

In order to observe the effect of DVFS of each of the major components (big CPUs, LITTLE CPUs, GPU and memory) of the MPSoC the power consumption was recorded while operating each of these components in their maximum operating frequency and minimum operating frequency consecutively to measure the percentage of total power consumption that is attributed to the maximum and minimum frequency. Fig. 1.1.(b) illustrates the percentage of total power consumption of big CPUs, LITTLE CPUs, GPU, memory and rest of the components in the Exynos 5422 MPSoC while executing Streamcluster benchmark (in native mode) from the PARSEC benchmark suite [Bienia, 2011a]. The average power consumed by the big CPUs, LITTLE CPUs, GPUs, Memory and rest of the components of the Exynos 5422 MPSoC while executing Streamcluster benchmark is 10.11 watts (W). Streamcluster benchmark was chosen because it reflects a mixed workload (both compute intensive and memory intensive) [Dey et al., 2019c] to mimic the workload of most of the popular applications used by the users. From Fig. 1.1 one interesting observation is that in a mixed workload application the big CPU, LITTLE CPU, GPU and memory can contribute to 68%, 4%, 7% and 19% of the average power consumption respectively, which constitutes a majority of the power consumed on the platform, and hence, DVFS in CPU, GPU and memory plays an important role towards the total power consumption of the device. Note that in Fig. 1.1.(a), the rest of the components such as the fan (active cooling), hardware storage & on-chip communication network of the Exynos 5422 MPSoC separate to the big CPU, LITTLE CPU, GPU and memory while idle might be consuming almost 46% of the average power consumed but in reality the rest of the components are consuming only 1.62 watts (W) as the average power consumption of the Exynos 5422 MPSoC while idle is 3.53 watts.

On the other hand, power consumption in these mobile platforms utilizing MPSoC has a direct correlation with the heat dissipation in such devices [DeVogeleer et al., 2014, De Vogeleer et al.,]. Therefore, increased power consumption in these MPSoCs leads to an increased heat dissipation, which retrospectively increases the peak temperature of the processing elements. Moreover, according to studies [Chantem et al., 2010, Coskun et al., 2007, Zhou et al., 2015, Singh et al., 2020] an increase in the operating temperature by 10-15° centigrade in the MPSoC could reduce the lifespan of the MPSoC by 2×. Additionally, an increase in peak temperature of the processing elements such as CPU

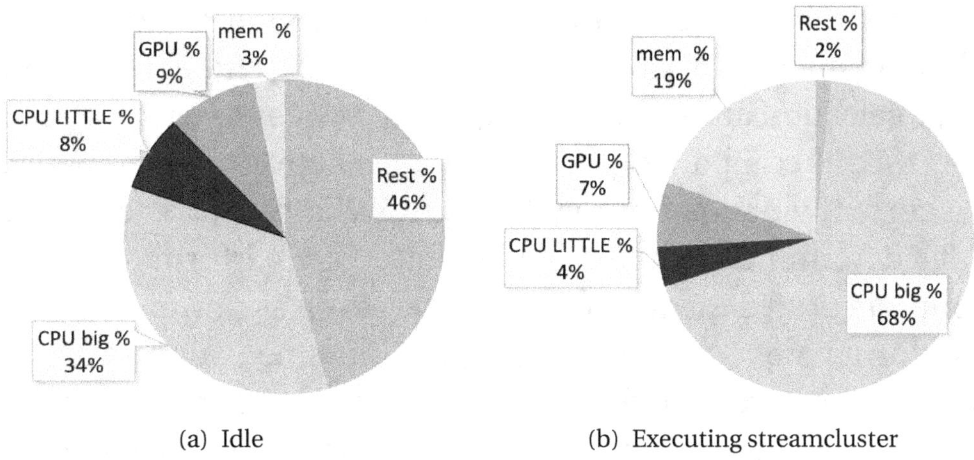

(a) Idle

(b) Executing streamcluster

Figure 1.1: Percentage of average power consumed by the big CPUs, LITTLE CPUs, GPUs, Memory and rest of the components such as the fan (active cooling), hardware storage & on-chip communication network of the Exynos 5422 MPSoC while idle vs executing streamcluster benchmark

in the MPSoC could also expose vulnerabilities related to thermal side-channel attack [Hutter and Schmidt, 2013, Masti et al., 2015, Bartolini et al., 2016], compromising sensitive data such as password while processing information on the DVFS enabled CPUs. Therefore, given these pieces of evidence, it is crucial to perform DVFS in mobile MPSoCs such that the performance requirement of the executing applications could be achieved while reducing power consumption, peak temperature of the device and improve security against thermal side-channel attack.

That said, the majority of traditional approaches to perform DVFS include dynamic power or thermal management or both [Singh et al., 2020]. Dynamic power and thermal management could be of two types, *Proactive* and *Reactive*. In Proactive, the methodologies try to pro-actively determine the future state(s) of the system and take actions to optimize either power consumption or thermal behaviour or both, whereas, in Reactive, the methodologies are reactive in nature and only take actions in order to perform optimizations when a certain state is met. For proactive management, the state could be future temperature by using a temperature estimation model or future workload by using workload estimation model, and actions could be resource selection and/or operating voltage (V) or operating frequency (F) control. In comparison, the state for reactive management could be the current workload or temperature. Whatsoever, these states are typically determined with the help of hardware performance monitoring counters providing data about metrics such as power consumption and performance. Moreover, these performance counters are special registers in the hardware that hold the value for the respective state(s) and are usually manufacturing vendor locked to be accessible. This makes it particularly difficult to perform DVFS for different types of applications (workloads) in the software layers of the OS if access to these performance counters is not accessible. Additionally, incorporating these hardware performance counters are expensive and increases the size of the MPSoC, especially in consumer devices such as smartphones. Therefore, this calls for an approach capable of performing DVFS based on the type of application (workload) without the need to access such performance counters.

Moreover, when it comes to consumer devices such as smartphones, user's satisfaction in terms of Quality of Service (QoS) plays an important role [Pathania et al., 2014, Sahin and Coskun, 2015, Shafik et al., 2016, Peters et al., 2016, Bhat et al., 2018]. At the same time on such devices, most of the existing methodologies related to optimizing performance [Pathania et al., 2015, Gupta et al., 2017] only consider performance and power consumption together in a metric such as Performance Per Watt (PPW) while not considering temperature into such metrics. This calls for an approach which is capable of performing DVFS while taking QoS, performance, power consumption and thermal behaviour into consideration. Additionally, all the published studies and methodologies only perform DVFS on CPU or GPU or memory or a combination of these but not on all of them together. Therefore, it is crucial to be able to perform DVFS on all these components of the MPSoC to achieve better performance, power and temperature optimization.

On the other hand, performing DVFS on processing cores leads to heat dissipation and propagation on the core, which can be observed over time in order to deduce security flaws. This type of an attack is called temperature based side-channel attack and could be directly correlated to DVFS since increased operating frequency on a processing core leads to increased heat dissipation as pointed out in [Hutter and Schmidt, 2013, Masti et al., 2015, Bartolini et al., 2016]. Henceforth, devising DVFS approaches to secure against such attack is very important while catering for the performance requirements of the executing application on the MPSoC.

To address the aforementioned shortcomings we need unorthodox approaches to perform DVFS in MPSoCs and this book introduces such approaches. In the following subsection, we will explore some of the key challenges in MPSoCs that this book is trying to address.

1.2 Key Challenges

Reduced power consumption. Most of the smartphones and smart wearables utilizing MPSoCs operate by stand-alone power supply like battery and henceforth, this calls for power optimization on such devices in order to increase the operational time of the systems and reduce the power consumption costs in the process.

Reduced peak temperature. An increase in temperature of the processing elements in the MPSoC in smartphones and smart wearables could lead to the reduction of lifespan of the device. Moreover, an increase in the peak temperature could also increase the overall thermal behaviour of the device itself and hence, contributing to discomfort of the user. Therefore, this calls for optimization of peak temperature of the processing elements of the MPSoC.

Improved security against thermal side-channel attack. Compute intensive tasks such as encryption and decryption on the processing elements in the MPSoC could lead to surge in the peak temperature, which exposes vulnerability to temperature based side-channel attacks. Such an attack in the smartphones and smart wearables could be exploited by Malwares or hackers and henceforth, this calls for an approach to secure such devices from thermal side-channel attack.

1.3   Contributions

To address the aforementioned key challenges, the main contributions of this book are fourfold, which have been made during the course of this research, and are summarized as follows:

1. Given the fact that smartphone users are ever increasing along with an increased availability of mobile applications [Cruz et al., 2019], different types of applications demand different performance and power consumption requirements. We developed the first ever methodology to classify applications automatically into the three categories: compute intensive, memory intensive and mixed workload; such that DVFS could be performed on the CPU to reduce the power consumption of the device while executing the application.

2. Smartphones and smart wearables come equipped with touch enabled display, on which the user interacts to perform a task. Throughout the day, the user's interaction behaviour with the application on these devices through touch interaction changes over time, and henceforth, DVFS needs to be performed to consider the user's interaction with the applications. We developed the first approach to perform DVFS on CPU and GPU while considering the user's mobile usage behaviour, performance of the executing application, power consumption and temperature of the device. We also introduce a metric based on performance, power consumption and thermal behaviour as well.

3. Although for most applications, which are compute intensive and mixed workload, performing DVFS on CPU and GPU could lead to massive reduction in power consumption and peak temperature of the device, however, for many applications, which are

more memory intensive, performing DVFS on RAM along with DVFS on CPU and GPU could lead to more power saving and reduction in thermal behaviour. To address this, we developed the first approach to perform DVFS on CPU, GPU and RAM.

4. Temperature based side-channel attack could be a real threat on smartphones and smart wearables. We developed the first machine learning based mechanism to perform temperature side-channel attack in a real smartphone platform and then developed an approach to secure such devices from these types of attacks. We also proposed a metric to evaluate security of such devices against temperature side-channel attacks.

1.4   Book Outline

The remainder of this book is organized as follows:

Chapter 2 (Background): We review the existing relevant literature that serves as the background for the research conducted in this book. We start by examining the role of DVFS in the reduction of power consumption and peak temperature on mobile platforms employing MP-SoC and explore the related proposed approaches in this area.

Chapter 3 (Performing DVFS on CPU): We introduce an automated technique to classify applications and then perform DVFS on CPU to cater for the performance requirement of the executing application along with reduced power consumption.

Chapter 4 (Performing DVFS on CPU and GPU): We introduce a software agent that performs DVFS on CPU and GPU while taking the user's interaction with the touch enabled mobile device into consideration such that power consumption and peak temperature of the device could be reduced while catering for performance.

Chapter 5 (Performing DVFS on CPU, GPU and RAM): We introduce a software agent that performs DVFS on CPU, GPU and RAM to cater for the performance requirement of the executing application while consuming the least power and reducing peak temperature in the process.

Chatper 6 (DVFS & Temperature Side-Channel Attack): We introduce
a novel machine learning approach to perform temperature based
side-channel attack in real mobile platforms utilizing MPSoC to explore the threat of such attacks. We then introduce a mechanism to
secure such devices against temperature based side-channel attacks
using DVFS approach.

Chatper 7 (Conclusion): We conclude this work in this chapter, providing a summary of the key contributions made throughout this book.
Additionally, potential future directions as an extension are also provided.

1.5   Publications

The research conducted in this book has resulted in several peer-
reviewed publications listed below in chronological order:

1. **Somdip Dey**, Amit Kumar Singh, Klaus McDonald-Maier, "Energy Efficiency and Reliability of Computer Vision Applications on Heterogeneous Multi-Processor Systems-on-Chips (MP-
   SoCs)", presented at MaRIONet Summer School, Glasgow, UK,
   16-20th July, 2018.

2. **Somdip Dey**, Grigorios Kalliatakis, Sangeet Saha, Amit Ku-
   mar Singh, Shoaib Ehsan, and Klaus McDonald-Maier. "MAT-
   CNN-SOPC: Motionless Analysis of Traffic Using Convolutional
   Neural Networks on System-On-a-Programmable-Chip", 2018
   NASA/ESA Conference on Adaptive Hardware and Systems (AHS
   2018), 2018.

3. **Somdip Dey**, Enrique Zaragoza Guajardo, Karunakar Reddy
   Basireddy, Amit Kumar Singh and Klaus McDonald-Maier,
   "EdgeCoolingMode: An Agent Based Thermal Management
   Mechanism for DVFS Enabled Heterogeneous MPSoCs", The
   32nd International Conference on VLSI Design and 18th Inter-
   national Conference on Embedded Systems (VLSID), 2019.

4. Samuel Isuwa, **Somdip Dey**, Amit Kumar Singh and Klaus McDonald-Maier, "TEEM: Online Thermal- and Energy-EfficiencyManagement on CPU-GPU MPSoCs", 2019 Design, Automation, and Test in Europe Conference (DATE), 2019.

5. **Somdip Dey**, Sangeet Saha, Xiaohang Wang, Amit Kumar Singh and Klaus McDonald-Maier, "RewardProfiler: A Reward Based Design Space Profiler on DVFS Enabled MPSoCs", 5th IEEE International Conference on Edge Computing and Scalable Cloud (IEEE EdgeCom), 2019.

6. **Somdip Dey**, Amit Kumar Singh, Xiaohang Wang and Klaus McDonald-Maier, "DeadPool: Performance Deadline Based FrequencyPooling and Thermal Management Agent in DVFS Enabled MPSoCs", 5th IEEE International Conference on Edge Computing and Scalable Cloud (IEEE EdgeCom), 2019.

7. **Somdip Dey**, Amit Kumar Singh and Klaus McDonald-Maier, "P-EdgeCoolingMode: An Agent Based Performance Aware Thermal Management Unit for DVFS Enabled Heterogeneous MPSoCs", IET Computers & Digital Techniques, 2019.

8. **Somdip Dey**, Amit Kumar Singh, Xiaohang Wang and Klaus McDonald-Maier, "User Interaction Aware Reinforcement Learning for Power and Thermal Efficiency of CPU-GPU Mobile MPSoCs", 2020 Design, Automation and Test in Europe Conference (DATE 2020).

9. **Somdip Dey**, Amit Kumar Singh, Klaus McDonald-Maier, "New approaches to DVFS in mobile MPSoC for power-, thermal-efficiency and reliability", presented at 16th International Summer School on Advanced Computer Architecture and Compilation for High-performance Embedded Systems (ACACES 2020), Fiuggi, Italy, 12-18 July, 2020.

10. **Somdip Dey**, Amit Kumar Singh, Dilip Kumar Prasad and Klaus McDonald-Maier, "SoCodeCNN: Program Source Code for Visual CNN Classification Using Computer Vision Methodology", IEEE Access. [**Most popular paper of IEEE Access & IEEE Xplore Digital Library from December, 2019 to August, 2020**]

11. Khadidja Gaffour, Mohammed Kamal Benhaoua, **Somdip Dey**, Amit Singh and Benyamina Abou El Hassan, "Dynamic clustering approach for Run-time Applications Mapping on NoC-Based Multi/Many-core systems", Second international conference on Embedded & Distributed Systems (EDiS'2020), 2020.

12. Amit Kumar Singh, **Somdip Dey**, Karunakar Reddy Basireddy, Klaus McDonald-Maier, Geoff Merrett, Bashir Al-Hashimi, "Dynamic Energy and Thermal Management of Multi-Core Mobile Platforms: A Survey", IEEE Design & Test. [**One of the most popular paper of IEEE Design & Test magazine in IEEE Xplore Digital Library since October, 2020**]

13. **Somdip Dey**, Amit Singh, Dilip Prasad, Klaus McDonald-Maier, "Temporal Motionless Analysis of Videos", 31st IEEE International Conference on Application-specific Systems, Architectures and Processors (ASAP 2020). [**One of the most popular paper of ASAP conference series in IEEE Xplore Digital Library since August, 2020**]

14. **Somdip Dey**, Amit Singh, Dilip Prasad, Klaus McDonald-Maier, "IRON-MAN: An Approach To Perform Temporal Motionless Analysis of Video using CNN in MPSoC," in IEEE Access. [**Most popular paper of IEEE Access on September, 2020**]

15. **Somdip Dey**, Suman Saha, Amit Kumar Singh, and Klaus McDonald-Maier, "FruitVegCNN: Power- and Memory-Efficient Classification of Fruits & Vegetables Using CNN in Mobile MP-SoC", 2020 IEEE 17th India Council International Conference (INDICON 2020), 2020.

16. **Somdip Dey**, Amit Kumar Singh and Klaus McDonald-Maier, "ThermalAttackNet: Are CNNs Making It Easy To Perform Temperature Side-Channel Attack In Mobile Edge Devices?" in Future Internet 13, no. 6: 146. [**Most viewed paper of Future Internet since June, 2021**]

17. **Somdip Dey**, Amit Kumar Singh, Xiaohang Wang and Klaus McDonald-Maier, "DATE: Defense Against TEmperature Side-Channel Attacks in DVFS Enabled MPSoCs." (**Under revision**)

18. **Somdip Dey**, Samuel Isuwa, Amit Kumar Singh and Klaus McDonald-Maier, "Asynchronous Hybrid Deep Learning: A Deep Learning Based Resource Mapping in DVFS Enabled Mobile MP-SoCs", 2021 IEEE 7th World Forum on Internet of Things (WF-IoT). IEEE, 2021.

19. **Somdip Dey**, Samuel Isuwa, Suman Saha, Amit Kumar Singh and Klaus McDonald-Maier, "CPU-GPU-Memory DVFS for Power-Efficient Mobile MPSoC" in Future Internet.

20. Samuel Isuwa, **Somdip Dey**, Andre P. Ortega, Amit Kumar Singh, Bashir Al-Hashimi and Geoff Merrett, "QUAREM: Maximising QoE through Adaptive Resource Management in Mobile MPSoC Platforms" in ACM Transactions on Embedded Computing Systems.

Chapter 2

Background

Multi-core embedded mobile platforms such as smartphones and smart wearables are on the rise as they enable efficient parallel processing to meet ever-increasing performance requirements. However, since these platforms need to cater for increasingly dynamic applications (workloads), efficient dynamic resource management is desired mainly to enhance the power and thermal efficiency for better user experience with increased operational time and lifetime of these mobile devices. Moreover security, especially against temperature side-channel attack, is one of the key requirements in such platforms. In this chapter, we first discuss some of the key concepts related to dynamic power and thermal management approaches along with the importance of security approaches against temperature side-channel attack, and then we explore the related published works for multi-core mobile platforms.

2.1   Introduction

Multi-Processor System-on-a-Chip (MPSoC) consists of different components such as microprocessors, memory chips, etc. developed through CMOS (Complementary Metal Oxide Semiconductor) technology. The total power consumption (P_{total}) in a CMOS integrated circuit is dependent on two components, as shown in Eq. 2.3 [Basireddy, 2019]:

- Static power consumption (P_{static}), which is the power consumed when the transistors are not in the process of switching (activity). It is represented by Eq. 2.1, where V is the operating voltage and $I_{leakage}$ is the leakage current [Jan et al., 2003].

- Dynamic power consumption ($P_{dynamic}$), which is the sum of transient power consumption and capacitive load power. Transient power is the power consumed when the circuit changes logic states such as 0 bit to 1 bit or vice-versa, whereas the capacitive load power is the power used to charge the load capacitance. Dynamic power is represented by Eq. 2.2, where α is the activity factor [1], C is the capacitance, V is the operating voltage, and F is the operating frequency [Jan et al., 2003].

$$P_{static} = V \times I_{leakage} \tag{2.1}$$

$$P_{dynamic} = \alpha \times C \times V^2 \times F \tag{2.2}$$

$$P_{total} = P_{static} + P_{dynamic} \tag{2.3}$$

Therefore, when an application is executing on the MPSoC, the total energy (E_{total}) consumption in the system is represented by the product of total power consumption and the execution time (T_{app}) of the application, as shown in the following equation.

$$E_{total} = P_{total} \times T_{app} \tag{2.4}$$

Moreover, as mentioned in section 1.1, DVFS performs power management of the processing elements by varying the operating voltage (V) and frequency (F) of the respective processing elements dynamically based on the current workload and performance requirements,

---

[1] The activity factor (α) is a dimensionless quantity, ranging from 0 to 1, that represents the average switching activity of a digital circuit or processor. It is used to capture the dynamic behavior of the circuit and estimate the dynamic power consumption.

the total power consumption (P_{total}) is also affected by the the operating voltage (V) and frequency (F). As shown in the above equations 2.1, 2.2 and 2.3, dynamic power ($P_{dynamic}$) is proportional to the square of the voltage and directly proportional to the frequency, while static power (P_{static}) is directly proportional to the voltage. Therefore, scaling both voltage and frequency concurrently by performing DVFS provides a more effective way to reduce power consumption. That said, we need to keep in mind that in most of the modern MPSoCs such as Exynos 5422 [Prakash et al., 2015], the operating voltage and frequency come paired together for each type of processing elements such as CPUs & GPUs, thus, by scaling the operating frequency the operating voltage is automatically scaled alongside.

Modern embedded mobile platforms ranging from smartphones to wearable devices employ heterogeneous Multi-Processor Systems-on-Chips (MPSoCs), which utilizes several types of processing cores such as ARM's big.LITTLE with DVFS capabilities are available within a single chip, to deliver performance as well as power efficient computing.

Previously simply increasing the operating frequency of a single-core processor was able to cater for performance criteria of mobile applications, however, with time we could notice a paradigm shift to the adoption of multi-core systems in mobile devices to satisfy the needs of more complex applications. Additionally, simply increasing the operating frequency of single core leads to high power consumption and heat dissipation.

In order to overcome the challenges associated with power consumption, heat dissipation and performance requirement of executing applications on mobile platforms, chip manufactures are integrating multiple processing cores (processing elements) operating at low frequencies, where the cores can cohesively communicate with each other [Singh et al., 2017a]. Over the decades, thanks to Moore's Law, now we cannot just fit many cores on a single chip but also cores of different processing capabilities onto the same chip to better fit our needs. The hardware (H/W) layer in Figure 2.1 shows an example chip containing many cores (resources) of different capabilities (colors). Such systems with multiple processing cores enable us to leverage the increased parallelism of the platform by partitioning applications (shown in the Appl. layer in Figure 2.1) into many small tasks and assigning the tasks to different cores (by H/W resource selection in Figure 2.1) in order to perform parallel executions towards satisfying the increased performance requirements, power consumption and heat dissipation [Hanumaiah and Vrudhula, 2012].

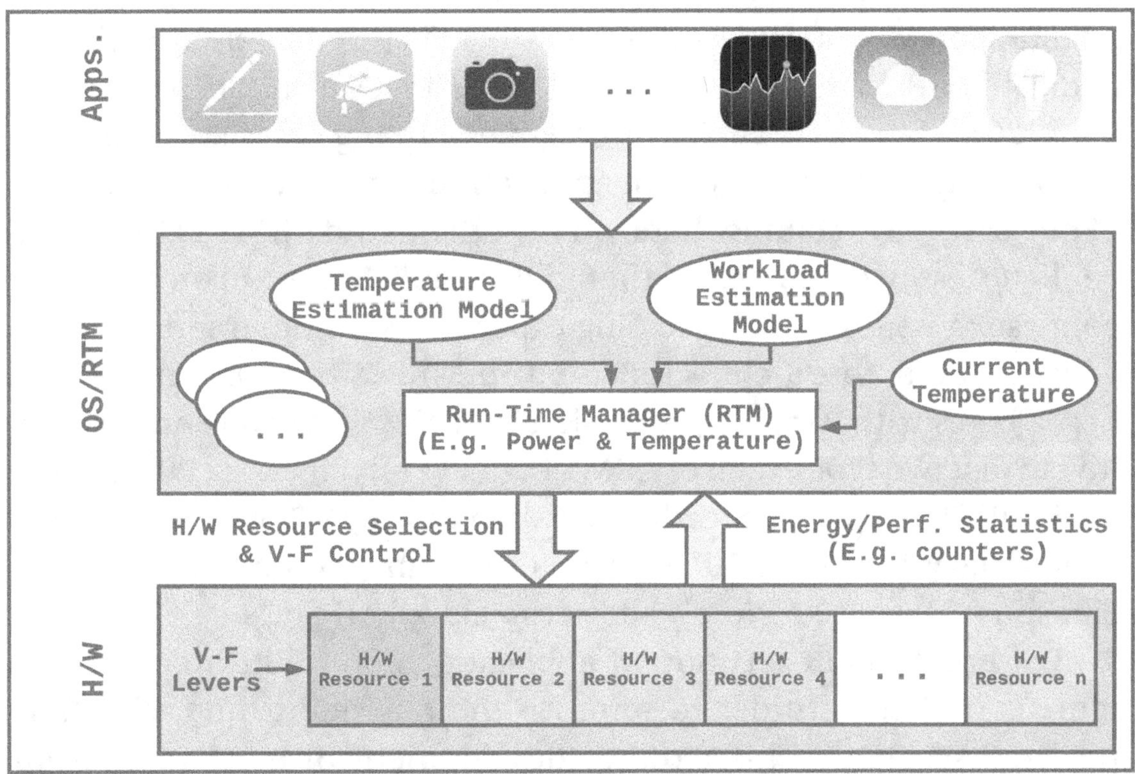

Figure 2.1: Resource management [Singh et al., 2020]

In these systems, the partitioning of applications is referred to as functional partitioning [Singh et al., 2017a]. This kind of procedure requires in-depth application knowledge and involves finding the tasks, adding synchronization and inter-task communication in the tasks, management of the memory hierarchy communication and checking of the parallelized code (tasks) to ensure for correct functionality. When heterogeneous multi-core system is in place, a task binding process, which specifies the types of cores on which the tasks can be allocated along with the allocation cost, is required [Smit et al., 2005]. In order to compute the allocation cost of the task, the binding process analyzes the implementation cost such as performance, power consumption and resource utilization of each task on supported heterogeneous cores such as general purpose processor (GPP), digital signal processor (DSP), graphics processing unit (GPU) and coarse grain re-configurable hardware. At the moment, the most popular mobile platforms such as Samsung Exynos 5410, Exynos 5422 and Qualcomm's Snapdragon MPSoCs host ARM's big and LITTLE GPPs along with other dedicated GPUs and DSPs [Dey et al., 2019d, Dey et al., 2019b, Pathania et al., 2014, Tan et al., 2018]. Although ARM's big cores are sometimes too powerful for some types of applications and end up wasting a lot of power while executing them, on the other hand ARM's LITTLE cores could be less powerful to run the similar applications. In order to overcome such issues with processing capabilities, future trend in heterogeneous multi-core architecture is heading towards having more number of cores with variable processing capacities, which is not just limited to just two types such of ARM's big.LITTLE [Lin et al., 2016, Rupley et al., 2016], as we can already observe in Exynos 9825 (powering Samsung Galaxy 10 & Note 10 devices) [exy, c] and Exynos 990 (powering Samsung Galaxy 20 & Note 20 devices) [exy, d] MPSoCs.

Power efficient execution of applications on multi-processor systems is desired in order to improve the operation time of battery-powered systems. This requires development of efficient run-time management (RTM) approaches, as shown in the OS/RTM layer of Figure 2.1. For decades several research and implementation works have focused on optimizing power at circuit, architecture and system levels. On the other hand, on systems utilizing MPSoCs if proper power consumption control measures are not taken then it could lead to heat generation in the system. The availability of multiple PEs on the system in comparison with uniprocessors can lead to more nonuniformity of heat generation & dissipation, leading to spatial temperature gradients (STGs) across the chip. Additionally, the variety of the workloads, which could be processed at the same time, may cause large temporal heat generation/dissipation leading to temporal thermal gradients (TTGs) at a single point on the chip. In the meantime, STGs, TTGs and thermal cycles lead to reduced performance and reliability of the system over the period of time [Iranfar et al., 2018]. If there is an increase of 10 °C to 20 °C for metallic structures then the lifetime reliability may decrease up to 16 times, thus, optimizing thermal behaviour of the mobile platform is very important for such devices. Not to mention, STG and TTG on the PEs in the chip could also expose vulnerabilities related to temperature (thermal) side-channel attacks [Hutter and Schmidt, 2013, Masti et al., 2015, Bartolini et al., 2016].

In this chapter, we explore the approaches available for dynamically optimizing power consumption and thermal behaviour on multi-core mobile platforms. First, we observe some of the recent trends in power and thermal management in MPSoCs. Also, given the fact that power consumption and heat dissipation on MPSoC devices could also lead to temperature side-channel attacks, we also explore studies related to that topic. We have segregated the surveyed methodologies into three categories: *Dynamic Power Management, Dynamic Thermal Management, & Dynamic Power and Thermal Management*; where each of the categories has two sub-categories: *Proactive*, where the methodologies are trying to pro-actively determine the future state and take actions to optimize either power consumption or thermal behaviour or both; & *Reactive*, where the methodologies are reactive in nature and only take actions to optimize either power consumption or thermal behaviour or both when a certain state is reached. Keep in mind, though power and energy consumption are distinct from each other, power consumption of executing apps are evaluated over the execution time of such apps (see Eq. 2.4) and hence, we use the term "energy" in some context when we observe the power consumption over the execution time period.

For proactive management, the state could be future temperature by using a temperature estimation model or future workload by using workload estimation mode and actions could be resource selection and/or voltage-frequency (V-F) control, as shown in Figure 2.1. In contrast, the state for reactive management could be current workload or temperature, as shown in Figure 2.1. The states are typically determined with the help of performance monitoring counters providing statistics about metrics such as power and performance. After we have explored the approaches on dynamically optimizing power consumption and thermal behaviour, we explore approaches related to temperature side-channel attacks.

Chapter organization: For ease of navigation within this chapter, the rest of the chapter is organized as follows. Recent emerging technologies in power and thermal management in MPSoCs are discussed in Sec. 2.2. Existing work on *Dynamic Power Management* (discussed in Sec. 2.3), *Dynamic Thermal Management* (discussed in Sec. 2.4) and *Dynamic Power and Thermal Management* (discussed in Sec. 2.5) are segregated into *Proactive* and *Reactive* approaches. In Sec. 2.6 we explore existing work on thermal side-channel attack, and finally, the chapter is concluded in Sec. 2.7.

2.2   Recent Emerging Technologies in Power and Thermal Management in MPSoC

Before we explore some of the existing works in power and thermal management, let us explore some of the emerging technologies that are being used for power and thermal management in MPSoCs. In this section, we explore some of these recent emerging technologies as they evolve. The rationale for discussing these emerging technologies in this section is to establish their relevance as they will be subsequently employed within the research presented throughout this book.

2.2.1 Heterogeneity in Processing Cores in the Machine Learning Era

As already mentioned most of the modern MPSoCs come equipped with heterogeneous processing elements such as big CPUs, LITTLE, CPUs, GPUs and DSPs [Dey et al., 2019d, Dey et al., 2019b, Pathania et al., 2014, Tan et al., 2018], however, with the evolution and popularity of machine learning algorithms in recent times we can also see emergence of neural processing units (NPUs), which are specifically integrated into the chip circuit that implements all the necessary control and arithmetic logic to execute machine learning algorithms [Patterson et al., 2012, Bouvier et al., 2021]. With rise in complexity in homogeneity in the processing elements in the MPSoC, several methodologies have been proposed to optimize either performance, power consumption, temperature and reliability of the MPSoC or a multiple of these objectives together.

2.2.2 Convolutional Neural Networks and Deep Learning

A Deep Learning (DL) model [Krizhevsky et al., 2017] consists of an input layer, several intermediate (hidden) layers stacked on top of each other and an output layer. Fig. 2.2 shows a representative diagram of DL model. In the input layer, which is the first layer of the model, the raw values of data features are fed into it. In each of the hidden layers a mathematical operation called convolution is applied to extract specific features, which is then utilized to predict the label of the raw data in the last (output) layer of the DL network. Most of the time, if a model utilizes an input layer, a hidden layer and an output layer then the model is denoted as Convolutional Neural Network (CNN) model or simply, CovNet. If such a model uses a lot of stacked hidden layers only then it is denoted as a DL model or Deep Neural Networks (DNN).

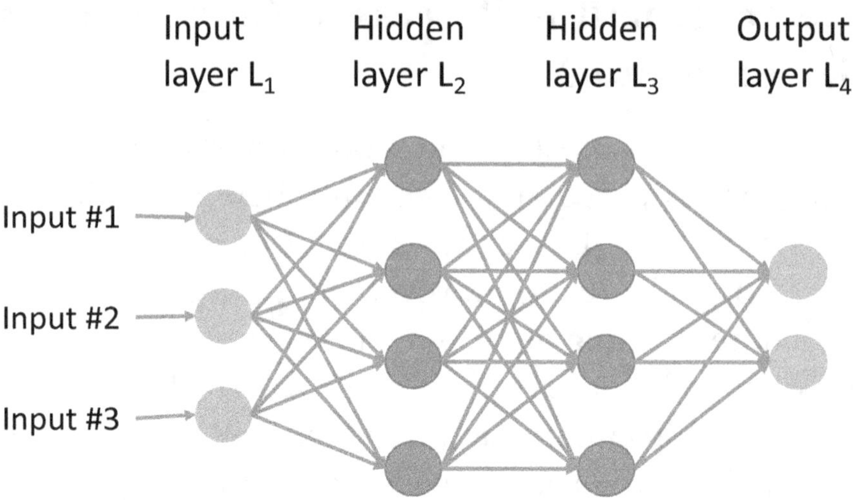

Figure 2.2: Representative diagram of Deep Learning model

2.2.3 Reinforcement Learning

Reinforcement learning (RL) [Sutton and Barto, 2018] is a type of machine learning algorithm where an intelligent agent, which is a computing system that perceives its environment to take actions autonomously in order to achieve cumulative rewards based on the knowledge gathered from the environment. Fig. 2.3 shows a representative diagram of an intelligent agent. Here, reward could be optimizing performance or power consumption or thermal efficiency or combination of these together. Several studies [Shafik et al., 2016, Maurer et al., 2020, Yu et al., 2020] on utilizing reinforcement learning for computing resource management have been proposed. One of the biggest advantage of using RL for resource management is that the system is capable of learning autonomously how to manage the resources online dynamically.

2.3 Dynamic Power Management

In this section, we explore the dynamic power management approaches that are currently available in MPSoCs. The studies mentioned in this section only focus on dynamic power management with-

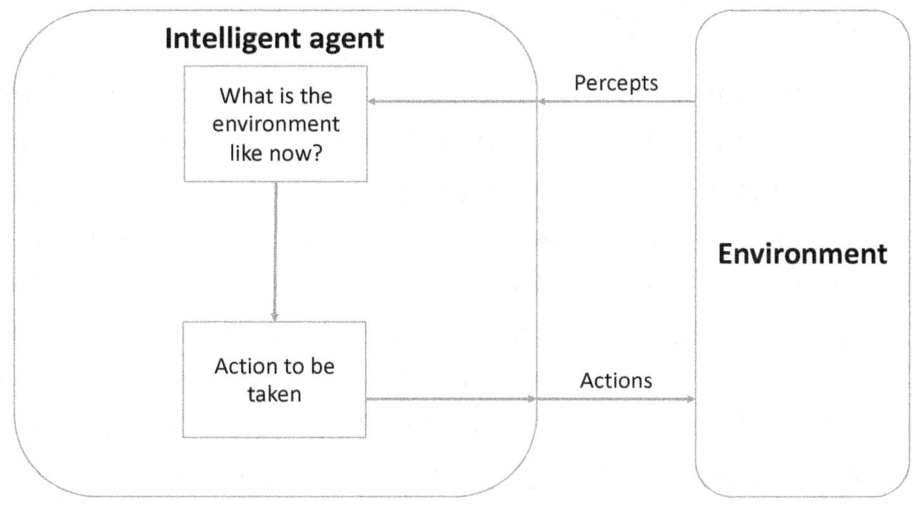

Figure 2.3: Representative diagram of intelligent agent

out explicitly considering dynamic thermal management on the MP-SoC.

To improve power consumption and/or to meet performance constraint in multi-core mobile platforms, various approaches for DVFS and/or mapping have been proposed using offline, online or hybrid (online optimization facilitated by offline analysis results) optimization for resource management [Goraczko et al., 2008, Singh et al., 2017a, Singh et al., 2017b, Basireddy et al., 2018, Reddy et al., 2017, Quan and Pimentel, 2015, Gupta et al., 2017, Shafik et al., 2016, Cochran et al., 2011, Van Craeynest et al., 2012, Aalsaud et al., 2016b, Sozzo et al., 2016, Donyanavard et al., 2016, Petrucci et al., 2015, Schranzhofer et al., 2010, Hölzenspies et al., 2008, Quan and Pimentel, 2013, Stamoulis and Marculescu, 2016, Mandal et al., 2019]. Depending on the control mechanism, runtime power management approaches can be further classified into two categories: proactive [Shafik et al., 2016, Hölzenspies et al., 2008, Gupta et al., 2017] and reactive [Goraczko et al., 2008, Schranzhofer et al., 2010, Quan and Pimentel, 2013, Weissel and Bellosa, 2002, Singleton et al., 2005, Mandal et al., 2019].

2.3.1 Proactive Approaches

To adapt to dynamic application workloads efficiently, proactive
control-based approaches have also been investigated [Shafik et al.,
2016, Hölzenspies et al., 2008, Gupta et al., 2017]. An online reinforcement learning based proactive DVFS approach targeting frame-based
applications is presented to improve energy efficiency [Shafik et al.,
2016]. More about the process of reinforcement learning is mentioned
earlier in Sec. 2.2.3. The efficacy of [Shafik et al., 2016] is proved on
DM3730 SoC. In [Hölzenspies et al., 2008], an online spatial mapping
for streaming applications is presented for a multi-core system and
the experiments were performed on hypothetical MPSoC with MON-
TIUMS with 2 ARM processors.

The study in [Quan and Pimentel, 2013] proposed scenario-based
hybrid mapping approaches targeting homogeneous multi-core platforms in which mappings derived from design-time DSE are stored for
runtime mapping decisions. Above discussed approaches target only
homogeneous multi-cores and thus may not be efficient for heterogeneous multi-cores. Similar to [Van Craeynest et al., 2012], some works
have used workload memory-intensity as an indicator to guide task
mapping [Petrucci et al., 2015]. [Petrucci et al., 2015] was evaluated
on 64bit x86 quad-core processors with varying operating frequencies.
A domain-specific hybrid task mapping is presented in [Quan and Pimentel, 2015], which depends heavily on offline results. [Quan and Pimentel, 2015] is implemented on Sesame system level simulator. However, approaches presented in [Van Craeynest et al., 2012, Quan and
Pimentel, 2015] do not consider DVFS, thereby missing on power saving opportunities. On the other hand, techniques proposed in [Sozzo
et al., 2016, Donyanavard et al., 2016, Aalsaud et al., 2016b, Gupta et al.,
2017, Reddy et al., 2017] use DVFS, but they have several shortcomings.
In [Sozzo et al., 2016], the design space is explored for a single application and applying it to concurrent execution of applications would be
inefficient due to huge design space. Donyanavard *et al.* [Donyanavard
et al., 2016] take applications with only one thread, so only one type
of core for each application is used. In *et al.* [Aalsaud et al., 2016b],

the study considered concurrent execution and mapping of application threads onto more than one type of cores. However, it requires extensive offline and/or online exploration for building regression models for performance and power consumption for all possible mappings and DVFS levels, which is non-scalable. Further, it does not apply online periodic adjustment of DVFS level, which is essential for adapting to workload variations and achieving better power savings.

Approaches presented in [Reddy et al., 2017, Gupta et al., 2017] address the above problem, but they also depend on extensive offline results, and in particular, [Gupta et al., 2017] requires application instrumentation to guide the runtime selection. In [Basireddy et al., 2019], the dependency on the application-dependent offline results is removed by online mapping and adapting to application arrival/completion times. The works presented in [Reddy et al., 2017, Gupta et al., 2017, Basireddy et al., 2019] were implemented on Samsung Exynos 5422 MPSoC.

2.3.2 Reactive Approaches

Reactive approaches that use offline-optimization require extensive design space exploration of the underlying hardware and application(s). The techniques proposed in [Goraczko et al., 2008, Schranzhofer et al., 2010, Quan and Pimentel, 2013] are used for DVFS and/or task mapping. In [Goraczko et al., 2008], a resource model is presented to improve the accuracy of existing models considering the time and energy costs of runtime mode switching. Given an application, the software partitioning problem (assign parts of an application to each processor to achieve maximum system lifetime without sacrificing application performance) has been formulated as an Integer Linear Programming (ILP) problem. The approach presented in [Schranzhofer et al., 2010] generates multiple mappings for each application offering a trade-off between resource requirements and throughput. Evidently, these techniques consume more time, and cannot cope with dynamic application behavior, especially when multiple applications are run concurrently.

To handle dynamic application workloads, pure online optimization-based approaches, performing all processing at runtime, have also been investigated [Weissel and Bellosa, 2002, Singleton et al., 2005]. In [Weissel and Bellosa, 2002], the online algorithm utilizes hardware performance monitoring counters (PMCs) to achieve energy savings without recompiling the applications. In [Singleton et al., 2005], the study presented an accurate run-time prediction of execution time and a corresponding DVFS technique based on memory resource utilization. Online approaches do well for even unknown applications, but may result in inefficient results as optimization decisions need to be taken quickly without prior knowledge about the application [Quan and Pimentel, 2015]. This can be overcome by using hybrid approaches, which usually provide better performance results than pure online optimization as they take advantage from both offline and online computations.

Among hybrid approaches, the reactive control mechanism is used in [Cochran et al., 2011]. In [Cochran et al., 2011], thread-to-core mapping and DVFS is performed based on power constraint. In [Sasaki et al., 2013], first thread-to-core mapping is obtained based on utilization and then DVFS is applied depending upon the surplus power. However, [Sasaki et al., 2013] is not implemented on mobile platform and was validated on a 64-core platform. Due to better power-performance trade-offs, heterogeneous architectures become prevalent across different computing domains [Van Craeynest et al., 2012, Aalsaud et al., 2016b, Sozzo et al., 2016, Donyanavard et al., 2016]. These approaches usually consider multi-threaded application to exploit the available hardware parallelism efficiently. For multi-threaded applications, most approaches tend to allocate whole application onto only one type of processing core(s) [Van Craeynest et al., 2012, Sozzo et al., 2016, Donyanavard et al., 2016]. Although it simplifies the mapping problem but cannot benefit from the power-performance trade-offs offered by simultaneously mapping application threads onto multiple types of cores. In [Van Craeynest et al., 2012], a performance impact estimation technique is discussed to predict which application-to-core mapping is likely to provide the best performance to map the application onto the most appropriate core type. This work was evaluated on CMP$im simulator with 4 big and 4 small processors. In [Mandal et al., 2019], the study proposed a practical imitation learning (IL) framework for dynamically controlling the type (Big/Little), number, and the frequencies of active cores in heterogeneous multi-core mobile processors. In this work, linear regression (LR) and regression tree (RT) algorithms are employed to generate policies with minimal storage compared to techniques based on reinforcement learning (RL), and also has minimal runtime decision-making overheads. This work was implemented on Samsung Exynos 5422 MPSoC.

2.4 Dynamic Thermal Management

In this section, we explore the dynamic thermal management approaches that are currently available in MPSoCs. The studies mentioned in this section only focus on dynamic thermal management without explicitly considering dynamic power management.

Several dynamic proactive and reactive thermal management mechanisms have been proposed over the years. However, majority of the studies are focused on many-core (more than 16 cores) general purpose processors and Network-on-chips (NoCs) on contrary to multi-core mobile platforms. Techniques in [Peters et al., 2016, Dey et al., 2019f, Dey et al., 2019e] are solely focused on optimizing thermal behaviour during runtime on mobile platforms. Note that this section covers approaches considering only thermal management but not both thermal and power management that are provided in the next section 2.5.

2.4.1 Proactive Approaches

In [Peters et al., 2016], the study proposed a power management strategy for mobile games based on frame- and thread-based workload prediction on MPSoC. This work manages power by using the frame rate and thread workload as metrics to evaluate the appropriate workload predictors, and apply thread-to-core mapping along with DVFS to cater for frames per second constraint. The efficacy of the technique was proved on Samsung Exynos 5422 MPSoC.

2.4.2 Reactive Approaches

Reactive techniques focus on reducing the temperature of the core/die when a certain temperature threshold is reached and are already implemented in the governors of mobile Linux kernel. Examples of actions taken when the thermal threshold is reached could vary from switching on the active cooling of the device such as fan or throttling the operating frequency of the cores.

In [Dey et al., 2019f], the study presented a dynamic thermal management technique using frequency scaling to meet the performance deadline of the executing application. This technique maps the operating frequency of the cores to a temperature while executing an application and uses the mapping to select the appropriate frequency to cater for the performance deadline while keeping the operating temperature lower than the threshold. The efficacy of the technique is proved on Samsung Exynos 5422 MPSoC. In another work [Dey et al., 2019e], the study presented a dynamic thermal management technique where design space exploration is used to first reduce the number of possible frequencies to only four and then selecting the most appropriate frequency to meet the desired reward, which is the thermal constraint for an example.

2.5 Dynamic Power and Thermal Management

In this section, we explore the dynamic power and thermal management approaches that are currently available in MPSoCs. The studies mentioned in this section focus on both power and thermal management.

Reactive power and thermal management methodologies focus on reducing the temperature of the die/individual core and reduce the power consumption after a certain temperature threshold and/or power consumption threshold is reached. The time period between two temperature or power consumption check is usually short to avoid exceeding the thresholds. Reactive techniques are already implemented in the governors of mobile Linux kernel. When the temperature goes up and reaches the threshold and/or when the power consumption reaches a threshold the Linux kernel throttles the operating frequency of PEs as means of reactive measures. On the other hand, proactive methodologies usually adjust the workloads or operating frequencies of the die/core by predicting the future power consumption or temperature behaviour. Proactive methodologies have higher performance overhead in general when compared to reactive ones due to the computation of predicting temperature and power consumption increase.

2.5.1 Proactive Approaches

In [Prakash et al., 2016], the study estimated the temperature of the CPU and GPU for a cooperative CPU-GPU thermal management on a multi-core mobile platform (Samsung Exynos 5250 MPSoC). Their technique utilizes the actual temperature readings of the CPU and GPU along with the cores' utilization to set the operating frequency setting for the next time interval.

On the other hand [Singla et al., 2015] proposed a predictor using power sensors and thermal sensors to predict the next power consumption based on the following operating frequency setting. This work computes a power budget using the predicted temperature and controls the operating frequencies along with the types and number of processing cores. Their experiments were performed on Samsung

Exynos 5410 MPSoC to prove the efficacy of the technique and an extension of this paper has also been published in [Bhat et al., 2017b].

In [Bhat et al., 2018], the study proposed an approach to achieve dynamic power-thermal management in heterogeneous MPSoCs by adapting models for performance, power consumption and temperature of various processing elements in the SoC. This work predicts temperature and power consumption through online learning of GPU frame processing time, GPU power consumption and power-temperature dynamics of a SoC, and the experiments were performed on Qualcomm Snapdragon 810 and Samsung Exynos 5422 MPSoCs.

In [Wächter et al., 2019], the study proposed predictive thermal and power management approach by predcting thermal behaviour for heterogeneous mobile platforms combining with application mapping and DVFS to reduce the energy consumption. The efficacy of the technique was proved on Samsung Exynos 5422 MPSoC.

2.5.2   Reactive Approaches

In [Bhat et al., 2017a], the study proposed power-temperature stability and safety analysis technique, which is based on a formula to compute the stable fixed point and maximum thermally safe power consumption at runtime. The efficacy of the technique is proved on Samsung Exynos 5422 MPSoC. In [Bhat et al., 2019], the study proposed a power and thermal management governor using the power-thermal dynamics on smartphones, where throttling on individual cores is performed based on the application being executed. This technique moves the most power-hungry process, which cause thermal violation, to low power processors, and throttle the cores to manage temperature and power consumption.

In [Dey et al., 2019a], the study proposed a technique to reduce temperature and power consumption of the device by dynamically selecting the appropriate operating frequency based on linear relationship between frequency and operating temperature, to improve the decision-making time of choosing the frequency. In this work, a linear relationship is deuced between frequency and temperature of the device while executing applications and at runtime the frequency-temperature mapping is used to maintain the desired temperature while reducing power consumption at the same time. The efficacy of the technique is proved on Samsung Exynos 5422 MPSoC. An extended version of the work is provided in [Dey et al., 2019b] where performance of the executing application is given priority.

The researchers in [Isuwa et al., 2019] proposed a dynamic thermal- and energy-management approach for CPU-GPU based MPSoCs by managing resources, frequency scaling and thread-partitioning of executing applications on CPU and GPU. The experiences were performed on Samsung Exynos 5422 MPSoC. In [Angioletti et al., 2019], the study presented a dynamic thermal and power management policy where parallel applications are mapped to the cores by profiling the through-put at different operating frequencies and then selecting the cores and relevant frequency to achieve close-to-optimal execution based on Quality of Service (QoS). If more than one mapping configuration is available, then power consumption is estimated between the big cores and GPU to select the appropriate option. In case big cores are chosen then power consumption of the subset of the big cores are estimated to limit maximum temperature. This work was evaluated on Samsung Exynos 5422 MPSoC.

2.6   Temperature Side-Channel Attacks

As low power mobile computing systems such as smartphones and wearables become more and more ubiquitous, security issues in these and similar systems become more paramount. These embedded systems have to face hostile security threats [Ambrose et al., 2015, De Haas, 2007, Hutter and Schmidt, 2013, van Elsloo, 2016] such as physical, logical / software-based and side-channel/lateral attacks. Amongst these, side-channel attack is a popular security threat due to ease of access to the physical hardware [Kocher et al., 1999, Koc, 2009, Kong et al.,

2008, Wang and Lee, 2007, Wang and Lee, 2008, Masure et al., 2020, Ambrose et al., 2015, De Haas, 2007, Hutter and Schmidt, 2013], where attacks are performed by observing the properties and behavior of the system such as power consumption, thermal dissipation, electromagnetic emission, etc.

Comparatively a lot less documented studies are performed in temperature based side channel attacks [Ambrose et al., 2015, De Haas, 2007, Hutter and Schmidt, 2013, Gu et al., 2016, Long et al., 2018, Knechtel and Sinanoglu, 2017] in the embedded computing systems. Due to a rise in the use of heterogeneous multi-processors systems-on-chips (MPSoCs) [Reddy et al., 2017, odr, b] in the embedded systems and a rise in studies on thermal side channel attacks [Hutter and Schmidt, 2013, Masti et al., 2015, Bartolini et al., 2016], it is crucial that side channel attacks in such platform should be addressed with utmost importance [Bartolini et al., 2016]. Several studies [Hutter and Schmidt, 2013, Masti et al., 2015, Bartolini et al., 2016] have pointed out processor's core temperature could be used to carry out side channel attacks even when the system has strong spatial and temporal partitioning of resources such as separate partitioning of cache memory, bus bandwidth, etc. But all these studies are focused on general purpose processors (using Complex Instruction Set Computer (CISC) architecture) and not on embedded multi-processors (using Reduced Instruction Set Computer (RISC) architecture), which have different architecture and operating signature from the general purpose ones [Patterson and Ditzel, 1980]. On the other hand, we could also see several studies [Field et al., 2014, Georgiou et al., 2017] documenting power/energy consumption for different types of instructions. Since there is a direct correlation between power consumption and heat dissipation [DeVogeleer et al., 2014, De Vogeleer et al.,], and armed with the knowledge of power consumption of each instruction executed on processors, it is even easier to launch a side channel attacks on these systems.

In 1996, [Kocher, 1996] demonstrated that implementations of cryptographic algorithms leak information from different side channels in the device. In [Hutter and Schmidt, 2013], the study evaluated the data leakages of CMOS devices via the temperature side channel. This study shows that the temperature leakage is linearly correlated with the power leakage model, however, it is limited by the physical properties of thermal conductivity and capacitance of the CMOS device. In [Masti et al., 2015], the scholars demonstrated that even when strong spatial and temporal partitioning of the processing cores in a system are performed, processor core temperature can be used as a side channel as well as a covert communication channel. This study evaluated their methodology in Intel Xeon server platform, however, MPSoCs have very different system components' architecture in comparison and no study has been performed to observe how temperature side-channel attack differs in a system that of MPSoCs'. On the other hand, in [Bartolini et al., 2016], research only studied thermal covert channel attack, where covert communication is established over temperature leakage, on multi-core in a general purpose processing system.

In the study by [Gu et al., 2016], the scholars have proposed a thermal-aware hardware functional unit that introduces noise to mask activity of encryption and decryption in order to secure against temperature based side-channel attack. The experimental work was done in simulation and is not easily deployable on existing embedded platforms utilizing DVFS enabled multi-processors due to the proposed approach requiring special hardware modifications. On the other hand, in the study by [Long et al., 2018], the scholars have proposed an approach to apply multiple transmitter to one receiver by generating noise to mask temperature behavior on the main transmitter and also establishing a new communication protocol between the transmitter and receiver. In [Long et al., 2018], a transmitter is the CPU core, which is executing the main task or set of tasks such as encryption/decryption, whereas, a receiver is the CPU core, which is establishing the thermal side-channel attack. Although this approach is easily implementable in existing embedded mobile platforms, however, this methodology doesn't improve the spatial and temporal thermal gradient of the processing cores, which is also important for low power mobile computing systems. Moreover, [Long et al., 2018] evaluated their work in simulation platforms and not in real devices. In the study [Knechtel and Sinanoglu, 2017], the scholars exploited the specifics of material and structural properties in 3D integrated circuits during design time exploration, thereby decorrelating the thermal behavior from underlying power and activity patterns. However, this approach also requires special hardware modifications in order to be implemented and is not deployable in existing embedded mobile platforms. This approach also does not consider the spatial and temporal thermal gradient of the PEs as well.

To this extent, we first need to define the key factors affecting temperature side-channel attack in an embedded system utilizing DVFS enabled MPSoC and introduce a metric that is capable of reflecting the vulnerability towards such an attack. This also calls for approaches to secure against thermal side-channel attack that could be easily deployed in existing and future mobile computing systems while conforming to reduced spatial and temporal thermal gradient on the processing cores.

2.7   Summary

This chapter provided a survey of emerging technologies, dynamic power and thermal management approaches, and temperature based side-channel attacks for multi-core mobile computing platforms. The approaches performing proactive and reactive management while following some principles are surveyed. Open challenges are also identified based on the ongoing academic and industrial research activities. The identified emerging technologies are expected to advance in the future to address the challenges of dynamic computing resource management into the next era.

Chapter 3

Performing DVFS on CPU

Automated feature extraction from program source-code such that proper computing resources could be allocated to the program is very difficult given the current state of technology. Therefore, conventional methods call for skilled human intervention in order to achieve the task of feature extraction from programs. This chapter proposes a novel human-inspired approach to automatically convert program source-codes to visual images such that the images could be then utilized for automated classification by visual convolutional neural network (CNN) based algorithm. After the program is classified then DVFS is performed on the CPU of the mobile MPSoC to optimize power consumption.

3.1 Prologue to First Contributory Article

This contributory chapter is based on the following articles along with my personal contribution to these articles.

3.1.1 Article Details

1. ***Somdip Dey***, Amit Kumar Singh, Dilip Kumar Prasad, and Klaus Dieter Mcdonald-Maier. "SoCodeCNN: Program source code for visual cnn classification using computer vision methodology." IEEE Access 7 (2019): 157158-157172. [**Most popular paper of**

IEEE Access and IEEE Xplore from December, 2019 to August, 2020]

2. ***Somdip Dey***, Suman Saha, Amit Singh, and Klaus McDonald-Maier. "Asynchronous Hybrid Deep Learning (AHDL): A Deep Learning Based Resource Mapping in DVFS Enabled Mobile MP-SoCs." In 2021 IEEE 7th World Forum on Internet of Things (WF-IoT), pp. 303-308. IEEE, 2021.

Personal Contribution In The Articles: Conceptualization, methodology, experimental software design were performed by Somdip Dey. Validation of the methodology was performed by Somdip Dey and Amit Singh while formal analysis was done by Somdip Dey. Resources and data curation were also done by Somdip Dey along with the preparation of the original draft of the papers. Paper writing was reviewed by Somdip Dey, Amit Singh, Suman Saha, Dilip Kumar Prasad and Klaus McDonald-Maier. Visualization of data was also done by Somdip Dey.

3.1.2 Media coverage

Given the popularity of the methodology (SoCodeCNN) in this article, it is covered by media (news) outlets as follows.

1. *"Research could make robots more resilient than ever before"*, University of Essex. Article link

2. *"Research Could Make Robots More Resilient Than Ever Before"*, Robotics News. Article link

3.2   Introduction & Motivation

Recently, we could see the emergence of several machine learning based methodologies to map and allocate resources such as CPU, GPU, memory, etc. to applications on embedded systems in order to achieve power efficiency, performance, reliability, etc. Several studies, which are focused on extracting features from source code of an application and then utilizing several machine learning models [Taylor et al., 2017, Cummins et al., 2017, Allamanis et al., 2018, Ashouri et al., 2018] such as Support Vector Machines (SVMs), Nearest Neighbor, etc. to classify different set of applications and then deciding the resources that need to be allocated to such applications. Using such methodologies also have their own disadvantages. Depending on feature extraction such as number of code blocks, branches, divergent instructions, and then utilizing machine learning on them usually requires accurate identification of features from the training data and then feeding them to the model. Extracting features from a source code of a program and then feeding to the machine learning model so that further inference could be made is difficult in many ways.

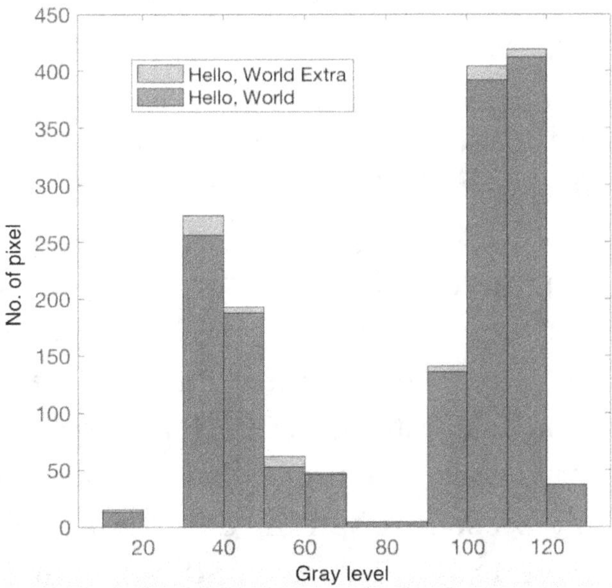

Figure 3.1: Histogram of source-code of "Hello, World" program vs Histogram of source-code of it with an additional integer variable initialization (Gray level vs Number of pixels)

It could be observed that with an addition of simple load & store instruction in a "Hello, World" program can lead to 16.98% difference

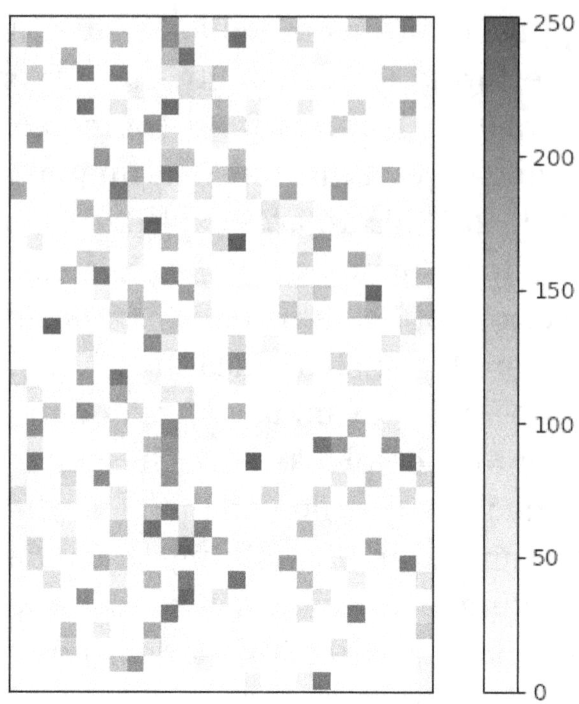

Figure 3.2: Differences in activation of neurons represented in shades of blue colour encoding

in the platform-independent LLVM intermediate representation (IR) code [Lattner, 2002, Ko et al., 2015], which is a platform-independent low-level programming language. This proves that there is a scope to find and learn the pattern from the program source code to build more intelligent information systems such that autonomy and ability to demonstrate close-to-human like intelligence could be demonstrated by the computing system. LLVM IR is a strongly typed reduced instruction set, very similar to assembly level language, used by the LLVM compiler to represent program source code. Fig. 3.1 shows the histogram of the IR code of a "Hello, World!" program written in C (see Program 1) and another C program with an addition of integer variable initialization code (see Program 2). When the source code of these programs are represented into visual images using our *SoCodeCNN* (Program **So**urce **Code** for visual Convolutional Neural Network (**CNN**) classification) approach and passed them through a visual CNN based model (as mentioned in Sec. 2.2.2, Chapter 2), VGG16 [Simonyan and

Zisserman, 2014], pre-trained with ImageNet dataset [Krizhevsky et al., 2012, Russakovsky et al., 2015], it is observed that there was 14.77% difference in activation of neurons in the last fully connected layer consisting of 1000 neurons. The difference between the activation of neurons for two different programs are evaluated by converting the activation of neurons for each program into visual images and then compared using Quality of Index methodology (Q) [Wang and Bovik, 2002]. Fig. 3.2 shows the differences in activation of 1000 neurons in the last fully connected layer of VGG16. In this figure, each cell in the matrix is represented as a colour ranging from 0 to 255, where each value ranges from white to different shades of blue. If the value is closer to 255 then the colour will be the darkest shade of blue whereas, the shade of blue fades away as the value is closer to 0. For the cells with white colour means that there was no difference (value equal to 0) in activation of neuron in that place for both the image representations of the programs (Program 1 and Program 2). However, if the cell has a colour other than white means that there is a difference between the activation of neurons in that place and the strength of the difference is represented by the darker shade of blue as mentioned earlier. The difference of neuron values are evaluated through the blue colour representation is by finding the difference in the neuron values and then normalizing the value ranging from 0 to 255 (similar to ASCII values), where each value represents a shade of blue as mentioned above. More details on evaluating the difference between two images as an image representation of different shades of blue is provided in Sec. 3.6.

Program 1: Pseudo-code for "Hello World!"	**Program 2:** Pseudo-code for "Hello World!" with additional load/store instruction
print("Hello, World!");	integer a = 3; print("Hello, World!");

In this chapter, the proposed methodology is inspired by the human being's ability to learn from its surrounding visually [Marr, 1982, Messaris, 1994, Dallow, 2009, Dillon and Spelke, 2017, Ahissar et al., 2009]. In [Marr, 1982, Messaris, 1994] it is evident that humans learn and interact with their surroundings based on their visual perception and eyes playing an important role in the process and have grown to be one of the complex sensory organs with millions of years evolution. In fact, most humans start to learn and educate based on the visual representation of knowledge, may that be in the form of languages in written form or associating words with the visual representation of objects. Most scientists have also adopted this ideology and tried to extract patterns so that machines could be taught in the same manner. This gave rise to the interdisciplinary research between computer vision and natural language processing (NLP) in the field of artificial intelligence [Wiriyathammabhum et al., 2017], where the main essence of the study is to teach computers to recognize, understand and learn human (natural) languages in the form of images. However, the trend in this interdisciplinary research is to understand patterns from human languages and then impart the knowledge to computers. For example, in order to teach computers to understand the digit '7', features from several human written forms of '7' are extracted and then imparted to the computer [Goodfellow et al., 2016]. This method of learning could be synonymous to the example where a non-English speaking foreigner learns English by first associating the English words to their mother tongue and then remembering the word to learn English [JANČOVÁ, 2010, Krajka, 2004]. Let's call this *learning approach 1*. In contrary, if we consider the example of how most human babies learn a language is through the process of associating phonetic words with the visual representation of objects first and then understanding the differences in features of different objects and remembering the associated words [Shinskey and Jachens, 2014, Dillon and Spelke, 2017, Thompson, 2001]. Let's call this *learning approach 2*. While it could be very intuitive to just take a picture of the program source-code (Program

1 & 2) and use NLP and visual CNN to classify the program, this approach would be similar to the *learning approach 1*. However, *learning approach 1* has its own limitations, especially when complex language frameworks are used in programs (more about this is discussed in Sec. 3.3).

Although it should be kept in mind that the learning process in a human being is much more complex than covered by just two examples mentioned above and includes knowledge and information gathered from all sensory organs [Thompson, 2001, Ahissar et al., 2009] such as eyes, ears, tongue, skin, and nose.

In this chapter, the same ideology of learning is adopted through visual representation (*learning approach 2*) by converting the program source code into machine understandable intermediate representation and then trying to extract patterns and learning from them such that DVFS could be performed based on the type of the program applications.

3.2.1 Contributions

To this extent the main contributions of this chapter are as follows:

1. Proposed **SoCodeCNN**, a way to convert program source code into more machine understandable visual representation (images) such that it makes the process of feature extraction from such images completely automated by utilizing the inherent feature extraction of visual deep convolutional neural network (DCNN) based algorithms, taking the expert skillful human effort out of the context.

2. Proposed a new metric index named **Pixelator: Pixel** wise differ-**entiator**, to understand the differences between two images pixel by pixel in a visually representative way such that we can quantitatively evaluate the proposed SoCodeCNN method.

3. Provided a methodology to utilize **SoCodeCNN** for application classification in embedded devices and then perform CPU

DVFS to optimize power consumption. The approach uses **SoCodeCNN** based classification to predict the types (*Compute intensive, Memory intensive, Mixed workload*) of different benchmark applications along with their probability of being a certain type, and then utilizing our heuristic based power management technique to save power consumption of the embedded device (Samsung Exynos 5422 multi-processor system-on-a-chip [exy, a]). To the best of our knowledge, this is the first work to convert program source code to a more machine understandable visual image and then classify into the type of program using CNN model in order to optimize power consumption.

The rest of the chapter is organized as follows. Sec. 3.3 the opportunity of automating feature extraction from program source code with a case study. Sec 3.4 mentions the preliminary concept that we need to know in order to under the proposed methodology. In Sec. 3.5, we explain our proposed methodology - SoCodeCNN, while Sec. 3.6 explains the process of Pixelator view. Sec. 3.7 shows the efficacy of SoCodeCNN via experimental validation while Sec. 3.8 shows an exemplar application of SoCodeCNN to perform DVFS on CPU in devices. Finally, Sec. 3.9 discusses the future scope of this research and Sec. 3.10 summarizes the chapter.

3.3 Motivational Case Study

3.3.1 Traditional Feature Extraction from Source Code

Let us discuss the traditional approach of using machine learning on program source code with an example. Let's assume that there is a simple program, which is capable of executing on several CPUs using OpenMP [ope,] programming framework. If we consider the following programs in Program 3 and Program 4 then if a skillful human without a knowledge of OpenMP is given the task of extracting features such as how many parallel executions of for loops are there or how many for loops are there in the programs, that person would classify both the programs (3 & 4) as the same, having two *for* loops in each algorithm. Whereas, Program 3 has one general *for* loop and one parallel *for* loop capable of executing on multiple threads. Therefore, the human being has to have special technical skills in order to understand such differences. In the study [Cummins et al., 2017], the authors proposed a heuristic based deep learning methodology for allocating resources to executing applications by utilizing feature extraction from source code and then training a deep neural network (DNN) model to take decisions on resource allocation. Their proposed methodology requires special technical skill-set as described earlier.

Program 3: An OpenMP example of partial program	**Program 4:** An example of partial program

``
#pragma omp parallel
{
    #pragma omp for
    for (i=0; i<N; i++) {
        c[i] = a[i] + b[i];
    }
}
for (i=0; i<M; i++) {
    d[i] = a[i] + b[i];
}
``
	``
	for (i=0; i<N; i++) {
	    c[i] = a[i] + b[i];
	}
	for (i=0; i<M; i++) {
	    d[i] = a[i] + b[i];
	}
	``

On the other hand if we consider that a program consists of 1000 features such as number of code blocks, branches, divergent instructions, number of instructions in divergent regions, etc. and each feature extraction requires 3 seconds for a human being then such program would consume 3000 seconds or 50 minutes for complete feature extraction so that those features could be further used in machine learning algorithm. Since feature extraction from program source-code using NLP is heavily utilized in compiler optimization and thus someone could argue that the field of compiler optimization has improved a lot in past couple of years [Namolaru et al., 2010, Leather et al., 2014]. However, given the emergence of specialized frameworks and directives such as OpenMP, OpenCL, OpenVX, modern automated code feature extraction methods [Taylor et al., 2017, Cummins et al., 2017, Allamanis et al., 2018, Ashouri et al., 2018] are still lacking in pace in terms of accurately extracting such features in a completely automated manner. Therefore, human intervention for improved accuracy in feature extraction is always required. However, if the **SoCodeCNN** methodology of converting the program source code to images is utilized and then use the images in visual convolutional neural networks (CNNs) then it does not require any human intervention in the process and could end up saving 50 minutes in manual feature extraction such as the case for the example mentioned above.

3.3.2 Filling up the gap

Instead of identifying features from source code by the user and then feeding them to machine learning models as in the conventional approaches, with our approach the machine learning model is able to understand and learn from the patterns in the source code of the program by themselves. One of our important observations which has led to the proposal of our methodology, "SoCodeCNN", human evolution inspired approach to convert program **So**urce **Code** to image for **CNN** classification/prediction, is that when the two different source codes (Program 1 & 2), where the difference is only of that of an additional load/store instruction, are compared there was a difference of 16.98% between the images using the Quality of Index methodology (Q) [Wang and Bovik, 2002], and a Mean Squared Error (MSE) value of 7864.3. In Fig. 1, the histogram of two different aforementioned source codes are shown, which highlights the fact that even for a minute difference such as introducing a simple instruction is capable of creating a different pattern. The main motivation of this study is to fill up the gap in the usual conventional approaches by employing "SoCodeCNN" to automate feature extraction from program source-codes and using visual based machine learning algorithm to understand the inherent differences in patterns of source codes of different programs so that further learning and classification could be performed on such programs.

In this proposed methodology, an effective way of converting source codes to visual images are introduced such that they could be fed to different computer vision based Deep Convolutional Neural Network for training and classification purposes.

3.4 Preliminaries

3.4.1 Pre-trained Networks and Transfer Learning

A conventional approach to enable training of Deep Neural Network/Convolutional Neural Network (DNN/CNN) on relatively small datasets is to use a model pre-trained on a very large dataset, and then use the CNN as an initialization for the applicative task of interest. Such a method of training is called *"transfer learning"* [Pan and Yang, 2009] and the same principle has been followed here. The chosen CNN models mentioned in Sec. 3.7 are pre-trained on ImageNet.

3.5 SoCodeCNN: How it Works

Many human beings are not able to read or write using written languages, yet intelligent capacity of human brain and sophistication of visual capacity make the same human being intelligent enough to learn about the surrounding through visual representation of every object. For example, a human being might not be able to read or write "car" or "truck", yet when he/she sees one, the person instantly can differentiate between a car and a truck based on obvious visual features of each of these objects.

The same kind of intelligence is tried to be imparted to a computing machine by representing each source-code of applications in the form of visual images. *SoCodeCNN* is not just a methodology but also a software application that processes source-codes to be represented as visual images, which is understandable by computing machines. It has two parts (*Pre-process Source-Code* and *Process Source-Code IR*), which are achieved through three distinct modules (refer to

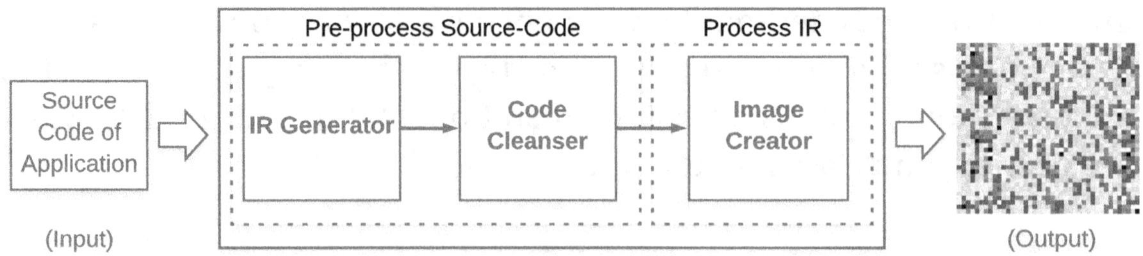

Figure 3.3: Block diagram of *SoCodeCNN*

Fig. 3.3) accomplishing separate tasks on their own in order to achieve the accumulated goal. The three modules are as follows: *IR Generator, Code Cleanser & Image Creator*. *IR Generator* and *Code Cleanser* pre-process the source-code of the application in order to generate platform-independent intermediate representation code so that the visual image could be created, whereas the *Image Creator* actually processes the intermediate representation code of the program source-code to create a visual image. The overview of *SoCodeCNN* is provided in Algorithm 5. Next, more details of steps *Pre-process Source-Code* and *Process Source-Code IR* are provided below.

3.5.1 Pre-process Source-Code

The algorithm of this part is provided in Algo. 5 (from line 4 to 11).

3.5.1.1 IR Generator

In this intermediate step, the LLVM intermediate representation (IR) [Lattner, 2002, Ko et al., 2015] of the source code of an instance of an application (App_i) is generated. LLVM IR is a low-level programming language, which is a strongly typed reduced instruction set computing (RISC) instruction set, very similar to assembly level language. The importance of converting to LLVM IR is that the code is human readable as well as easily translatable to machine executable code, which is platform independent. This means that LLVM code could be used to build and execute an application instance (App_i) on any operating system such as Windows, Linux, Mac OS, etc. LLVM also provides a methodology to create optimized IR codes, where the IR code is optimized even further such as not including unused variables, memory optimization, etc. The *IR Generator* generates the optimized IR code from the program source-code for further processing.

For example: When the Program 1 is converted to LLVM IR code the IR code is generated, as shown in the snapshot in Fig. 3.4.(a). It could be noticed that the first four lines consist of meta-data about the program itself such as the name of the program, related meta-information, etc. Although it should be noted that regardless of the target platform and the platform OS information is available in the LLVM IR code as meta-information, however, the variables and other instructions generated as part of the IR code is platform independent.

3.5.1.2   Code Cleanser

The main job of the *Code Cleanser* module is to get rid of the redundant part of the IR code, which does not add any value in the process of understanding the implementation of the application. Such redundant part of the code consists of initializing the name of the application and on which platform the LLVM IR code is built for or comments in the IR, etc. Once the redundant part of the LLVM IR code is removed the IR is ready to be utilized for visual image creation by the *Image Creator*.

For example: Fig. 3.4.(b) shows the IR code after *Code Cleanser* processes the IR code which is generated from the *IR Generator* module.

3.5.2   Process Source-Code IR

The algorithm of this part is provided in Algo. 5 (from line 12-34).

Image Creator

The *Image Creator* module first gets the total number of characters in the file consisting of optimized LLVM IR code (as mentioned in Sec. 3.5.1.2) and the number of characters ($SizeOf(IR)$) in line 14 of Algo.

```
; ModuleID = 'hello.c'
source_filename = "hello.c"
target datalayout = "e-m:o-i64:64-f80:128-n8:16:32:64-S128"
target triple = "x86_64-apple-macosx10.13.0"

@.str = private unnamed_addr constant [14 x i8] c"Hello, World!\00", align 1

; Function Attrs: noinline nounwind optnone ssp uwtable
define i32 @main() #0 {
  %1 = call i32 (i8*, ...) @printf(i8* getelementptr inbounds ([14 x i8], [14 x i8]* @.str, i32 0, i32 0))
  ret i32 0
}

declare i32 @printf(i8*, ...) #1

attributes #0 = { noinline nounwind optnone ssp uwtable "correctly-rounded-divide-sqrt-fp-math"="false" "disable-t
"unsafe-fp-math"="false" "use-soft-float"="false" }
attributes #1 = { "correctly-rounded-divide-sqrt-fp-math"="false" "disable-tail-calls"="false" "less-precise-fpmad

!llvm.module.flags = !{!0, !1}
!llvm.ident = !{!2}

!0 = !{i32 1, !"wchar_size", i32 4}
!1 = !{i32 7, !"PIC Level", i32 2}
!2 = !{!"clang version 6.0.1 (tags/RELEASE_601/final)"}
```

(a) Snapshot of LLVM IR Code of Program 1 generated by *IR Generator* module

```
@.str = private unnamed_addr constant [14 x i8] c"Hello, World!\00", align 1
define i32 @main() local_unnamed_addr #0 {
  %1 = call i32 (i8*, ...) @printf(i8* getelementptr inbounds ([14 x i8], [14 x i8]* @.str, i32 0, i32 0))
  ret i32 0
}
declare i32 @printf(i8* nocapture readonly, ...) local_unnamed_addr #1
attributes #0 = { noinline nounwind optnone ssp uwtable "correctly-rounded-divide-sqrt-fp-math"="false" "disable-t
"unsafe-fp-math"="false" "use-soft-float"="false" }
attributes #1 = { nounwind "correctly-rounded-divide-sqrt-fp-math"="false" "disable-tail-calls"="false" "less-prec
!llvm.module.flags = !{!0, !1}
!llvm.ident = !{!2}
!0 = !{i32 1, !"wchar_size", i32 4}
!1 = !{i32 7, !"PIC Level", i32 2}
!2 = !{!"clang version 6.0.1 (tags/RELEASE_601/final)"}
```

(b) Snapshot of LLVM IR Code of Program 1 after *Code Cleanser* module processed the IR code

Figure 3.4: Processing of LLVM IR Code of Program 1 by *IR Generator* and *Code Cleanser* modules

5) is denoted by $totalSize$. The $totalSize$ would be used to evaluate the height and width of the visual image to be created and the relationship between the height, width and $totalSize$ is provided in Eq. 3.1. The height and width of the image are determined such that $|height - width|$ (see Eq. 3.1) is the least from all the possibilities of a set (F) of factors, $F = \{f_1, f_2, ... f_n\}$ (where $f_1, f_2, ... f_n$ are all possible factors of $totalSize$), of $totalSize$, and $height$ and $width$ belong to the set F.

$$totalSize = height \times width \tag{3.1}$$

When the $height$ and $width$ is evaluated, the *Image Creator* module creates an instance of an empty image matrix (Img_i) as $0_{M_{height \times width}}$. The *Image Creator* then parses through the file containing the LLVM IR code and reads the file character by character and fetches the ASCII value (a) of those characters. Since each unique character will have a unique ASCII value (number), the IR code will be converted to their equivalent number representatives, which are correspondingly processed by the computing system. After fetching the ASCII value (a_j) of the character at position j of $totalSize$, the value at the corresponding position on the image matrix (Img_i) is replaced with the ASCII value of the character (as shown in line 28 to 31 in Algo. 5) since $totalSize$ follows a relationship with $height$ and $width$ as shown in Eq. 3.1. The image matrix could be denoted by the formula portrayed in Eq. 3.2.

$$Img_i = (a_{height,width}) \in \mathbb{R}^{heigth \times width}$$
$$\text{and } a_{height,width} = ASCII(\, a_j \,) \forall \, j \in \mathbb{R} \, \& \, 0 \le j \le totalSize \tag{3.2}$$

For example: After *Image Creator* processes the optimized LLVM IR code of Program 1, a visual image is generated as the Output in Fig. 3.3.

Note that for some programs/applications the total number of characters of the optimized IR code ($totalSize$) could be a prime number, which means that the either the height or width in Eq. 3.1 can be represented as $1 \times primenumber$ (as shown in Eq. 3.3).

$$totalSize = 1 \times primenumber \qquad (3.3)$$

In case, the $totalSize$ is a prime number as in Eq. 3.3, the generated image from the *Image Creator* module will be an image where the height is equal to 1 and the width is the prime number (or can also be interchanged depending on implementation such that $height = primenumber$ & $width = 1$). Even if the generated image from the *Image Creator* module is oddly shaped, where $height = 1$ & $width = primenumber$, this would not change the performance while the image is being used to train CNNs as the input images in CNNs are reshaped depending on the CNN's architecture regardless [Manaswi and Manaswi, 2018, Ghosh et al., 2019]. This is also true if $height >> width$ or $width >> height$ in Eq. 3.1.

3.6   Pixelator: Pixel Wise Differentiator of Images

3.6.1   Overview of Pixelator

A special algorithm is designed, which is capable of showing pixel wise difference between two separate images in the form of different colour shades. This algorithm is called as Pixelator view (**Pixel** wise differ-**entiator** view). In the Pixelator view, two images are compared pixel by pixel where each difference in the pixel value is evaluated using Eq. 3.4 and the difference is shown in a cell in the matrix representation. Each pixel of first image (P^1), which is being compared, is converted into its equivalent integer value. Since, each pixel of the image has a Red-Green-Blue (RGB) value associated with it, the formula of $(R \times 2^{16} + G \times 2^8 + B)$ is used to convert the associated RGB value of the pixel of the first image to its corresponding integer, and then compared with the integer value (RGB to integer) of the corresponding pixel in the second image (P^2), where the difference in the value only ranges from 0 to 255 similar to ASCII values. Each value, ranging from 0 to 255, represents a shade of blue. Since, most of the program source codes are written in the English language where each character in the code could be represented by a unique ASCII value ranging from 0 to 255, henceforth, the range of difference between the pixels is chosen to be within that.

$$int(P') = \left| int(P^1_{i,j}) - int(P^2_{i,j}) \right| \, mod \, 255 \qquad (3.4)$$

If we assume that h and w are the height and width of the referenced (original) image respectively then the *Pixelator* also integrates (adds) the difference between corresponding pixels to quantify the difference between two separate images using the Eq. 3.5. In 3.5, the h and w corresponds to the height and width of the image (P') respectively. We have given the index in Eq. 3.5 the same name as the approach itself for ease of naming convention. If the value of the index, *Pixelator*, using Eq. 3.5 is high then it means that the difference between the two images is also high and directly proportional.

Note: If the size of the images (P^1, P^2) are different then the pixel value of the smaller image (P^{small}, where $P^1 \leq P^{small} \leq P^2$) is compared with corresponding pixel value of the larger image (P^{large}, where $P^1 \leq P^{large} \leq P^2$) till the difference of all the pixel values of dimension ($h^{small} \times w^{small}$) of P^{small} are evaluated, where h^{small}, w^{small} corresponds to the height and width of P^{small} respectively.

The reason to have both a quantitative value and a visual image to understand the difference between two images, pixel by pixel, is to make it easier for both human and machine to understand the differences between the images. Although it is easier and intuitive to understand the differences of the images just by visualizing and inspecting the difference by a human being, however, for a machine it is not easy to achieve such level of capability without some complex computation. Whereas, machines can process numbers faster and hence having a quantitative value (number) associated to measure the difference between two images is more readily understandable by the machine.

$$Pixelator = \sum_{1,1}^{h,w} int(P') \qquad (3.5)$$

3.6.2 Comparison of Pixelator with other popular methodologies

Some of the popular approaches for assessing perceptual image quality to quantify the visibility of errors (differences) between a distorted image and a reference image includes Mean Squared Error (MSE) [Martens and Meesters, 1998], Quality of Index (Q) methodology [Wang and Bovik, 2002] and Structural Similarity Index (SSIM) [Wang et al., 2004] for measuring image quality.

A widely adopted assumption in image processing is that the loss of perceptual quality is directly related to the visibility of the distorted image. An easy implementation of this concept is visualized in the MSE [Martens and Meesters, 1998], where the differences between the distorted image and reference image is quantified objectively. But two distorted images with the same MSE may have very different types of distortion, where some of the distortions are much more visible than others. To overcome this issue in the study, Quality of Index (Q) methodology [Wang and Bovik, 2002], Wang et al. developed an approach, which would quantify the distortion by modeling it as a combination of three factors: loss of correlation, luminance distortion, and contrast distortion. Hence, quantifying distortion in images as a number does not truly reflect the exact area on the image where distortion happened nor reflects the kind of distortion that took place. In contrast in SSIM [Wang et al., 2004] approach, Wang et al. developed a framework for quality assessment based on the degradation of structural information by computing three terms: the luminance, the contrast and the structural information. The overall SSIM is a multiplicative combination of the aforementioned three terms and represents the structural distortion appropriate for human visual perception. However, for minuscule distortions in one of the colour channels out of the RGB channels of the image, SSIM fails to represent such minimal distortion which could be differentiated for human visual perception (see example in Sec. 3.6.2.1).

In order to overcome the drawbacks of MSE, Q and SSIM, *Pixelator* is developed, which is not just able to quantify the distortion but at the same time represent the exact distortion area in an image representation, which is suitable and comprehensive for human visual perception. *Pixelator* is developed, especially to understand differences in images (example result as Output in Fig. 3.3) created from the *SoCodeCNN* approach such that we could understand and visualize minuscule modifications in these visual images due to minuscule changes in the program source-code, which might not be visualized easily in general.

3.6.2.1   An example demonstrating the importance of Pixelator

The Lena image (refer to Fig. 3.5.(a)) is chosen, which is popularly utilized in image processing, to demonstrate the effectiveness of *Pixelator* over approaches such as MSE, Q and SSIM. Only one of the colour channels of the Lena image is chosen and for the pixel values in that channel representing 94, 95, 96, 97 and 220, the corresponding values are incremented by 2 (distorted Lena image is shown in Fig. 3.5.(b)). The reason to choose the aforementioned pixel values is that from the histogram of the image it could be observed that these pixel values were the most frequently occurring values in the chosen Red channel. When the difference between distorted Lena image and the referenced Lena image are evaluated using MSE, Q, SSIM and Pixelator, we could visualize that Pixelator is able to quantify and reflect the differences in the form of an image with respect to human visual perception (refer to Fig. 3.5.(d)), and at the same time outperforms the popular approaches. By differentiating the distorted and referenced images MSE gave a value of 9.7221, Q index evaluated to be 0.99984 (approx.), SSIM was evaluated to be 0.9959 (approx.) and *Pixelator* was evaluated to be 30533.43457. However, *Pixelator* is able to represent the differences more prominently in the form of visual representation

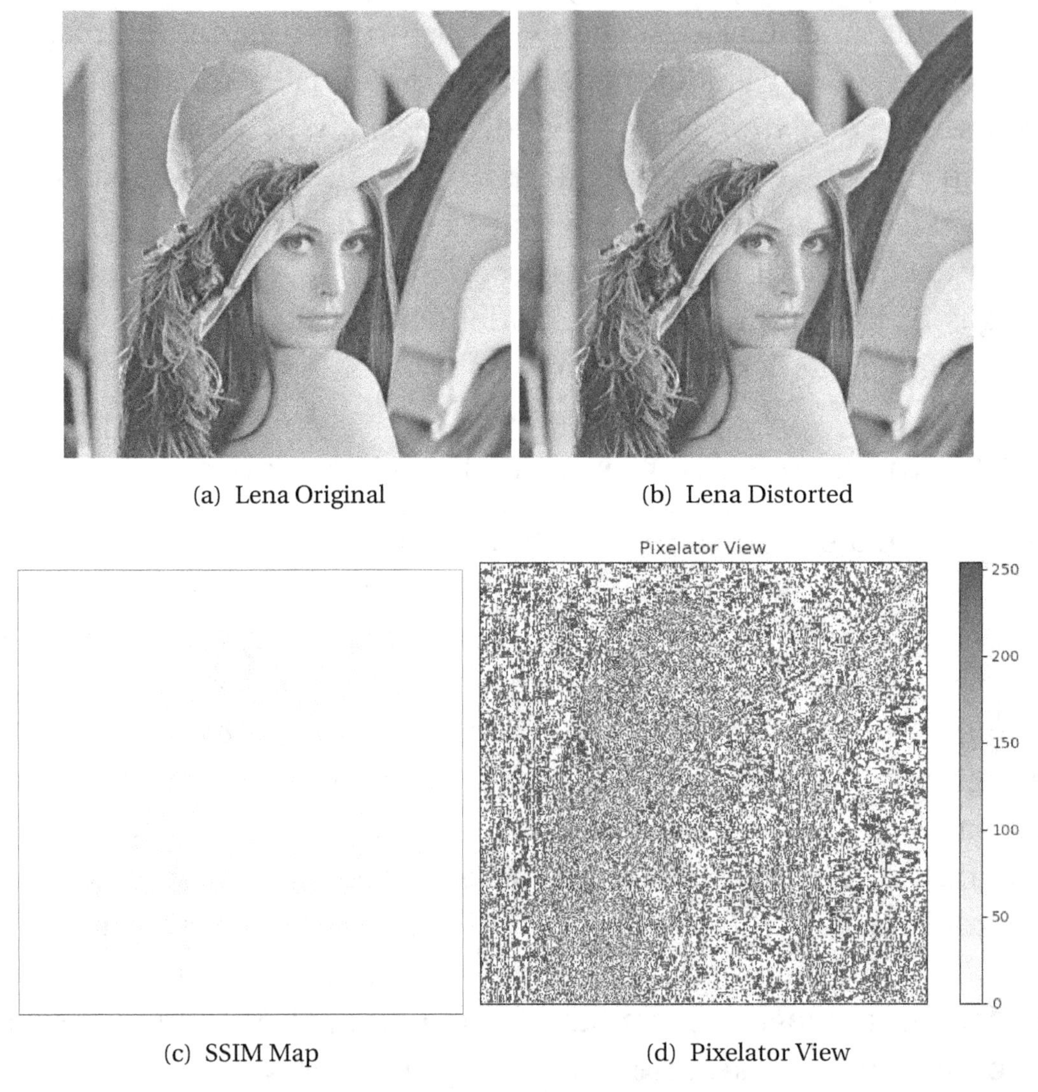

(a) Lena Original   (b) Lena Distorted

(c) SSIM Map   (d) Pixelator View

Figure 3.5: Highlighting differences between distorted Lena and reference Lena images using SSIM and Pixelator

image than SSIM, which is shown in Fig 3.5 as SSIM map. It could be noticed that regardless of having a SSIM value of 0.9959 (approx.), the approach is not able to represent the differences visually in SSIM map (refer to Fig. 3.5.(c)), whereas *Pixelator* is able to highlight the difference in each pixel wherever there is one.

Therefore, using *Pixelator* we are able to both visualize the difference between the original and distorted image, and quantify the difference at the same time, which could not be achieved by other popular methodologies such as MSE, Q and SSIM.

3.7 Experimental Results of SoCodeCNN

3.7.1 Experimental Setup

Several sets of experiments were run to evaluate the potential and efficacy of utilizing *SoCodeCNN* and scale its usability. The first experiment denoted as *Exp. 1* was performed to see how much difference could be there in the visual images with the slightest modification in the program source code. Several simple programs have been chosen with slight modifications to convey the efficacy of utilizing the *SoCodeCNN* methodology. In this experiment, the base program (denoted as *1st program*) is a "Hello, World!" program, which just prints out "Hello, World!" on the terminal (see Program 1). An additional load/store instruction in the base program (1st program) was added, where an integer value is initialized into a variable and this program is denoted as the *2nd program* (see Program 2). In the next program, an additional code was added to the base program to print out three integer values and we denote this program as *3rd program* (see Program 6). In the *4th program*, also denoted as the same name in figures and tables, has some additional load/store codes to initialize three integer variables whereas one of the variables is the sum of the other two and the result of the summation is printed out on the terminal (see Program 7). *SoCodeCNN* was used to convert these program source-codes to visual images and compared the differences using histogram, Mean

Squared Error (*MSE*) [Martens and Meesters, 1998] and Quality of Index (Q) methodology [Wang and Bovik, 2002].

Program 6: 3rd program pseudo-code	**Program 7:** 4th program pseudo-code

print("Hello, World!");
print(1 2 3);
	integer a = 3, b = 4, c;
	print("Hello, World!");
	c = a + b;
	print("Sum of " + a + " and " + b + " is " + c);

In the second set of experiments, denoted by *Exp. 2* VGG16 [Simonyan and Zisserman, 2014] Imagenet trained model was chosen with a custom classifier having only three classes: *Compute, Memory, Mixed*. According to several studies [Singh et al., 2013, Reddy et al., 2017] different workloads could be classified as compute intensive, memory intensive, and mixed (compute and memory intensive) based on the number of instructions per cycle or memory accesses. The purpose of *Exp. 2* is to show the efficacy of existing CNN models to classify programs based on images generated by *SoCodeCNN*. The classes (*Compute, Memory, Mixed*) of our classifier reflects the different types of workloads and hence denotes the type of program application. The class *Compute* refers to the programs, which are very compute intensive, but has low memory transactions (read/write, data sharing/exchange) in comparison, whereas the class *Memory* represents the programs, which have really high memory transactions in comparison to the computation performed in such programs. The class *Mixed* represents programs, which are both compute intensive and memory intensive. All the benchmarks of the PARSEC [Bienia, 2011a] benchmark suit were converted using the *SoCodeCNN* and passed the corresponding images through the pre-trained VGG16 to fetch the Deep Dream [Szegedy et al., 2015] images from the last fully connected layer of the model for each of the three classes to compare the visual differences between these classes if there is any.

In the third set of experiments (*Exp. 3*), *SoCodeCNN* was utilized to convert the program source-codes of all benchmarks from the

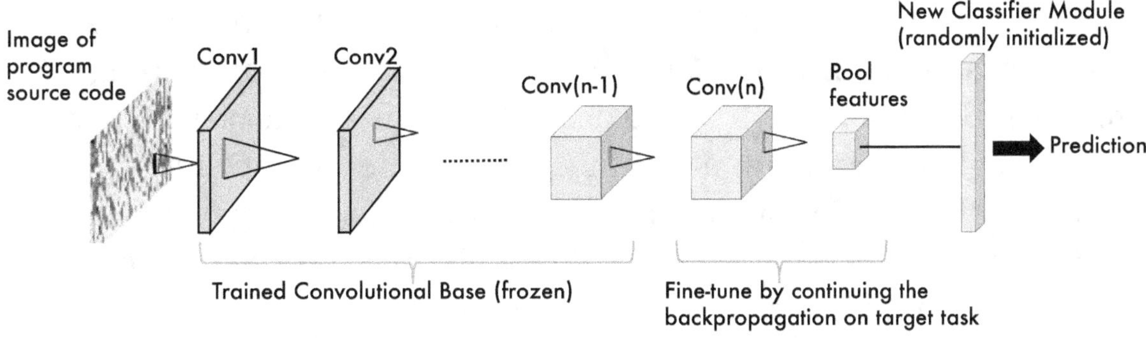

Figure 3.6: Network architecture used for fine-tuning

PARSEC, SPLASH-2 [Woo et al., 1995a] and MiBench [Guthaus et al., 2001] benchmark suit. The purpose of *Exp. 3* is to show scalability of *SoCodeCNN*'s application with CNN model by classifying programs from some of the popular benchmark suits. There were 28 individual images in total created from PARSEC and SPLASH-2 including P-thread and serial version of some of the benchmarks, and were segregated into three different classes (Compute, Memory & Mixed) based on the study [Bienia et al., 2008] comparing each benchmark with respect to their different number of instructions and memory transaction. To train and test the images for classification purposes VGG19 CNN model is used instead of VGG16 since it produced improved classification accuracy due to its deeper architecture. VGG19 CNN model was fine-tuned by adding our a new randomly initialized classifier, and training the last fully connected layer by freezing all the layers of the base model (frozen layers represented with gray colour in Fig. 3.6) and unfreezing the last fully connected layer (unfrozen layers represented with green colour in Fig. 3.6). In this way, only the weights of the last fully connected layer is updated and the classifier is trained with our images (see Fig. 3.6 for the CNN architecture used for fine-tuning). The source-code of benchmarks of MiBench are used for cross-validation purpose and testing the trained VGG19 CNN with our defined classes. The 28 images from PARSEC and SPLASH-2 were utilized to train the classifier and the last fully connected layer of the VGG19 pre-trained CNN using transfer learning [Pan et al., 2010] so that during prediction we could classify a program source-code image using a visual based

CNN model such as VGG16/19. The *Compute* and *Mixed* classes have 10 images each, and the *Memory* class has 8 images for training. Due to the imbalance in the training dataset, weights of the classes were set accordingly to facilitate fair training. It should be kept in mind that training of the CNN model could be performed on any type of computing system and then the trained model could be used on the mobile computing system such as Odroid XU4 (utilizing Exynos 5422 MPSoC) for evaluation.

Program 8: Execute power of 2 for 100,000 numbers iteratively on 4 different threads

```
function evaluatePowerOf2() {
    foreach i in 100,000 do
        | Compute i²;
    end
}
Execute evaluatePowerOf2() on
    Thread 1;
Execute evaluatePowerOf2() on
    Thread 2;
Execute evaluatePowerOf2() on
    Thread 3;
Execute evaluatePowerOf2() on
    Thread 4;
```

Program 9: Execute power of 2 for 100,000 numbers iteratively and add the result with itself in a separate variable

```
function
  doubleSumOfPowerOf2() {
    foreach i in 100,000 do
        | z = Compute i²;
        | y = z;
        | x = y + z;
    end
}
```

Since most of the benchmarks from MiBench are mixed load and, sometimes the benchmark programs are complicated to be segregated into either of the three different classes. Hence, to show the efficacy of using *SoCodeCNN* approach in CNN based algorithm we wrote simple programs, which would directly reflect either compute intensive or memory intensive or mixed workloads, and evaluate the classification outcome of such programs in *Exp. 3*. We wrote a simple program (see Program 8), which computes power of 2 for 100,000 numbers iteratively on 4 different threads and hence it could be classified as 'Compute'. We also slightly modified the program to make it more memory intensive by initializing the value of the power of 2 in a separate variable and then adding the result with itself in another separate variable (see Program 9). In Prog. 9 instead of executing the computation function on four different threads, we execute it only on one thread, making it more memory intensive. We further slightly modified Prog. 9 to make it mixed workload (compute and memory intensive) by executing the memory intensive function iteratively on 4 separate threads (see Program 10). We fed the source-code of the Prog. 8, 9 and 10 to the trained CNN in order to verify the output classification.

3.7.2   Experimental Results

Table 3.1 shows the result from *Exp. 1*, where different programs are compared using MSE and Q methodologies. From the table, it is evident that the visual representation of different program source-codes have different image representation and hence a potential playground for pattern recognition using visual CNN and image processing methodologies. Fig. 3.7 shows the histograms of four different programs (Program 1, 2, 6 and 7) of *Exp. 1*, where the X-axis represents the gray level of the visual images of the corresponding program and Y-axis represents the number of pixels for the corresponding gray level. Fig. 3.8 shows the Pixelator view of the differences in the visual images of Program 1 and Program 2.

Fig 3.9 shows the Deep Dream images of three different classes (Compute, Memory & Mixed) of program source-codes from *Exp. 2*, which proves that each class has different features that could be extracted to differentiate between program source-code in a visual manner. Fig. 3.2 shows the difference in activation of neurons of the VGG16 CNN when 1st Program and 2nd Programs are passed through the CNN model of *Exp. 2*.

In *Exp. 3*, after training the VGG19 CNN the CNN achieved a validation prediction accuracy of 55.56% and when we passed the program source-code of Program 8, the trained CNN was able to classify the program as Compute intensive with the confidence probability of each class as shown in Table 3.2. From Table 3.2 we could also notice that although the CNN classified Program 8 as compute intensive but the probability of memory intensive is also high and that is because when the power of 2 is computed iteratively, the values are still stored in the memory and hence has moderately high memory transaction as well. Table 3.3 shows the classification prediction for Program 9 and Table 3.4 shows the classification prediction for Program 10. While evaluating/validating the trained CNN on Exynos 5422 the average time to classify each image of the respective program was 0.83 seconds while consuming 5.34 watts (W) of power on an average.

In order to verify whether Program 8, 9 & 10 are Compute, Memory intensive and Mixed workload respectively we used MRPI [Singh et al., 2013] methodology for cross-validation. In [Singh et al., 2013] workloads are classified based on **Memory Reads Per Instruction** metric ($MRPI = \frac{\text{L2 cache read refills}}{\text{Instructions retired}}$). The workload is quantified by MRPI, where high value of MRPI signifies low workload on the processing core and vice-versa. For Program 8, 9 & 10 MRPI values were 0.018, 0.031 and 0.028 on average respectively, proving the correctness of workload classified by our trained CNN model. Therefore, for our chosen programs (Program 8, 9 & 10) we could notice that the CNN classifier is able to predict the label for each program source-code with high probability. Fig. 3.10 shows the classification (confidence in percentage) of some of the chosen popular benchmarks from MiBench benchmark suits.

From the aforementioned experiments we noticed that compared to conventional methodologies [Taylor et al., 2017, Allamanis et al., 2018], where skilled human is required to extract features from program source-code to determine whether a program is compute intensive or memory intensive or mixed, our approach is able to avoid such manual feature extraction and still able to classify programs into their corresponding classes accurately in an automated manner using visual based CNN algorithm.

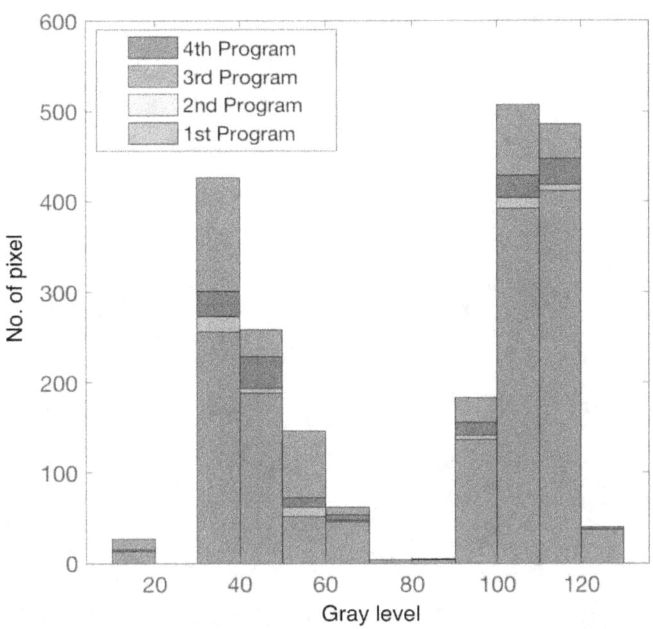

Figure 3.7: Histogram of source-code of 1st, 2nd, 3rd and 4th Program

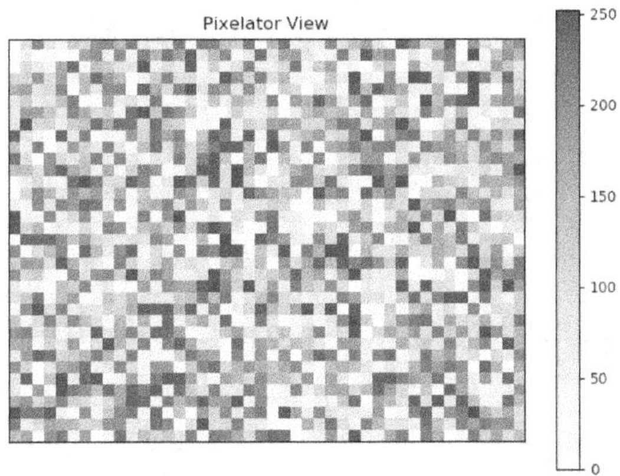

Figure 3.8: Differences in pixel of 1st and 2nd Program using Pixelator view

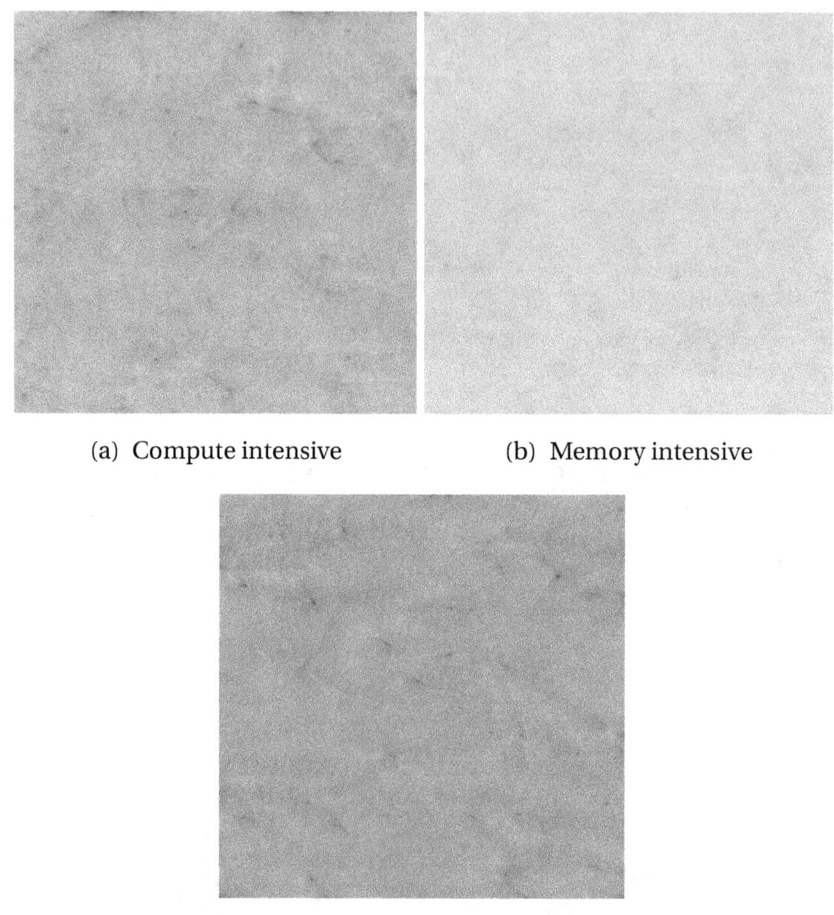

(a) Compute intensive   (b) Memory intensive

(c) Mixed load

Figure 3.9: Deep Dream Images of three different types of program source-codes: Compute, Memory & Mixed

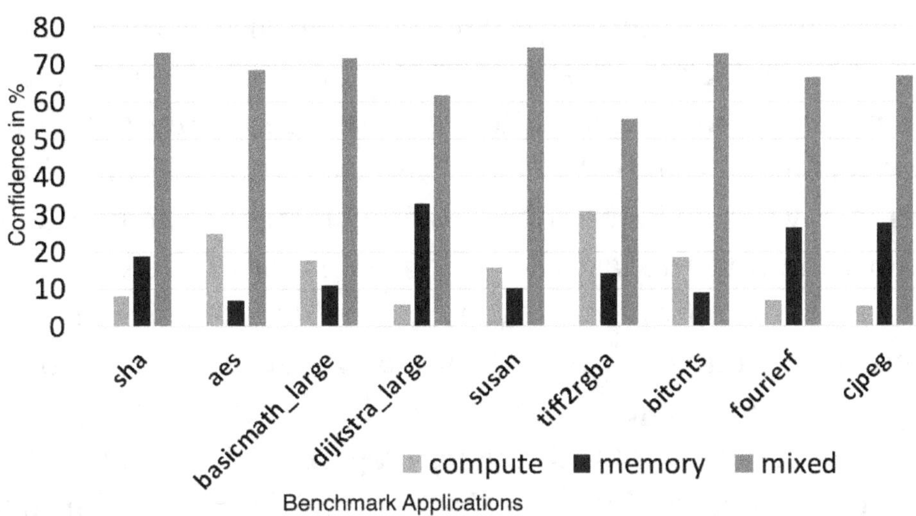

Figure 3.10: Classification of MiBench [Guthaus et al., 2001] benchmark suits (Benchmark vs Confidence in % for a specific class)

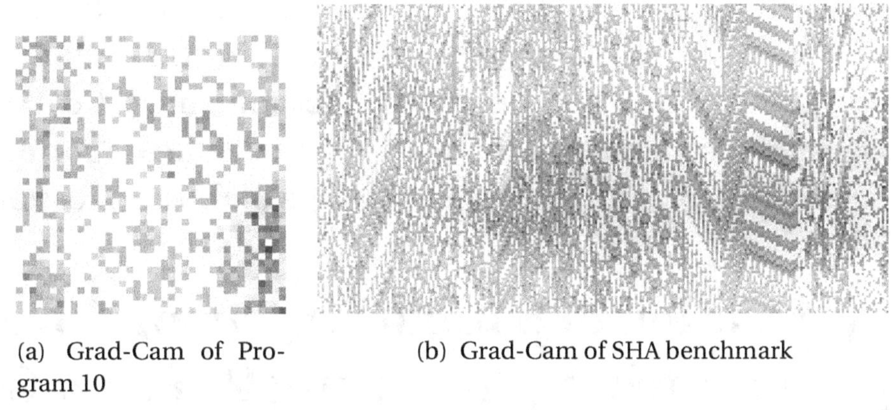

(a) Grad-Cam of Program 10

(b) Grad-Cam of SHA benchmark

Figure 3.11: Grad-Cam visualization

3.7.3   Where the CNN is looking

In order to verify whether the VGG19 CNN of *Exp. 3* is extracting the correct features to be able to predict the type of the application (program) Grad-Cam [Selvaraju et al., 2017] was utilized to visualize which area of the program-source code image is the model focusing on to make a decision (predict). In Grad-Cam the visual-explanation of decision made by the CNN model is provided by using the gradient information flowing into the last convolutional layer of the CNN model to understand the importance of each neuron for a decision made.

When Grad-Cam was utilized for classification of Program 10 and SHA benchmark application of MiBench by CNN we got Fig. 3.11.a and Fig. 3.11.b respectively to notice which regions are highlighted, reflecting the regions focused by the CNN to make the prediction decision. In Fig. 3.11.a and Fig. 3.11.b the regions highligted as red are the most important feature-extraction regions by the CNN, whereas the yellow regions are less significant and the blue ones are the least significant regions influencing the prediction decision.

When we referred back the red-highlighted regions of Fig. 3.11.a and Fig. 3.11.b we can notice that the CNN is focusing on the code for separate thread executions of Program 10, and parts of the functions named *sha_transform* and *sha_final* of SHA benchmark of MiBench. Upon inspecting Grad-Cam visualization of Program 10 and SHA benchmark it re-instated our confidence in the performance of the CNN in order to make a prediction decision since the aforementioned code regions in those programs are actually the important code-regions which are required to deduce the type of the application.

3.8   Application of SoCodeCNN in optimizing power consumption using DVFS on CPU

To prove the efficacy of utilizing SoCodeCNN we use the CNN model from the *Exp. 3* mentioned in Section 3.7.1 to develop an automated power management agent, which uses the CNN model to decide the

operating frequency of the processing elements (CPU) by performing
DVFS based on the type of the program being executed on the computing system. To implement the automated power management agent
we chose Odroid XU4 [odr, b] development board (see Fig. 3.13), which
employs the Samsung Exynos 5422 MPSoC platform. The Exynos 5422
MPSoC is used in several modern Samsung smart-phones and phablets
including Samsung Galaxy Note and S series devices.

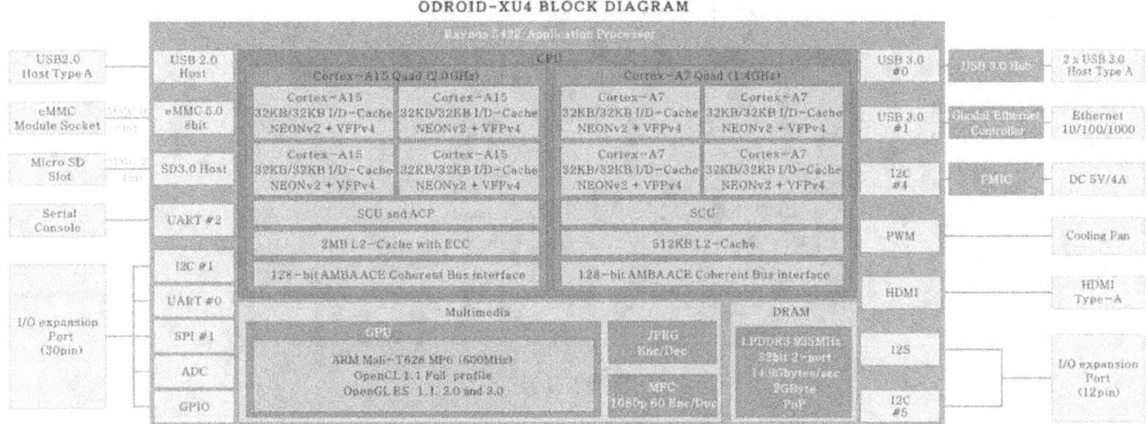

Figure 3.12: Odroid XU4 [odr, b] MPSoC block diagram highlighting
major components

3.8.1   Hardware & Software Infrastructure

Nowadays heterogeneous MPSoCs consist of different types of cores,
either having the same or different instruction set architecture (ISA).
Moreover, the number of cores of each type of ISA can vary based
on MPSoCs and are usually clustered if the types of cores are similar.
For this research, we have chosen an Asymmetric Multicore Processors
(AMPs) system-on-chip (AMPSoC) [Dey et al., 2019e], which is a special
case of heterogeneous MPSoC and has clustered cores on the system.
Our study was pursued on the Odroid XU4 board [odr, b], which employs the Samsung Exynos 5422 [exy, a] MPSoC (as shown in Fig. 3.12
and Fig.3.13.b) and is popularly used in Samsung mobile devices, especially Samsung Galaxy S5. Exynos 5422 MPSoC is based on ARM's

(a) Odroid XU4 in action

(b) Exynos 5422 MPSoC on Odroid XU4 development board

Figure 3.13: Odroid XU4 development board and Exynos 5422 MPSoC

big.LITTLE technology [arm,] and contains cluster of 4 ARM Cortex-A15 (big) CPU cores and another of 4 ARM Cortex-A7 (LITTLE) CPU cores, where each core implements the ARM v7A ISA. This MPSoC provides dynamic voltage frequency scaling feature per cluster, where the big core cluster has 19 frequency scaling levels, ranging from 200 MHz to 2000 MHz with each step of 100 MHz and the LITTLE cluster has 13 frequency scaling levels, ranging from 200 MHz to 1400 MHz, with each step of 100 MHz. Additionally, each core on the cluster has a private L1 instruction and data cache, and a L2 cache, which is shared across all the cores within a cluster.

Since Odroid XU4 board does not have an internal power sensor onboard, hence an external power monitor [odr, a] with networking capabilities over WIFI is used to take power consumption readings. Although the ARM Cortex-A7 (LITTLE) CPU cores on Odroid XU4 do not have temperature sensor but there are individual temperature sensors on each of the ARM Cortex-A15 (big) CPUs and a temperature sensor on the GPU. Our intelligent power management agent approach is scalable and works for heterogeneous cluster cores. We have run all our experiments on UbuntuMate version 14.04 (Linux Odroid Kernel: 3.10.105) on the Odroid XU4.

3.8.2 DVFS on CPU utilizing SoCodeCNN in MPSoCs

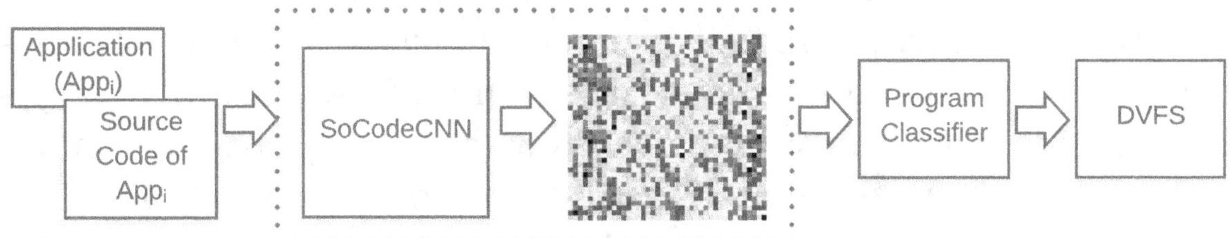

Figure 3.14: Block diagram of power management agent, APM, using SoCodeCNN

Fig. 3.14 shows the block diagram of the implementation of the automated power management agent. When an instance of an application (App_i) is executed, the program source code of the application is fed to the *SoCodeCNN* to create the image representing the platform-independent IR code of App_i, which will be used by the CNN model (called as "*Program Classifier*" in Fig. 3.14) for classification purpose. If App_i has been executed before on the platform, then the image representation created by *SoCodeCNN* during its first execution is already saved on the memory and used only for classification purpose for future executions. The *Program Classifier* will classify based on what type of application is being executed at the moment such as App_i is of compute intensive or memory intensive or mixed load, and *DVFS* module is used to set the operating frequency of the CPUs of the Odroid as required by the type of executing application.

We refer to this proposed automated power management agent as *APM*. In the APM implementation we specify if an application is compute intensive then the maximum operating frequency of the big CPU cluster of the Odroid should be set to 2000 MHz and for the LITTLE cluster's frequency to 1400 MHz, whereas if the application is memory intensive then the maximum operating frequency of the big cluster to be set to 900 MHz and the LITTLE cluster's frequency to 600 MHz. If the executing application is of mixed workload, then the maximum operating frequency of the big cluster to be set to 1300 MHz and the LITTLE cluster's maximum operating frequency to 1100 MHz. Through our experiments we have found that if an application is memory intensive or mixed load then most of the time running the CPUs at high frequency only wastes energy while not utilizing the maximum cycles per second capacity of the CPUs. Hence, we chose the associated operating frequencies as mentioned earlier through several experimentations. In the next sub-section, we show the power consumption difference between execution of Program 9 and Program 10 on UbuntuMate's (Linux) ondemand governor and on our APM implementation in a graphical representation. We also evaluated the difference in terms of power consumption while executing several benchmark applications of MiBench using Linux's ondemand, performance and APM.

Most MPSoCs in modern smartphones and wearables come equipped with limited hardware performance counters compared to general purpose computing systems such as PCs & workstations, and the access to the hardware performance counters could also vary from the device model to another. Implementation of the automated power management agent (APM) is introduced to provide an alternative approach to perform DVFS without the need of accessing hardware performance counters on mobile computing systems.

3.8.3   Results

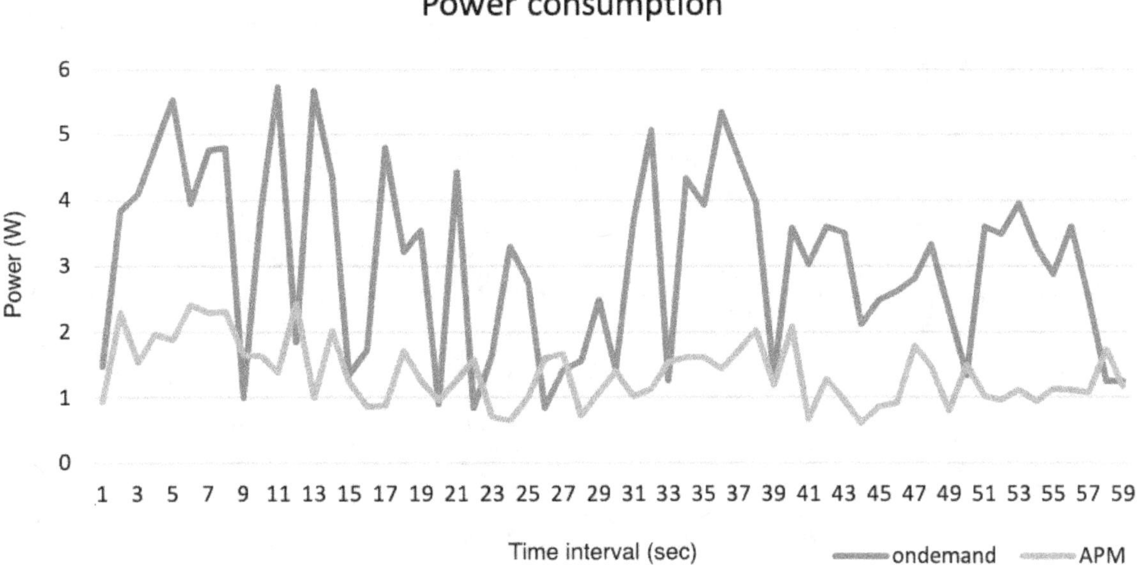

Figure 3.15: Power consumption of executing Program 9 on ondemand vs APM

Fig. 3.15 and Fig. 3.16 show the power consumption over time of execution of Program 9 and Program 10 respectively while executing on Linux's ondemand governor and on our APM. In the figures, the Y axis is denoted by power consumption in watts (W) vs time interval in seconds. In Fig. 3.15, using APM we are able to save 49.52% of power on average over the time period (APM power consumption: 1.372 W vs ondemand power consumption: 2.718 W). Using APM we only sacrificed 1.8 secs of execution time compared to ondemand's execution

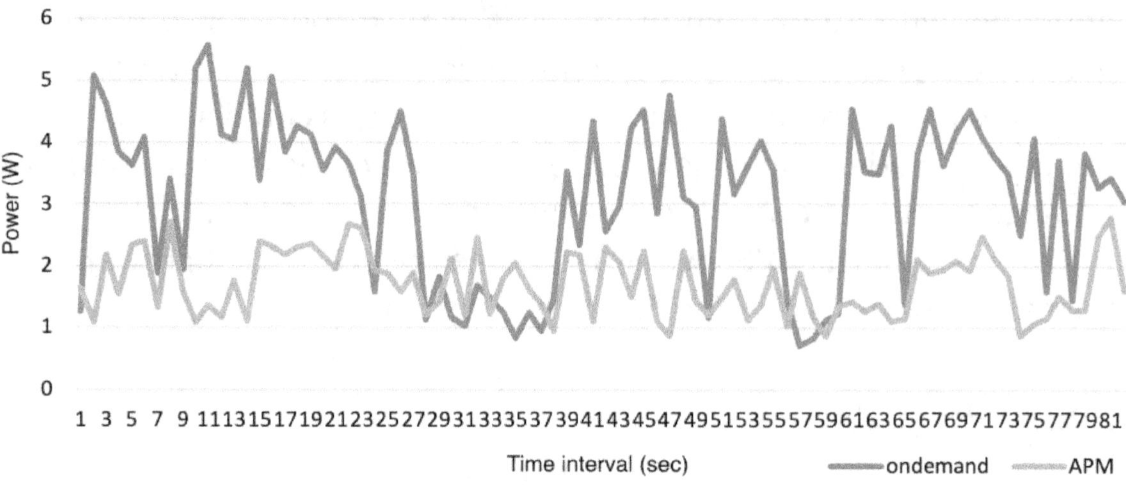

Figure 3.16: Power consumption of executing Program 10 on ondemand vs APM

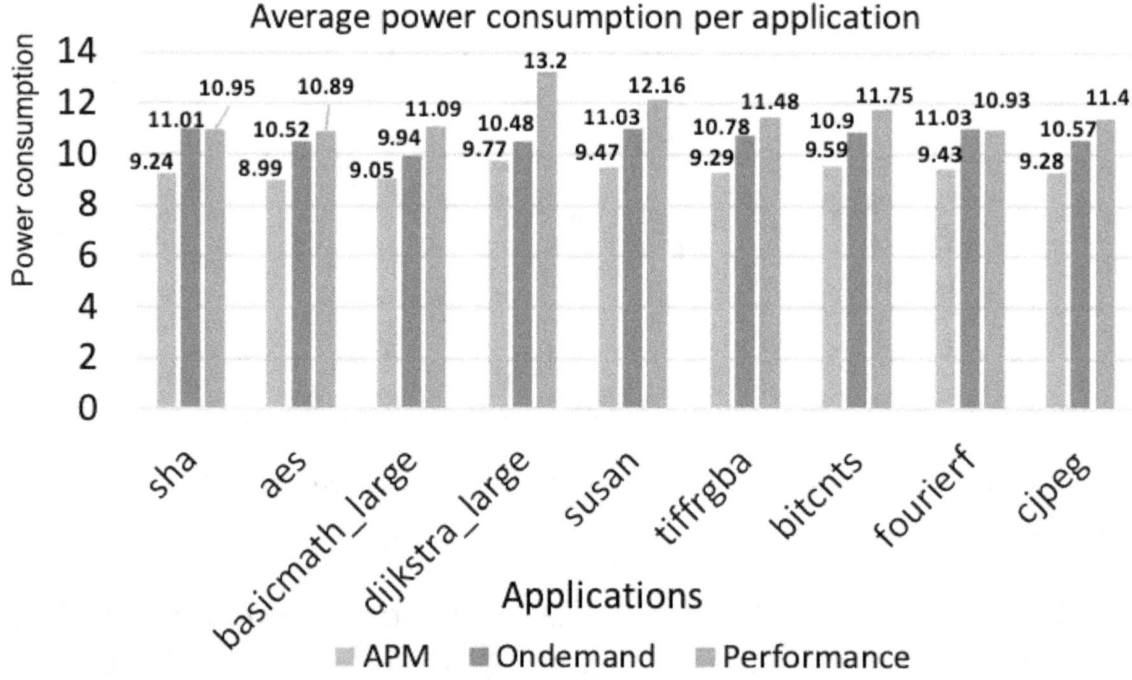

Figure 3.17: Power consumption of executing Program 10 on ondemand vs APM

time of 58.2 secs while achieving 49.52% more power consumption reduction. In Fig. 3.16, using APM we are able to save 43.48% of power on average (APM power consumption: 1.716 W vs ondemand power consumption: 3.036 W). Using APM we only sacrificed 3.1 secs of execution time compared to ondemand's execution time of 80.4 secs while achieving 43.48% more power consumption reduction.

As Program 9 is classified as memory intensive (refer to Table 3.3) in the Program Classifier module of APM, the APM forces the big CPU cluster and the LITTLE CPU cluster to operate at the maximum frequency of 900 MHz and 600 MHz respectively. This means that for memory intensive applications such as Program 9 APM forces the big CPU cluster to operate within 200 MHz to 900 MHz and forces the LITTLE CPU cluster to operate within 200 MHz to 600 MHz. On the other hand, the ondemand scheduler is capable of scaling the frequency of the big CPU cluster from 200 MHz to 2000 MHz and scaling the frequency of the LITTLE cluster from 200 MHz to 1400 MHz based on the performance demand of the executing application/program. Because APM only allows scaling of the frequency of the big and LITTLE clusters for limited frequency levels, APM enables more power saving compared to ondemand scheduler. This is evident from Fig. 3.15, where we can observe that while executing Program 9 on ondemand scheduler, the power consumption peaks (up to 5.8 W) and drops downs (to 1 W) repeatedly throughout the execution of the program. Whereas, while executing Prog. 9 on APM, the power consumption remains more stable and varies between 0.9 W to 2.4 W throughout the execution of the program.

Similarly, while executing Program 10 on APM, which classifies the program as mixed workload (refer to Table 3.4), then the maximum operating frequency of the big cluster is set to 1300 MHz and the LITTLE cluster's maximum operating frequency to 1100 MHz by the APM. Thus, enabling more power saving compared to ondemand scheduler (as shown in Fig. 3.16).

When we evaluated the power consumption of executing several benchmark applications of MiBench using ondemand, performance governors and APM, we noticed that APM is able to achieve more than

10% power saving on average over the time period compared to on-demand and performance while sacrificing only less than 3% of performance on average in terms of execution time. Fig. 3.17 shows the average power consumption of different benchmarks while using on-demand, performance and APM. In Fig. 3.17 the X-axis denotes the name of the benchmark and the Y-axis denotes the average power consumption.

It should also be noted that when a new application is executed on the platform, the average time taken to create the visual image from the source-code of the application using *SoCodeCNN* is less than 2 seconds (depending on the size of the program). Image creation is only performed once if the new application is executed for the first time using APM, otherwise, the inference of the image for classification and setting the operating frequency appropriately takes less than 150 milliseconds.

3.8.4   Advantage of SoCodeCNN based DVFS

In the methodology proposed in [Taylor et al., 2017], the authors define a machine learning based system which selects the appropriate processing elements and the desired operating frequency of the processing elements by extracting the features from the program source code and then evaluating the feature values by a predictor. However, the features from the program source code has to be manually selected by skilled people having experience with the programming language framework. In another study [Cummins et al., 2017], the authors utilize similar feature extraction methodology from source code to be fed to a DNN model to make decisions and this approach also requires the intervention of a skilled person to perform the manual feature extraction. On the other hand, studies [Singh et al., 2013, Reddy et al., 2018, Wachter et al., 2017] which include hybrid scheduling/resource mapping where the methodology is partly dependent on offline and online training of the executing application to decide the appropriate processing elements and their operating frequencies, also has its own limitations. In case a new application is being executed on the device, we need to perform an offline training on this new application in order to achieve an improvement on the main objective of scheduling/resource mapping to optimize performance, power efficiency, etc.

From the application of APM using *SoCodeCNN* to use DVFS of the processing elements we could notice that we do not require a skilled person to extract features manually from the source code to be fed to the software agent to decide the operating frequency of the system. At the same time in case a new application is installed and executed on the system then the APM is capable of classifying the application using *SoCodeCNN*'s image conversion methodology and trained CNN model, and then appropriately deciding the operating frequency of the processing elements based on the type of application being executed. The most advantage of utilizing *SoCodeCNN* is that we can design power and thermal management agents which are automated in nature with an overhead of at most 150 ms during classification and setting the operating frequency.

3.9   Discussion

Although using SoCodeCNN we are able to classify program applications automatically into Compute intensive, Memory intensive and Mixed workload to perform DVFS on CPUs, applications do not just rely on CPUs to meet the performance requirements. Often times, portions of the program of the executing application could heavily rely on other PEs such as GPUs, which could potentially affect the performance of the executing application. However, given the current state of sophistication of the SoCodeCNN approach it is not able to classify program applications in a fine-grained level where it could deduce whether the application requires more CPU or GPU or other types of PEs. Henceforth, this calls for approaches where DVFS could be performed on CPU and GPU automatically.

3.10 Summary

In this chapter, we have proposed *SoCodeCNN* (Program **So**urce **Code** for visual **CNN** classification) capable of converting program source-codes to visual images such that they could be utilized for classification by visual CNN based algorithm. Experimental results also show that using *SoCodeCNN* we could classify the benchmarks from PARSEC, SPLASH-2, and MiBench in a completely automated manner and with high prediction accuracy for our chosen test cases. We also demonstrate an approach to use *SoCodeCNN* to classify programs and then perform DVFS on CPUs in mobile MPSoC to optimize power consumption.

Moreover, most modern smartphones that utilize MPSoC, come equipped with touch screen enabled display, which requires other types of PEs than CPU such as GPU to execute the workloads. In the next chapter, we propose a novel methodology to perform DVFS on CPU and GPU to undertake the workloads executed on modern smartphones.

Algorithm 5: SoCodeCNN: The Methodology

Input:
$S(App)$: set of source-code of applications, where source-code of each application instance is represented as App_i

Output: I: set of visual images, each representing each App_i in $S(App)$

1   **Initialize:**
2   $height_{imageMatrix} = 0$;
3   $width_{imageMatrix} = 0$;

4   **Preprocess Source-code:**

5   **foreach** App_i in $S(App)$ **do**
6   Generate LLVM IR using *IR Generator* module;
7   Generate LLVM Optimized IR using *IR Generator* module;
8   Strip all the program related metadata using *Code Cleanser* module;
9   Strip all the comments using *Code Cleanser* module;
10   Store the IR in a set $S(IR)$;
11   **end**

12   **Process Source-code IR using *Image Creator* module:**

13   **foreach** IR_i in $S(IR)$ **do**
14     $totalSize = SizeOf(IR_i)$;
15   **foreach** $Byte$ in IR_i **do**
16   Store in $imageArray[totalSize]$ as an integer value;
17   **end**
18     $lengthOfFactorArray$ = Total number of factors of $totalSize$;
19   Factorize $totalSize$ and store in
      $factorArray[lengthOfFactorArray]$;
20   **foreach** $Factor$, f, in $factorArray[lengthOfFactorArray]$ **do**
21       $divisor = totalSize/f$;
22   **if** $(f - divisor)$ $is\ least$ **then**
23         $height_{imageMatrix} = f$;
24         $width_{imageMatrix} = divisor$;
25   **end**
26   **end**
27   Create an image matrix, Img_i with height, $height_{imageMatrix}$, and
      width, $width_{imageMatrix}$; **foreach** $ASCII$ $Integer\ value$, a_i, in
      $imageArray[totalSize]$ **do**
28   **foreach** $Cell$, c_i, in Img_i **do**
29   Store a_i in c_i;
30   **end**
31   **end**
32   Store Img_i in I;
33   **end**
34   return I;

```
function doubleSumOfPowerOf2() {
foreach i in 100,000 do
    z = Compute i²;
    y = z;
    x = y + z;
end
}
Execute doubleSumOfPowerOf2() on Thread 1;
Execute doubleSumOfPowerOf2() on Thread 2;
Execute doubleSumOfPowerOf2() on Thread 3;
Execute doubleSumOfPowerOf2() on Thread 4;
```

Table 3.1: MSE and Q values of *SoCodeCNN* of different
programs compared to 1st Program

Frequency Levels	MSE	Q
1st Program	0.0	1.0
2nd Program	7864.280746459962	0.830200472952753
3rd Program	6436.206069946288	0.871193634636040
4th Program	8134.392196655273	0.833703260745370

Table 3.2: Classification probability of Program
8 for different
classes: Compute, Memory & Mixed

Class Name	$Probability$
Compute	**0.5661**
Memory	0.3085
Mixed	0.1253

Table 3.3: Classification probability of Program 9 for different
classes: Compute, Memory & Mixed

Class Name	*Probability*
Compute	0.0774
Memory	**0.8236**
Mixed	0.0990

Table 3.4: Classification probability of Program 10 for different
classes: Compute, Memory & Mixed

Class Name	*Probability*
Compute	0.0071
Memory	0.1339
Mixed	**0.8590**

Chapter 4

Performing DVFS on CPU and GPU

In the Chapter 3, we presented a methodology to perform DVFS on CPU of the mobile MPSoC to optimize power consumption on a mobile platform based on the type of executing application. However, for smartphones, apart from reduced power consumption, thermal efficiency and Quality of Service (QoS) are important factors as well. Moreover, most of the applications do not just rely only on CPUs to meet the performance requirement but rely on CPUs and GPUs to provide a more enriched visual experience to the user. Most smartphones come equipped with MPSoC, which allows DVFS capability on both CPU and GPU to cater for performance requirement of the executing applications. On such smartphones the mobile user's usage behaviour changes throughout the day and the desirable QoS could thus change for each session. In this chapter, a QoS aware agent is proposed to monitor the mobile user's usage behaviour to find the target frame rate, which satisfies the desired user's QoS, and applies reinforcement learning based DVFS on the CPU-GPU to satisfy the frame rate requirement.

4.1 Prologue to Second Contributory Chapter

This contributory chapter is based on the following article along with my personal contribution to this article.

4.1.1 Article Details

Somdip Dey, *Amit Singh, Xiaohang Wang, and Klaus McDonald-Maier. "User Interaction Aware Reinforcement Learning for Power and Thermal Efficiency of CPU-GPU Mobile MPSoCs." In 2020 Design, Automation & Test in Europe Conference & Exhibition (DATE), pp. 1728-1733. IEEE, 2020.*

Personal Contribution In The Article: Conceptualization, Somdip Dey; methodology, Somdip Dey; software, Somdip Dey; validation, Somdip Dey; formal analysis, Somdip Dey; investigation, Somdip Dey; resources, Somdip Dey; data curation, Somdip Dey; writing–original draft preparation, Somdip Dey; writing–review and editing, Somdip Dey and Amit Singh and Xiaohang Wang and Klaus McDonald-Maier; visualization, Somdip Dey; supervision, Somdip Dey; project administration, Somdip Dey.

4.1.2 Media coverage

Given the popularity of the proposed methodology in this article, it is covered by media (news) outlets as follows.

1. *"Smartphones could get smarter by learning user's habits"*, University of Essex. Article link

2. *"Smartphones get smarter with Essex innovation"*, Business Weekly. Article link

3. "Future smartphones 'will prolong their own battery life by monitoring owners' behaviour'", The i news. Article link

4.2   Introduction & Motivation

Due to fast advancement in chip integration technology in the past couple of decades, we can see an increased adaptation of heterogeneous multi-processor System-on-Chip (MPSoC) in Edge devices, especially in smartphones and tablets. Market research performed by eMarketer [eMa,] shows that in 2018 mobile users in the USA spend 4 hours 16 minutes on an average on in-apps and mobile web with the availability of the mobile Internet on their smartphones and tablets. This includes an average of 1 hour 56 minutes on the top 5 social media platforms: Youtube, Facebook, Snapchat, Instagram and Twitter [med,]. Another market research by Deloitte US and Rescue Time [del, , res,] shows that an average person picks-up/look at their phones 52 times during their workday, where 70% of the sessions are less than 2 minutes, 25% of the sessions lasting between 2 to 10 minutes and 5% of the sessions prolonged more than 10 minutes. Even the duration of the user picking-up/looking at their Edge device every time varies from user to user and hence, making the sessions stochastic in nature and furthermore making existing resource management (DPTM) techniques inefficient for real-world Quality of Service driven applications on Edge devices.

Fig. 4.1 shows the varying frames per second (FPS) generation (frame rate denoted as *schedutil FPS* in the primary vertical axis) while using home screen, facebook and spotify apps on Samsung Galaxy Note 9 [gal,], which employs Exynos 9810 MPSoC [exy, b], over a 5 minutes of session. *Frame rate* is the frequency at which a new frame is rendered. In Fig. 4.1, FPS is recorded and shown every 3 seconds to provide a holistic view on the variation of frame rate during the session, especially the frame rate could vary even for one application based on the user's usage behaviour. In Fig. 4.1, the secondary vertical axis shows the operating frequency of the big and LITTLE CPUs of Exynos 9810 MPSoC, where the *Freq. B. sched* denotes the operating frequency of the big cores, and *Freq. L. sched* denotes the operating frequency of

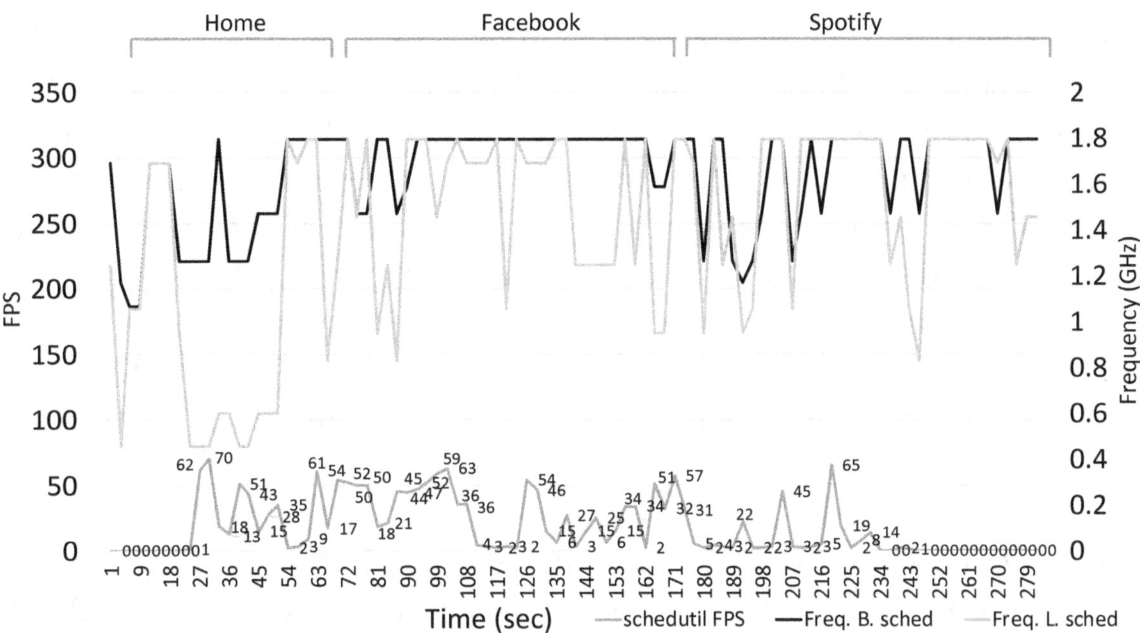

Figure 4.1: FPS generation, operating frequency of big and LITTLE CPUs in Samsung Note 9 while using home screen, Facebook and Spotify apps during a session on schedutil governor

the LITTLE cores. It should be kept in mind that the max operating frequency of the big cores is capped to 1794 MHz by vendor (Samsung) by default to reduce the overall power consumption of the MPSoC.

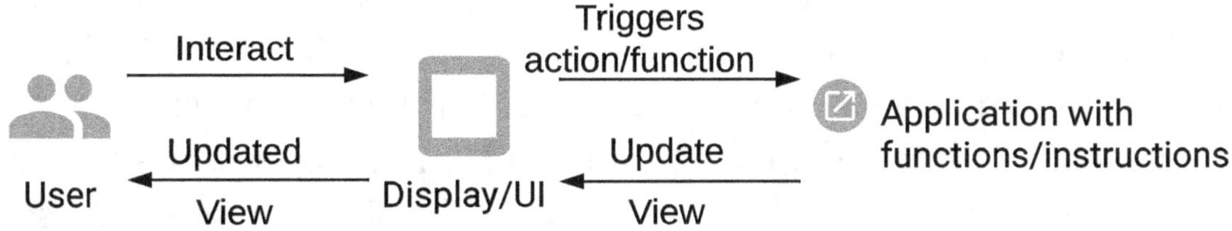

Figure 4.2: Interaction between the user and an app on a smartphone happens through display/UI

User experience or Quality of Service (QoS) of an application on an Edge device, especially smartphones, is often a measure of their frame rates. On modern smartphones, the user interacts with the display/UI which then triggers an event (action), which is again tied to some function(s) or instructions of the application with which the user is interacting [Johansson et al., 2016, Nilo et al., 2016], as shown in Fig. 4.2. Contrary to popular belief that the QoS of games or media applications, such as videos, are the only applications where the user experience is evaluated through their frame rates, the user's experience of any application on a modern smartphone with a touch screen display is measured with the frame rate as well. As the frame rate increases, the display experience tends to appear smoother and more fluid to the human eye and hence, very high frames-per-second (FPS) is often translated to a much richer experience for the user. Typically most commercial mobile devices render a maximum of 60 FPS to match their display's refresh rate of 60 Hz. A display *refresh rate* is the frequency at which the display is updated. Although at the moment there are some commercial devices which have higher display refresh rate such as 90 Hz and 120 Hz, however, 60 Hz display refresh rate continues to be the most popular mobile display refresh rate available in the majority of the devices.

The refresh rate and the frame rate are synchronized to update the display of the device through the process of Vertical Synchronization (VSync) [Johansson et al., 2016]. On the Android OS, 3 buffers consisting of 1 front buffer and 2 back buffers are used for VSync. CPU-GPU renders the new frames in the back buffers while the display shows the content of the front buffer. When a new frame is rendered in the back buffer, after each VSync the content of the back buffer is pushed to the front buffer and hence, the display outputs the front buffer content to the user. Since most displays have a 60 Hz refresh rate, the VSync is generated every 16.67 ms for such devices. The display is only refreshed on each VSync regardless of whether new frames are generated within the VSync period. When CPU-GPU fails to produce a frame within the VSync period, the front buffer is not updated and the display continues to render the previous frame, which results in a drop of the frame (*frame drop*) and hence, hindering the user experience. These frame drops lead to lag or stutter and hence, reduced QoS is achieved. Every mobile application on smartphones is a dynamic application consisting of periodic, aperiodic and sporadic tasks [Pillai and Shin, 2001], where the load of the application constantly varies based on the user interaction and the mechanics of the application itself.

For example, the primary vertical axis of Fig. 4.1 shows that for the same (intra-) mobile application (Facebook or Spotify) different FPS is generated at the different time period during the session based on varied interaction between the user and the application through the display/UI. If we take a closer look at the operating frequency of the big and LITTLE CPU cores (as shown in the secondary vertical axis of Fig. 4.1) of the Exynos 9810 MPSoC while using the applications (Facebook or Spotify) we could notice that the operating frequency remains relatively very high yet generating less FPS at certain occasions (as is evident in Fig. 4.1). This phenomenon is more evident while using the Spotify app during the session where the FPS drops close to 0 yet the operating frequencies of the big and LITTLE cores are very high, which results in high power consumption and operating temperature of the device.

Several power and thermal management schemes [Pathania et al., 2014, Sahin and Coskun, 2015, Shafik et al., 2016, Peters et al., 2016, Bhat et al., 2018, Dey et al., 2019a, Dey et al., 2019b, Isuwa et al., 2019, Dey et al., 2019e, Dey et al., 2019f, Dey et al., 2019c] for power and thermal efficiency while considering frame rate or QoS have been proposed over the years. However, neither of the techniques tries to improve power and thermal efficiency by taking user's interaction with the mobile into account to cater for improved QoS. Moreover, most of the existing studies focus on maximizing performance per watt (PPW), however, for a mobile platform reducing power consumption as well as the temperature of the device is very important while catering for the performance requirement and trying to maximize PPW is not enough for such platform. To overcome this limitation in this chapter we also introduce a new metric to incorporate performance, power consumption and thermal behaviour of the mobile device.

We propose a reinforcement learning based intelligent agent, called *Next* (Next generation user interaction aware DVFS), that learns the user's usage pattern of the mobile applications and then utilizes DVFS to save power and reduce the temperature during the mobile usage session while catering for the QoS required by the user. Reinforcement learning is a type of machine learning approach where the software agent takes actions in a system environment in order to maximize the cumulative reward [Sutton and Barto, 2018].

In order to determine the desired QoS for the user for each session, we also define a new metric, which is optimized by Next to improving the reward generated using reinforcement learning. Fig. 4.3 shows the average power consumption in the primary vertical axis and peak temperature of the big CPUs of Note 9 platform in the secondary vertical axis while utilizing the Next technique for a similar user session using home screen, Facebook and Spotify application. For the similar session using the Next technique we are able to save 41.88% more power (refer to primary vertical axis of Fig. 4.3) on an average over the time period when compared to default schedutil governor of Android, whereas we are also able to reduce the peak temperature of the big CPU cores by 21.02% (refer to secondary vertical axis of Fig. 4.3) compared to the temperature of the big cores while on schedutil governor. In mobile MPSoC, the big CPU cores consume the most power [Zhang et al., 2018] and are also the focus of hot spots on the chip, and hence in this case, we have focused on the thermal behaviour of the big cores for the comparative study.

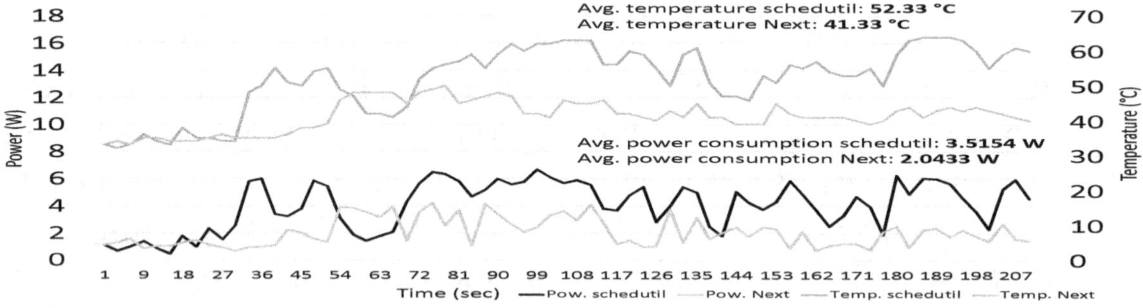

Figure 4.3: Power consumption and temperature of big CPUs on Samsung Note 9 while using home screen, Facebook and Spotify apps during a session on schedutil vs Next

4.2.1 Contributions

The concrete contributions of this chapter are the following.

- We define a new metric to optimize QoS based on power consumption and peak temperature obtained.

- We explore DVFS in mobile CPU and GPU based on user's interaction behaviour using a software agent based on reinforcement learning.

- We implement our power and thermal management technique - Next - in the application layer of the Android platform on Galaxy Note 9 smartphone utilizing Exynos 9810 MPSoC, and evaluate its efficacy with the latest popular applications from the Google Play store.

- We also show the scalability of our proposed approach by implementing it in the Odroid XU4 development platform and provide a comparative study with the state-of-the-art mechanisms to show its efficacy.

The rest of the chapter is organized as follows. In Sec. 4.3, we discuss the hardware and software platform used for our study as well as the problem that this study focuses on optimizing. In Sec. 4.4, we discuss the effect of DVFS on CPU and GPU towards power consumption and thermal behaviour as a motivational case study for the proposed methodology. In Sec. 4.5, we discuss the proposed methodology and its implementation. The efficacy of the proposed methodology, Next, is showcased in Sec. 4.6 while Sec. 4.7 shows the scalability of Next in other devices. Finally, Sec. 4.8 discusses the future scope of this research and Sec. 4.9 summarizes the chapter.

4.3 System, Metric and Problem Formulation

In this section, we explore the hardware & software infrastructure on which our proposed method is initially experimented. We also define the metric and problem formulation that form the foundation of our proposed approach.

4.3.1   Hardware & Software Infrastructure

We chose to execute our experimental evaluation on Galaxy Note 9 [gal,], which is one of the latest mobile device from Samsung and utilizes the Exynos 9810 MPSoC [exy, b]. The block diagram of Exynos 9810 is provided in Fig. 4.4. Exynos 9810 MPSoC has two CPU clusters, one for big CPU cores consisting of 4 Mongoose 3 CPU cores, and the other cluster for LITTLE CPU cores consisting of 4 Cortex A-55 CPU cores. The Mongoose 3 CPU cores allow cluster wise DVFS and has 18 frequency scaling levels ranging from 650 MHz to 2704 MHz (2704 MHz, 2652 MHz, 2496 MHz, 2314 MHz, 2106 MHz, 2002 MHz, 1924 MHz, 1794 MHz, 1690 MHz, 1586 MHz, 1469 MHz, 1261 MHz, 1170 MHz, 1066 MHz, 962 MHz, 858 MHz, 741 MHz, 650 MHz). However, at the OS level 4 Mongose 3 CPU cores can only be operated between 1794 MHz and 650 MHz as the rest of the frequencies are vendor locked. Similarly, the LITTLE Cortex-A55 CPU cores allow cluster wise DVFS and has 10 frequency scaling levels ranging from 455 MHz to 1794 MHz (1794 MHz, 1690 MHz, 1456 MHz, 1248 MHz, 1053 MHz, 949 MHz, 832 MHz, 715 MHz, 598 MHz, and 455 MHz). Exynos 9810 MPSoC also hosts ARM Mali-G72 MP18 GPU, which has 18 cores operating at a frequency range of 260 MHz to 572 MHz with 6 frequency scaling levels (572 MHz, 546 MHz, 455 MHz, 338 MHz, 299 MHz and 260 MHz). There are 5 thermal sensors on the device, out of which one is placed on the big CPU cluster, and one virtual sensor[1] is used for overall device temperature.

The Galaxy Note 9 was running on Android 9 (Pie) [and,] OS utilizing Linux kernel version 4.9.59, which has only one governor named *schedutil* based on Energy Aware Scheduling (EAS) [eas,].

---

[1] The overall temperature of the device is computed using the manufacturer's proprietor formula.

87

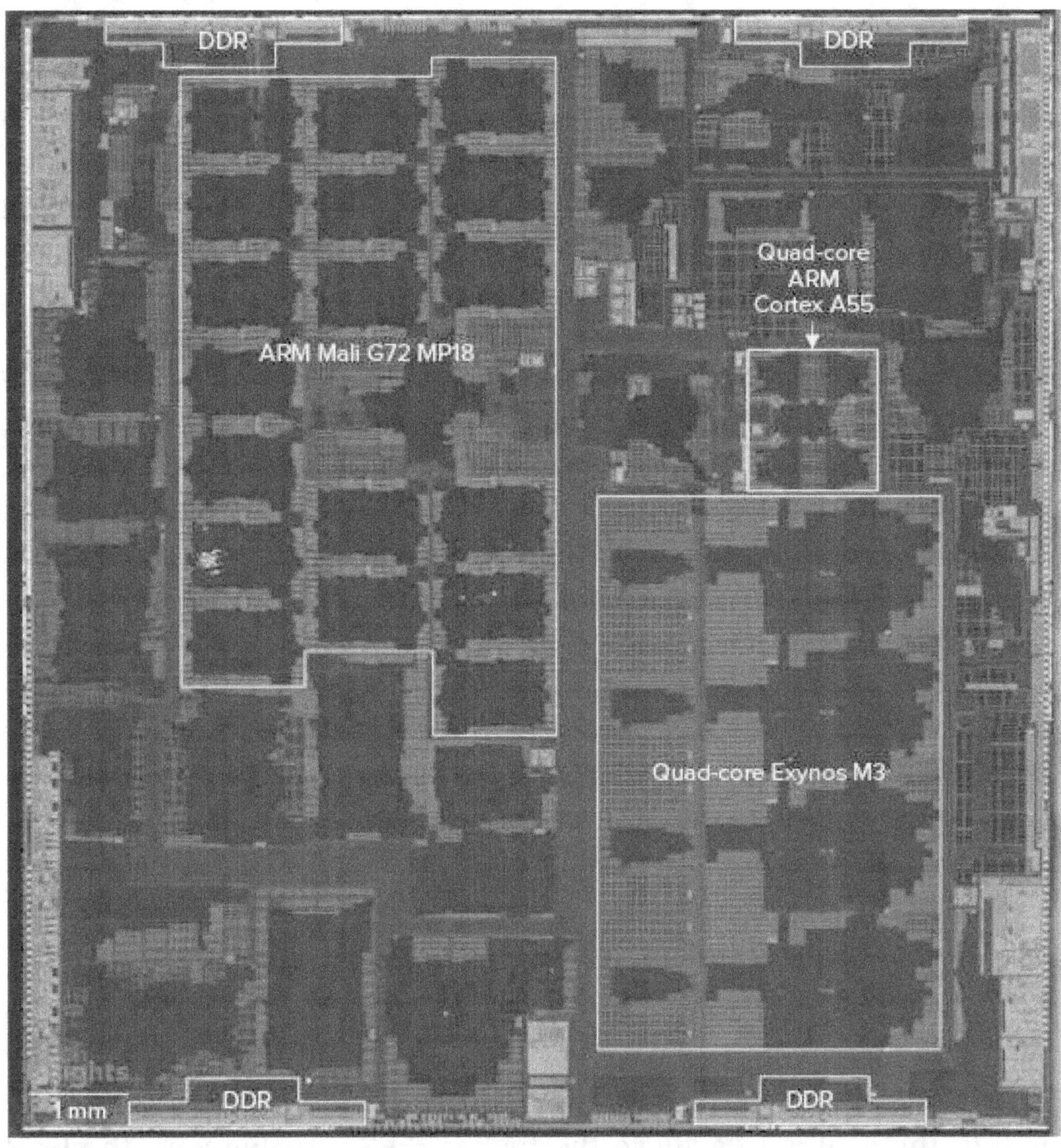

Figure 4.4: Exynos 9810 [exy, b] MPSoC block diagram highlighting major components

4.3.2 Metric and Problem Definition

The main focus of this work is to meet QoS while optimizing power consumption and peak thermal behaviour based on the user's interaction with the application. Most studies available at the moment focus on Performance per watt, however, there is no provision for thermal behaviour in the metric. Therefore, in this chapter we define a new metric, which incorporates both power consumption and peak temperature to evaluate the performance at a given time period. We call this metric *performance per degree watt* (PPDW), which is represented by the Eq. 4.1. In Eq. 4.1, $PPDW_i$ is the performance per degree watt at a time period i, FPS_i, P_i and T_i are the frames-per-second, power consumption and temperature respectively at that time, and T_a is the ambient temperature.

$$PPDW_i = \frac{FPS_i}{\Delta T \times P_i}, \text{where } \Delta T = T_i - T_a \tag{4.1}$$

The main objective is to minimize the value of PPDW, however, the optimum minimal value, which is $PPDW_{desired}$, needs to be between $PPDW_{worst}$ and $PPDW_{best}$ (refer to Eq. 4.4), which are defined as:

$$PPDW_{worst} = \frac{FPS_{least}}{(T_{max} - T_a) \times P_{max}}, \tag{4.2}$$

and

$$PPDW_{best} = \frac{FPS_{max}}{(T_{least} - T_a) \times P_{least}} \tag{4.3}$$

$PPDW_{worst}$ is obtained when FPS generated is least (FPS_{least}) while the maximum power (P_{max}) is consumed and the device reaches the maximum peak temperature (T_{max}) allowed on the device (as in Eq. 4.2); for example, generated FPS is 1 while executing all CPU and GPU cores at their corresponding maximum frequencies. On the other hand, the goal is to achieve the highest FPS possible with the least power consumed and least peak temperature achieved, which is denoted by $PPDW_{best}$ equation (Eq. 4.3), where FPS_{max} is the maximum FPS, T_{least} is the least peak temperature achieved and P_{least} is the least power consumed; for example, $PPDW_{best}$ is obtained when 60 FPS is achieved while consuming least power with no rise in temperature. Fig. 4.5 shows the general trend of PPDW value as the FPS scales along with power consumption and peak temperature of the big CPUs achieved on Exynos 9810 MPSoC while executing Lineage 2 Revolution mobile game, which is a very computationally intensive game. In Fig. 4.5, the PPDW values (for FPS: 0, 1, 10) marked by red colour are the worst values achieved for the corresponding FPS while consuming the most power and achieving the maximum peak temperature of the big CPUs.

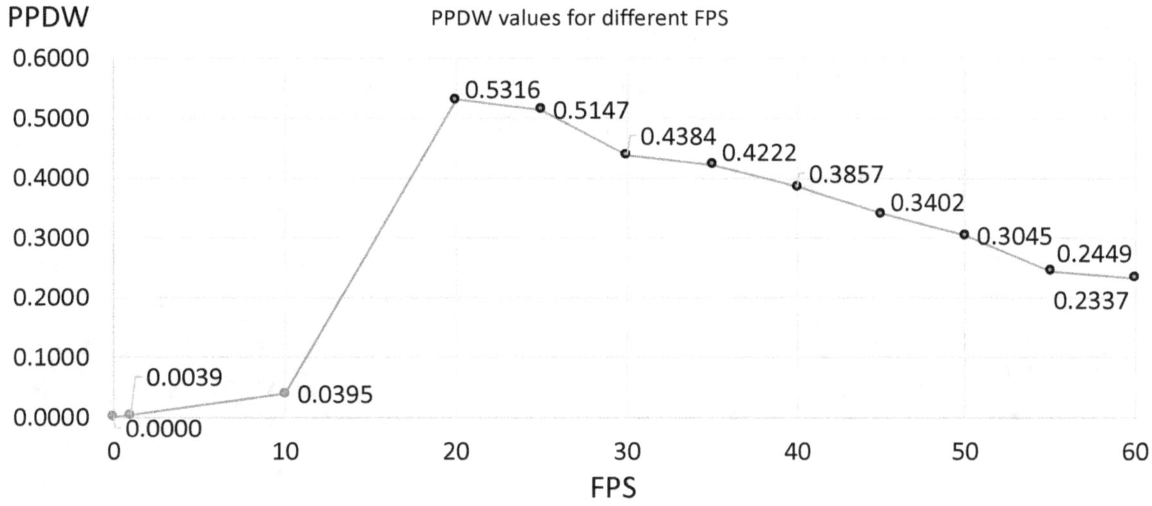

Figure 4.5: PPDW value trend as the FPS, peak temperature of big CPUs and power consumption scale accordingly

$$optimize(PPDW) \rightarrow PPDW_{best} \geq PPDW_{desired} > PPDW_{worst} \quad (4.4)$$

4.4 Motivational Case Study: Effect of DVFS on CPU & GPU in Note 9

Before we move into discussing our proposed methodology - Next, we need to understand how DVFS on the CPU & GPU in a mobile MPSoC such as Exynos 9810 that could affect the power consumption, thermal behaviour and generated FPS. To understand the effect of DVFS on CPU & GPU in Exynos 9810 MPSoC, a mobile application named 'EOptomizer Lite - Note 9' [eop,] is developed, which makes it easier for the user of the app to select the operating frequency of the LITTLE CPUs, big CPUs and GPUs on the MPSoC easily using drop-down list. Usually, majority of the researchers in this field of study write automated executable scripts with specified operating frequencies for the CPUs and GPUs to measure the effect of DVFS, and then update and execute the script as DVFS need to be performed with different operating frequencies. In comparison, 'EOptomizer Lite - Note 9' mobile app is developed to provide an easy to use GUI based interface for the researchers to select the desired operating frequency for the CPUs and GPUs and then monitor/recording different metrics such as power consumption, thermal behaviour, generated FPS easily.

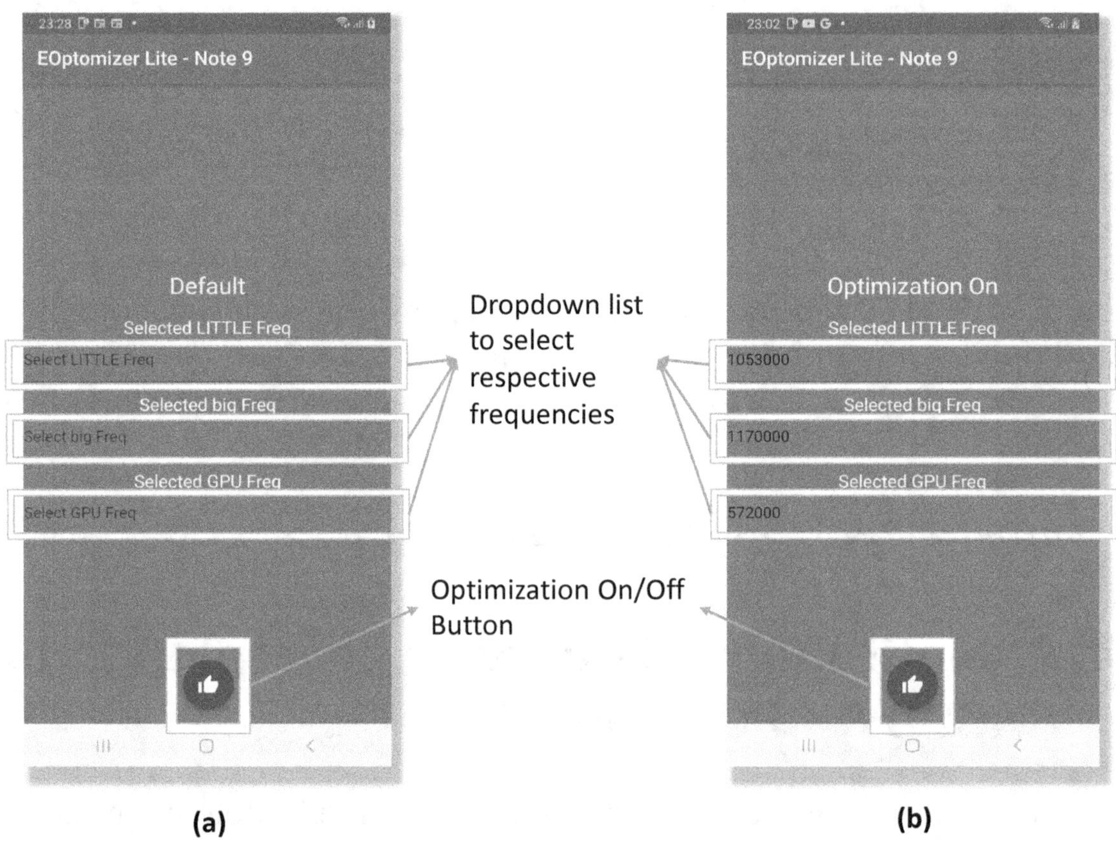

Figure 4.6: Graphical interface of 'EOptomizer Lite - Note 9' mobile app [eop,]. (a) shows the app UI when CPUs & GPUs operate on default frequencies of the *schedutil* governor; (b) shows the app UI when the CPUs & GPUs operate at a chosen frequency for LITTLE & big CPUs and GPUs respectively

Fig. 4.6 shows the interface of the 'EOptomizer Lite - Note 9' mobile app [eop,]. When the app loads for the first time (as shown in Fig. (a)) it shows "Default" as a label hinting that the OS is using the default governor, which is *schedutil* in Exynos 9810 MPSoC of the Galaxy Note 9, and run the CPUs and GPUs on default operating frequencies. The default *schedutil* can scale frequencies of the LITTLE CPUs, big CPUs and GPUs from 0.455 GHz to 1.794 GHz, 0.65 GHz to 1.794 GHz and 0.26 GHz to 0.572 GHz respectively. Fig. (a) shows the drop-down list for each of the LITTLE and big CPU and GPU clusters respectively and an "Optimization" button. When the desired operating frequency is selected for each of the CPU and GPU clusters and the "Optimization" button is pressed (as shown in Fig. (b)), in the background, the mobile app sets the *maxfreq* (maximum operating frequency) of each cluster according to the selected operating frequencies while recording the different metrics of the system such as power consumption, thermal behaviour and generated FPS in the background. The label on the app is also updated to "Optimization On " to hint that the *maxfreq* for the CPUs and GPUs are in fact set to the selected operating frequencies. This mobile app is developed using Flutter open-source framework [flu,], which is popularly used to develop cross-platform applications for Android, iOS, Linux, macOS, Windows, Google Fuchisa and the web from a single codebase. Note that the 'EOptomizer Lite - Note 9' mobile app can only be executed in *rooted* Android device, where the user has privileged root access.

Given, Exynos 9810 MPSoC has 11 operable frequency scaling levels for the big CPU cores, 10 operable frequency scaling levels for the LITTLE CPU cores and 6 operable frequency scaling levels for the GPU cores, the design space exploration taking all the operable frequencies into consideration is large. To understand the effect of DVFS on CPU and GPU in the Exynos 9810 MPSoC, the proposed mechanism from [Dey et al., 2019e] was used to select certain operating frequencies of the CPU and GPU cores to evaluate the difference in power consumption, thermal behaviour and generated FPS for those selected frequencies on the system. This reduces the exploration time for design space exploration as the number of frequencies-to-select reduces drastically.

For our experimentation, the following frequencies for LITTLE CPUs, big CPUs and GPUs as a group were selected such that we can compare the system metrics for those selected maximum operating frequency groups.

- **Default**: The maximum operating frequency of the LITTLE CPUs, big CPUs and GPUs are set to 1.794 GHz, 1.794 GHz and 0.572 GHz respectively.

- **HH**: The maximum operating frequency of the LITTLE CPUs, big CPUs and GPUs are set to 1.69 GHz, 1.69 GHz and 0.572 GHz respectively.

- **MH**: The maximum operating frequency of the LITTLE CPUs, big CPUs and GPUs are set to 1.053 GHz, 1.17 GHz and 0.572 GHz respectively.

- **ML**: The maximum operating frequency of the LITTLE CPUs, big CPUs and GPUs are set to 0.832 GHz, 0.962 GHz and 0.572 GHz respectively.

- **LL**: The maximum operating frequency of the LITTLE CPUs, big CPUs and GPUs are set to 0.455 GHz, 0.650 GHz and 0.572 GHz respectively.

- **LL2**: The maximum operating frequency of the LITTLE CPUs, big CPUs and GPUs are set to 0.455 GHz, 0.650 GHz and 0.338 GHz respectively.

- **LL3**: The maximum operating frequency of the LITTLE CPUs, big CPUs and GPUs are set to 0.455 GHz, 0.650 GHz and 0.26 GHz respectively.

The aforementioned maximum operating frequency groups (Default, HH, MH, ML, LL, LL2 & LL3) were selected to execute Lineage 2 Revolution mobile game (referred to as Lineage), Facebook app and Chrome web browser (referred to as Web Browser) on the Galaxy Note 9 to understand the difference in metrics such as power consumption, thermal behaviour and generated FPS. For each group of selected maximum operating frequencies Lineage, Facebook app and Chrome web browser were executed for at least 3 minutes per session and for 3 times to get an average of the different metrics. Between each session the smartphone was put on sleep for at least 30 minutes and the background processes on the device were also kept running to mimic the usage of a real smartphone user. It was made sure that the brightness of the system was set to 50% without auto-brightness switched on and an ambient temperature of 21°was maintained using a controlled thermostat. As part of the experimentation, the following execution metrics on the system were recorded every 200 milliseconds: max temperature of the big CPU cluster (denoted as **Max. Temp.** and measure in °C), average temperature of the big CPU cluster (denoted as **Avg. Temp.** and measure in °C), average power consumption of the system at the moment of executing applications (denoted as **Avg. Pow. Now** and measured in watts (W)), maximum operating frequency of the big CPU cluster (denoted as **Max freq. big** and measured in GHz), mode of the operating frequency of the big CPU cluster (denoted as **Mode freq. big** and measured in GHz), maximum operating frequency of the LITTLE CPU cluster (denoted as **Max freq. LITTLE** and measured in GHz), mode of the operating frequency of the LITTLE CPU cluster (denoted as **Mode freq. big** and measured in GHz), maximum operating frequency of the GPUs (denoted as **Max freq. gpu** and measured in GHz), mode of the operating frequency of the GPUs (denoted as **Mode freq. gpu** and measured in GHz), maximum of how busy the GPUs were during the execution of the respective app (denoted as **Max gpu busy** and measured in %), mode of how busy the GPUs were during the execution of the respective app (denoted as **Mode gpu busy** and measured in %), and mode of the generated FPS during the execution of the respective app (denoted as **Mode FPS**). Note that mode of the operating frequencies of the LITTLE and big CPU clusters were recorded to observe which operating frequencies for the respective CPU clusters were running most of the time during the execution of the respective app. For similar reason, mode of GPU busy was recorded to understand how busy the GPU was most of the time during the session and mode of the generated FPS was recorded to observe which FPS was generated most of the time for the selected operating frequencies while executing the respective app.

Table 4.1: Different metrics for Lineage while executing on different operating frequency groups - Default, HH, MH, ML, LL, LL2 & LL3

Lineage	Max. Temp. (°C)	Avg. Temp. (°C)	Avg. Pow. Now (W)	Max freq. big (GHz)	Mode freq. big (GHz)	Max freq. LITTLE (GHz)	Mode freq. LITTLE (GHz)	Max freq. gpu (GHz)	Mode freq. gpu (GHz)	Max gpu busy (%)	Mode gpu busy (%)	Mode FPS
Default	68	58.94	7.89	1.794	1.469	1.794	1.794	0.455	0.26	54	29	60
HH	63	56.27	7.5	1.69	1.17	1.69	1.69	0.455	0.26	58	32	60
MH	60	55.58	5.59	1.17	1.17	1.053	1.053	0.338	0.26	66	29	60
ML	57	53.85	4.25	0.962	0.962	0.832	0.832	0.338	0.26	53	30	50
LL	49	47.07	3.95	0.65	0.65	0.455	0.455	0.455	0.26	41	28	40
LL2	47	45.92	3.57	0.65	0.65	0.455	0.455	0.338	0.26	85	57	30
LL3	46	44.43	3.21	0.65	0.65	0.455	0.455	0.26	0.26	85	61	30

Table 4.2: Different metrics for Facebook while executing on different operating frequency groups - Default, HH, MH, ML, LL, LL2 & LL3

Facebook	Max. Temp. (°C)	Avg. Temp. (°C)	Avg. Pow. Now (W)	Max freq. big (GHz)	Mode freq. big (GHz)	Max freq. LITTLE (GHz)	Mode freq. LITTLE (GHz)	Max freq. gpu (GHz)	Mode freq. gpu (GHz)	Max gpu busy (%)	Mode gpu busy (%)	Mode FPS
Default	59	52.52	5.42	1.586	0.65	1.794	1.794	0.546	0.338	11	29	0
HH	55	50.97	5.14	1.69	0.65	1.69	1.69	0.572	0.546	18	1	0
MH	53	47.38	4.12	1.17	0.65	1.053	1.053	0.572	0.572	17	2	0
ML	48	46.44	3.95	0.962	0.65	0.832	0.832	0.572	0.572	16	3	0
LL	43	42.59	3.35	0.65	0.65	0.455	0.455	0.572	0.572	17	4	0
LL2	43	41.75	3.24	0.65	0.65	0.455	0.455	0.338	0.338	18	4	0
LL3	43	41.45	3.24	0.65	0.65	0.455	0.455	0.26	0.26	20	4	0

Table 4.3: Different metrics for Web Browser while executing on different operating frequency groups - Default, HH, MH, ML, LL, LL2 & LL3

Web Browser	Max. Temp. (°C)	Avg. Temp. (°C)	Avg. Pow. Now (W)	Max freq. big (GHz)	Mode freq. big (GHz)	Max freq. LIT-TLE (GHz)	Mode freq. LIT-TLE (GHz)	Max freq. gpu (GHz)	Mode freq. gpu (GHz)	Max gpu busy (%)	Mode gpu busy (%)	Mode FPS
Default	67	59.64	8.59	1.794	1.17	1.794	1.794	0.572	0.338	46	3	0
HH	67	59.06	8.7	1.69	1.69	1.69	1.69	0.572	0.572	63	6	0
MH	57	52.77	6.25	1.17	1.17	1.053	1.053	0.572	0.572	37	2	0
ML	54	51.01	5.67	0.962	0.962	0.832	0.832	0.572	0.572	27	3	0
LL	49	47.31	3.78	0.65	0.65	0.455	0.455	0.572	0.572	39	0	0
LL2	48	46.35	3.56	0.65	0.65	0.455	0.455	0.338	0.338	23	2	0
LL3	46	42.57	3.43	0.65	0.65	0.455	0.455	0.26	0.26	35	11	0

Table 4.1, 4.2 and 4.3 show the aforementioned observed metrics while executing Lineage, Facebook and Web Browser on the Galaxy Note 9 on the selected maximum operating frequency groups (Default, HH, MH, ML, LL, LL2 & LL3). From the tables one important observation is that for different mode FPS of executing apps, the selected maximum operating frequency could drastically affect the average power consumption & average temperature of the big CPUs. For example, in Table 4.1, for the Lineage app if the user's interaction with the device during the session is 40 FPS then LL maximum operating frequency group could be selected to operate the CPUs & GPUs to achieve the desired 40 FPS goal. However, if the average power consumption of the system and average temperature of the big CPU cluster are compared for these metrics while the operating frequencies of CPUs & GPUs are set to Default maximum operating frequency group then there is a power saving and temperature reduction of 49.93% and 20.13% respectively. For Lineage, if the user's session needed to generate the 30 FPS then LL3 maximum operating frequency group could be selected to operate the CPUs & GPUs. While Lineage is operated on LL3 maximum operating frequency group then the power saving and reduction in temperature compared to Default maximum operating frequency group are 59.31% and 24.61% respectively.

From table 4.2, we can also observe that for any selected operating frequency group (Default, HH, MH, ML, LL, LL2 & LL3) while using Facebook the mode FPS generated is always 0, so, to cater for the performance requirement of achieving the 0 FPS while trying to reduce power consumption and temperature reduction, it is better to operate the CPUs & GPUs at LL3 maximum operating frequency group instead. Therefore, for Facebook if LL3 maximum operating frequency group is selected for the LITTLE & big CPU cores and GPUs then there is a power saving and temperature reduction of 40.22% and 21.07% respectively compared to operating on Default maximum operating frequency group. The same is true for the Web Browser as well (refer to table 4.3) if LL3 frequency group is selected for the LITTLE & big CPU cores and GPUs then there is a power saving and temperature reduction of 60.07% and 28.62% respectively. From these analysed data we could notice that power saving and temperature reduction could be significantly different based on different maximum operating frequencies for the CPUs and GPUs.

These aforementioned sets of experiments motivated us to develop our proposed, Next, methodology such that the approach is capable of understanding what is the desired FPS, thermal behaviour and power consumption (as mentioned in the metric $PPDW_{desired}$ in eq. 4.4) while the user interacts with the app and then set the operating frequencies of the CPUs & GPUs accordingly.

4.5   Proposed Methodology: Next

In this section, we introduce our proposed approach, Next, in details.

4.5.1   Overview of Next

Next is a software agent that executes continuously on the application layer of the Edge device employing MPSoC and runs on the most power efficient CPU, which is the LITTLE CPU of Exynos 9810 MPSoC, in order to consume the least power while executing. Since the agent runs on the application layer, no modifications to the existing hardware/software of the device is required.

The most important part of the Next methodology is to understand the user's interaction behaviour with the display/UI and its effect on the frame rate. To achieve this, the agent continuously monitors the frame rate every 25 milliseconds (ms) for a window of n seconds. We call this virtual window of frame rates as *frame window*. From our empirical data we found that choosing the frame window for 4 seconds generates the best frame rate pattern analysis from user's interaction. Since, frame rate is usually denoted by frames per second (FPS), the agent has to scale the FPS accordingly due to monitoring of the frame rate every 25 ms. For 4 seconds of frame window, we are able to capture 160 distinct values of frame rate during the user's interaction for that 4 seconds. The agent now computes the mathematical mode operation of all the 160 distinct values, which actually determines the most possible frame rate suitable to provide the desirable QoS for the user during that session.

Now, as shown in Fig. 4.7, the mode value is fed to the reinforcement learning (RL) module of the agent as the target FPS to achieve till the target FPS changes during the next frame window of user's interaction. The target FPS is now used for training purposes by the RL agent, and more details are provided in section 4.5.2. If we consider that the MPSoC consists of m number of processing element (PE) clusters and the current operating frequency of each cluster for cluster wise DVFS is denoted by f_i^{CM}, where $M \in 1,2,...m$ then the frequency values are fed to the RL module of the agent as part of the states. In our implementation, Samsung Note 9 (Exynos 9810 MPSoC) has 3 PE clusters namely: big CPU, LITTLE CPU and GPU. Once the agent is aware of the frequency states of the PE clusters along with power consumption, temperature, current FPS (referred to as $FPS_{current}$), which is the frame rate of the front buffer of VSync, and target FPS (referred to as $Target\_FPS$), the agent takes action to maximize reward, which in our case is to achieve the target FPS along with the best PPDW value. Once the training is complete based on the states and action values, the agent selects the desired operating frequencies ($f_{desired}^{CM}$, where $M \in$ 1, 2, ...m) for the respective PE clusters and the *maxfreq* (maximum operating frequency) of each cluster is set to that desired operating frequency in order to achieve the target FPS and best PPDW for that FPS. Setting the *maxfreq* provides the flexibility for the PEs to operate within the range of maximum and minimum allowed operating frequencies.

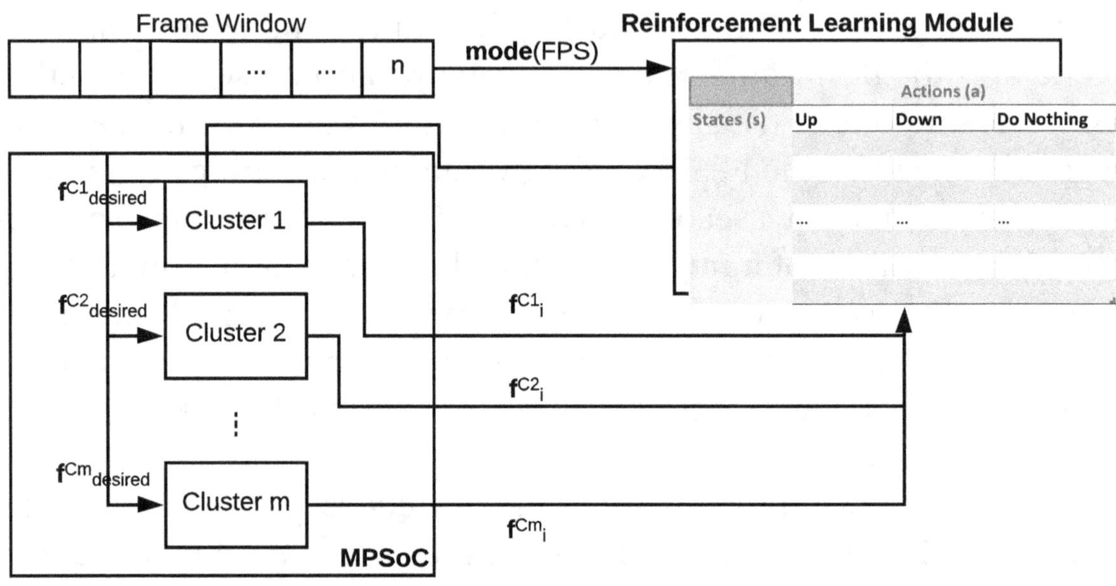

Figure 4.7: Block digram of Next agent

4.5.2 Online Reinforcement Learning

Next is modeled to follow Q-Learning of reinforcement learning (RL) [Watkins and Dayan, 1992]. RL agent defines an environment (ϵ), in which the agent observes the state (s_i) at a time instance i and performs an action (a_i), and receives a reward (r_i) for that instance. At every time instance (i^{th}), the agent chooses an action a_i from a predefined list of actions with $a_i \in 1, 2, ...K$, where K is the maximum number of actions allowed for a given state. Following the action at time i any changes are perceived in the ϵ are observed at time $i+1$, when the state of ϵ changes to s_{i+1}.

For our use case, if there are m number of PE clusters then for each cluster we would obtain 3 actions: Frequency up, frequency down, do nothing. Here, we are under the assumption that each cluster of PEs only allow cluster wise DVFS (operating frequency is allowed for the cluster and not individual PEs). In this applicative case, we have 3 PE clusters on Exynos 9810 MPSoC and hence, there are 9 actions: big frequency up, big frequency down, do not change big frequency, LITTLE frequency up, LITTLE frequency down, do not change LITTLE frequency, GPU frequency up, GPU frequency down & do not change GPU frequency. It should be noted that setting operating frequency (up, down and do nothing) means to set the *maxfreq* of the respective PE (big, LITTLE, GPU) to that operating frequency. Setting the *maxfreq* to a particular value also means that the frequency is free to operate between the minimum allowed frequency (*minfreq*) of the PE cluster and the set *maxfreq*. In Next, the environment ϵ is defined by the states such as frame rate, power consumption and peak temperature of the Edge device running an application. For our Next implementation on Exynos 9810 MPSoC the following states are chosen as input: big_CPU_{freq}, $LITTLE\_CPU_{freq}$, GPU_{freq}, $FPS_{current}$, $Target\_FPS$, $Power_{current}$, $Temperature_{big}$ and $Temperature_{device}$[2]. Here, the value of $Target\_FPS$ is the mode of FPS values achieved from the *frame window*. Next is invoked every 100 ms to record the states and take actions.

The goal of the RL agent is to maximize reward r_i in the future. The propagation of information from the future is discounted by a γ factor at every time step such that: $r_i = \sum_i^{i+n} \gamma_i r_i$ in order to dampen the rewards' effect on the agent's choice of action. For every time step the probability that the agent chooses an action at a given state is defined by a policy function. In this policy, the function which maximizes the agent's long term reward generation is called action-value function, which is defined by $Q(s_i, a_i)$ as shown in Eq. 4.5.

---

[2] $Temperature_{big}$ is the temperature of the big CPU cluster, whereas, $Temperature_{device}$ is the temperature of the overall device consisting of temperature of the battery and MPSoC, which could be captured from the device.

$$Q(s_i, a_i) = Q(s_i, a_i) + \alpha(r_i - Q(s_i, a_i) + \gamma max_a Q(s_{i+1}, a)) \tag{4.5}$$

In Eq. 4.5, α is the learning rate at which the agent learns new information. We have to keep in mind that the optimal action-value function could be obtained by iteratively updating $Q(s_i, a_i)$ in Eq. 4.5. Now, to maximize the reward generation we require a *reward function* ($R(s_i, a_i)$). For our *reward function* we use the Eq. 4.1 such that $R(s_i, a_i) = PPDW_i$. The agent's goal is to maximize reward, which means the agent has to optimize *PPDW* according to Eq. 4.4 and achieve $FPS_{current} = Target\_FPS$. The max reward generation could be represented using the following equation:

$$max\ R(s_i, a_i) = max(PPDW_i),$$

$$where \tag{4.6}$$

$$max(PPDW_i) = PPDW_{best} \geq PPDW_i > PPDW_{worst}$$

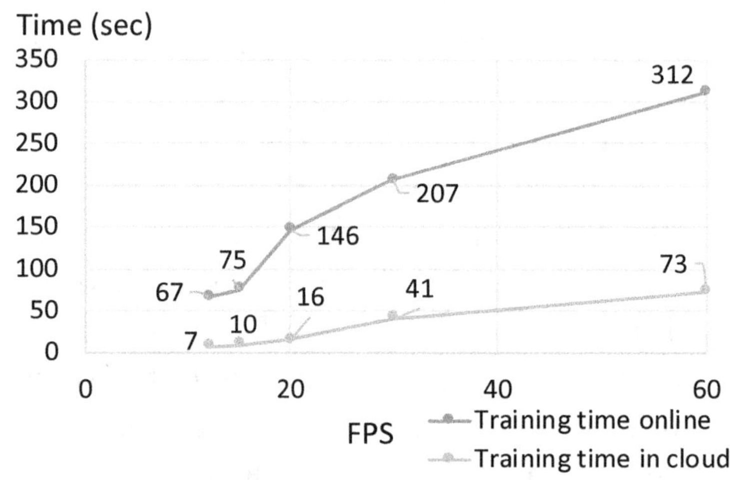

Figure 4.8: Increase in training time for online vs cloud (offline) as the frame rate increases at part of the chosen states

For each application the training needs to be performed in order for the agent to make a learned decision when the application is executed by referring to the action-values. It should be kept in mind that if we consider all the possible value of frame rates (FPS 0 to 60) as part of the states and reward generation as mentioned above then the training time would be significant and hence quantizing the frame rate would be desirable for improved training time. Data series for *Training time online* in Fig. 4.8 shows the increase in average training time required for different frame rates for each application on the device. If we choose 60 frame rate then no quantization is required since that is the highest frame rate at 60 Hz refresh rate, whereas, for other frame rates we quantize the frame rate range. In our experimentation, choosing 30 frame rate results in the best training period on the Note 9 device. Since, through empirical data the average training period lasts around 3 minutes 27 seconds for a new application, which has not been executed/trained before, the agent achieved the best reward (PPDW) for the amount of time spent in training. Due to the Next agent executing on LITTLE CPU, the average power consumption during the training time does not exceed more than 6% of the average power consumption while executing the mobile application in general. The training for every newly executing application is only performed once and the Q-table (action-value) results are stored on the memory so that later when the application is executed again the agent is able to refer to the Q-table to set the correct frequency of different clusters (CPU/GPU). Given the training time is not significant compared to daily usage of mobile applications (4 hours 16 minutes), no offline training is required and the whole training could be performed on the device.

4.5.3 Offline training using Federated Learning or in Cloud

Given the fact that each Edge device manufacturers generally produce several different Edge device models, which are capable of executing similar mobile applications, a new type of machine learning called *federated learning* [Konečný et al., 2016] could be utilized to train the agent more effectively by leveraging the computational power of the cloud. The training data from the Edge devices are sent back to the cloud server where the training of the agent happens. Once the training is complete the learned data (action-values) is sent back to the Edge devices, and hence, reducing the need of wasting local computing resource of the Edge device for training. Since cloud is computationally more powerful, the training period could significantly reduce to few seconds instead of minutes. Data series for *Training time in cloud* in Fig. 4.8 shows the reduced training time for different frame rate while the training is performed in a cloud system having Intel Xeon E7-8860V3 processor (16 cores) with 64 GB DDR3 RAM. Although it should also be noted that there was a maximum communication (to- and fro-) overhead of 4 secs between the device and the cloud system.

4.6   Experimental Results

4.6.1   Experimental setup

In this section, we compare the proposed Next methodology against the independent Linux CPU-GPU power management solution used in Android platforms by schedutil governor (we refer to it as *schedutil*) and QoS-aware power management methodology proposed by Pathania et al. [Pathania et al., 2014] (we refer to it as *Int. QoS PM*). Due to lack in manufacturer's support and vendor locking on Samsung Note 9 it was not possible to install additional libraries in the Android kernel to access performance counters. Moreover, such commercial devices also do not have a lot of hardware performance counters to save chip area, and hence, we were not able to compare Next with other state-of-the-art methodologies such as [Peters et al., 2016, Bhat et al., 2018], which mostly rely on performance counter values to optimize power consumption or thermal behaviour. To evaluate the efficacy of Next we chose different types of applications from Google Play store [goo,] to get a more holistic view on power saving and reduction of thermal behaviour for such applications. From the pool of most popular applications we chose the following to represent different types of apps that a user would normally use: Facebook, Spotify music app, Chrome web browser (referred to as *Web Browser*), Lineage 2 Revolution gaming app (referred to as *Lineage*), PubG Mobile gaming app (referred to as *PubG*) and Youtube video streaming app. All the applications were used between 1 minute 30 seconds to 5 minutes per session, which is the general usage pattern by users according to [res,], and the results reflect the average power consumption and peak temperature recorded during the sessions. For gaming applications (Lineage and PubG) each session lasted for 5 minutes, whereas, for other types of applications (Facebook, Spotify, Web Browser and Youtube) each session lasted between 1 minute 30 seconds to 3 minutes. For the results related to peak temperature observation, the experiments were all performed on the same day while the ambient temperature around the device was maintained around 21°C using controlled thermostat. All results for Next were observed when it was fully trained on the respective applications.

4.6.2 Power evaluation

Fig. 4.9 shows the average power consumption of Next, schedutil and Int. QoS PM for the chosen aforementioned applications. For Next approach the power savings for Facebook, Lineage, PubG, Spotify, Web Browser and Youtube compared to schedutil are 37.05%, 50.68%, 40.95%, 32.98%, 32.11% and 40.6% respectively. Since, Int. QoS PM is used for power management for mobile games and the methdology could not be extended to all applications, we could only evaluate the methodology for Lineage and PubG apps. The power savings of Int. QoS PM for Lineage and PubG compared to schedutil are 16.31% and 23.84% respectively, making Next more power efficient by 41.07% and 22.47% respectively for the gaming apps when compared to Int. QoS PM, proving the effectiveness of Next in terms of power saving over the state-of-the-art power management approach such as Int. QoS PM.

4.6.3 Thermal evaluation

Fig. 4.10 shows the average peak temperature of big CPU cluster and the Samsung Note 9 device in general using schedutil, Next and Int.

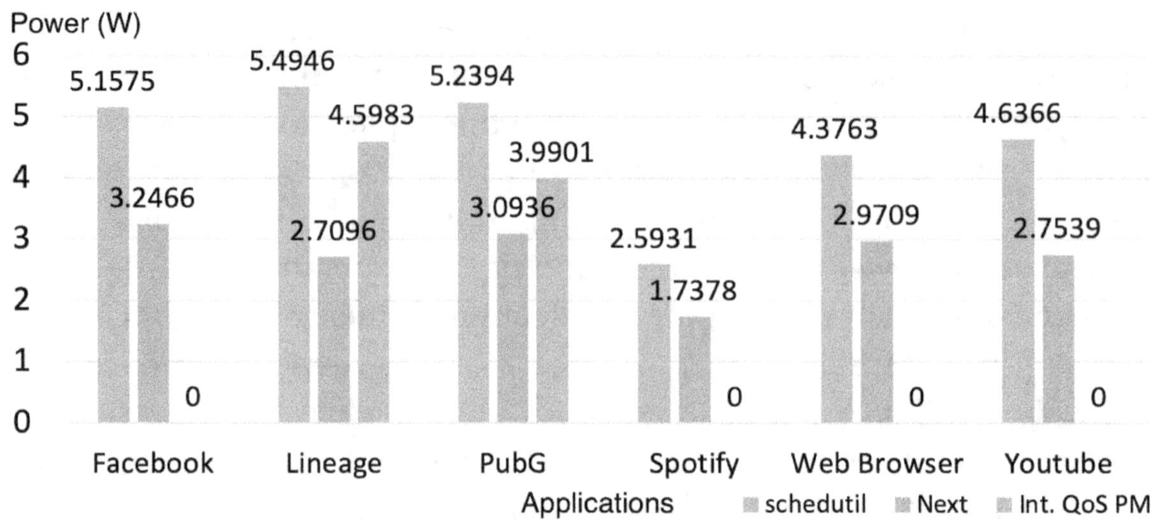

Figure 4.9: Average power consumption for different mobile applications using schedutil, Next and Int. QoS PM approaches

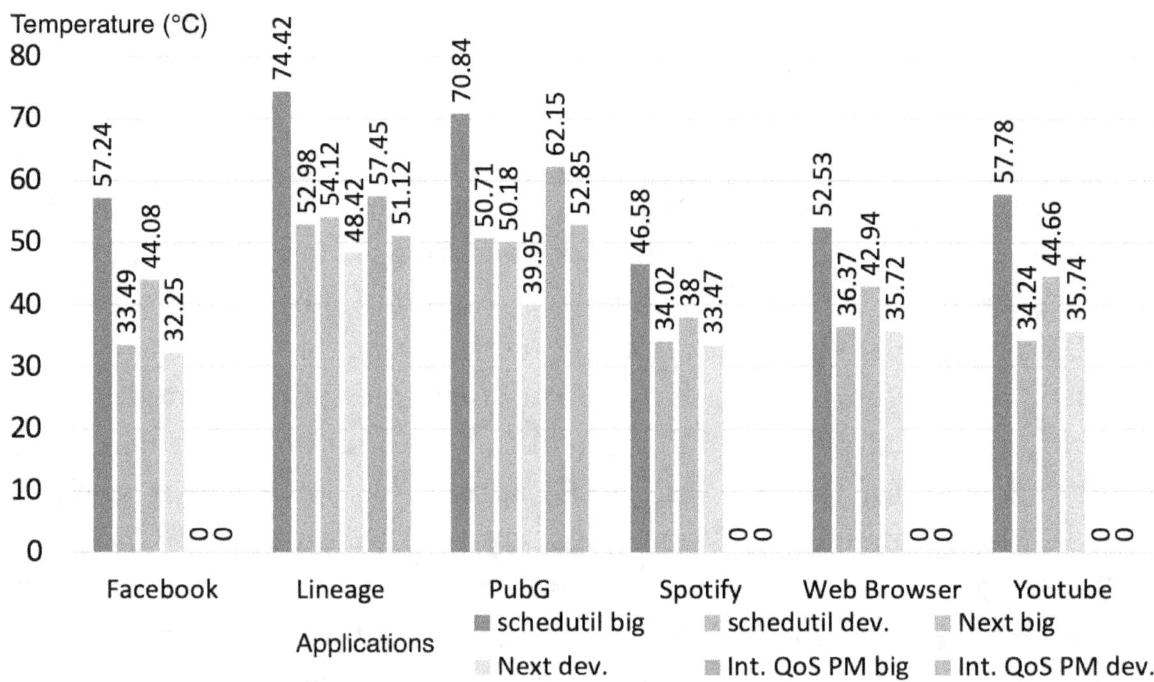

Figure 4.10: Average peak temperature of big CPUs and the device for different mobile applications using schedutil, Next and Int. QoS PM approaches

QoS PM. In the Fig. 4.10, *Int. QoS PM big* represents the average peak temperature of big CPU cluster using Int. QoS PM, *Int. QoS PM dev.* represents the average peak temperature of the device using Int. QoS PM, *Next big* represents the peak temperature of big CPU cluster using Next, *Next dev.* represents the peak temperature of the device using Next, *schedutil big* represents the peak temperature of big CPU cluster using schedutil, and *schedutil dev.* represents the peak temperature of the device using schedutil. From the Fig. 4.10 it is evident that comparing the results against schedutil Next is capable of reducing peak temperature by 29.16% (maximum) for big CPUs and 21.21% (maximum) for the device in general, whereas Int. QoS PM is only able to reduce the peak temperature by maximum of 22.80% for big CPU cluster and maximum of 3.51% for the device. This proves the effectiveness of Next over schedutil and state-of-the-art Int. QoS PM for its ability to reduce peak temperature of big CPUs and overall device.

4.6.4   Analysis of power and thermal evaluation

It is important to keep in mind that the proposed Next methodology (as mentioned in Sec. 4.5.2) monitors the $Target\_FPS$, which is the mode of FPS values achieved during the user's interaction session while executing the respective apps, and then performs DVFS on CPUs and GPUs to achieve the $Target\_FPS$. As we can notice from our observations from Sec. 4.4, depending on the $Target\_FPS$, performing DVFS on CPUs and GPUs accordingly could lead to significant power saving and temperature reduction compared to the default schedutil governor. Thus, as seen in Sec. 4.6.2 and 4.6.3, the proposed Next methodology was able to achieve impressive power and temperature reduction.

4.6.5   Overhead analysis

From our empirical data, we noticed that the maximum overhead required for computation by the Next agent is around 227 ns on an average, which is computed over a session lasting for at least 5 minutes.

4.7 Scalability of Next across MPSoC platforms

To show the efficacy and scalability of the Next agent we implemented the software agent in the Odroid XU4 development platform with slight modifications since, the provided Odroid XU4 experimental device didn't have a touch screen display, and performed a comparative study with the state-of-the-art approaches. More details on Odroid XU4 and the associated modifications of the Next method are as follows.

4.7.1 Hardware & Software Infrastructure

We utilized the Odroid XU4 development platform, which employs the Exynos 5422 MPSoC as described in Chapter 3, Sec. 3.8.1. The Exynos 5422 MPSoC comes equipped with a GPU cluster, called Mali-T628 MP6 GPU, consisting of 6 shader cores and has seven frequency scaling level as follows: 600, 543, 480, 420, 350, 266, 177 MHz respectively. On Exynos 5422 the 4 ARM Cortex-A15 (big) CPU cores have individual temperature sensors on them. In our experiments, we only observed the peak temperature of the 4 big CPUs.

The Odroid XU4 was running on UbuntuMate version 14.04 (Linux Odroid Kernel: 3.10.105) and executing the performance governor. During the time of implementing and conducting our experiments the average ambient temperature of the room was 21°C.

4.7.2 Modification of Next for Odroid XU4

We modified Eq. 4.1 to incorporate performance of all types of applications, not just FPS based ones, and the modified equation for $PPDW$ as shown in Eq. 4.7, where $Perf_i$ is the performance of the executing application at a given time period. All the states and actions taken, as mentioned in Sec. 4.5.2, during the exploration by the agent remains the same.

$$PPDW_i = \frac{Perf_i}{\Delta T \times P_i}, \text{where } \Delta T = T_i - T_a \qquad (4.7)$$

The objective is to maximize $PPDW_i$ such that $PPDW_{desired}$ is achieved. In Eq. 4.8, $Perf_{desired}$, $P_{desired}$ and $T_{desired}$ are the desired performance, desired power and desired peak temperature of the system while executing an application.

$$PPDW_{desired} = \frac{Perf_{desired}}{\Delta T \times P_{desired}}, \text{where } \Delta T = T_{desired} - T_a \qquad (4.8)$$

4.7.3 Experimental applications

To evaluate the efficacy of Next we modified some of the existing popular applications, which mimics mixed workload as utilized by users, such that the agent is capable of recording the performance output during the profiling step. The following applications were chosen for the experimental evaluation:

Face detection: Face detection using Haar-cascade [Soo, 2014] is utilized where faces are detected based on the presence of Haar features in the video image frame. This application is denoted as *face.*

YOLO object detection: Object detection using You Only Look Once (YOLO) approach [Redmon et al., 2016] is utilized where objects are detected based on different regions in the video image frame. This application is denoted as *yolo.*

Video rendering: Video rendering program is utilized, where each video image frame is converted to gray-scale image and then the text, "Hello, World!" is rendered on top of the video image frame to be shown as output. This application is denoted as *render.*

On-device streaming: A video streaming application is utilized, where the video is streamed from the on-device storage. This application is denoted as *stream.*

Traffic sign detection: An application to detect traffic signs using Haar-cascade [Kalafatić et al.,] is utilized, where Haar features for traffic signs are being detected. This application is denoted as *traffic.*

MobileNet object classification: An application to classify dogs and cats in video image frames using MobileNet CNN model [Howard et al., 2017] is utilized. This application is denoted as *classify*.

For the aforementioned applications, since all of them are computer vision based, we chose frames per second (FPS) to be the performance output. Since, Odroid XU4 doesn't come with an in-built touch-screen such that the user's behaviour could be observed by the Next agent, we fixed the $Perf_{desried}$ value for the PPDW equation (Eq. 4.8). In our experiments, we have chosen the desired FPS/performance ($Perf_{desried}$) to be 60 for *face, yolo, render, stream, traffic & classify* applications.

Additional benchmark applications: Since, benchmark applications from PARSEC and SPLASH-2 benchmark suits don't allow to observe the intermediate performance (execution time) of the application while executing without the use of performance counter, we executed blackscholes (denoted as blks.) from PARSEC, streamcluster (denoted as strm.) from PARSEC [Bienia, 2011b] and fft from Splash-2 [Woo et al., 1995b] 216 times. The minimum execution time out of 216 executions of the respective benchmark application (228.18 secs for blks., 368.15 secs for strm.& 12.58 secs for fft) is chosen as the $Perf_{desried}$ for that application. We chose to perform such experimentation to prove the scalability and efficacy of Next across different types of applications and not just for computer vision based applications on the Odroid XU4.

Exploration sessions for face, yolo, render, stream, traffic & classify applications for Next were 5 minutes, whereas, blks., strm. and fft were executed for their execution lifespan for Next and Next_Mod to explore. **Note**: Since, we have chosen the minimum (best) execution time for the additional benchmark applications and given the fact that the media based benchmark applications such as face, yolo, render, stream, traffic and classify don't have a specific execution time since they are continuously executing, the power consumption here is equivalent to the energy consumption (energy = power × execution time) for executing the respective applications since the execution time is constant here.

4.7.4 Experimental results and Comparative study

We evaluated Next while executing each of the aforementioned experimental applications and we show the average power consumption of the MPSoC and the average peak temperature of the big CPUs. We chose to observe the peak temperature of big CPUs since they tend to be the hottest hot spot in the MPSoC [Iranfar et al., 2018]. We also evaluated the average power consumption of the MPSoC and the average peak temperature of big CPUs achieved by the performance governor (denoted as performance), interactive governor (denoted as interactive) of Linux and the state-of-the-art approaches as proposed in [Reddy et al., 2017] and [Dey et al., 2019e]. In [Reddy et al., 2017], the study perform thread-to-core mapping and DVFS on the cores to workloads that are classified based on a metric, Memory Reads Per Instruction (MRPI) and we denote this methodology as MRPI. In [Dey et al., 2019e], the study perform DVFS on processing elements based on the desired reward, which is chosen to be reduced power consumption on the device in our case, and we denote this methodology as RewardProfiler.

Fig. 4.11 shows the average power consumption of the device (see Fig. 4.11.(a)) and the average peak temperature of big CPUs (see Fig. 4.11.(b)) while executing the aforementioned benchmark applications using different DVFS approaches: performance, interactive, MRPI, RewardProfiler and Next. It could be noticed that Next outperforms performance, interactive, MRPI and RewardProfiler for applications such as face, yolo, render, stream, traffic and classify. Interestingly, although Next outperforms performance and interactive governors for blks. strm., and fft applications, however, MRPI and RewardProfiler outperforms Next in some of the cases.

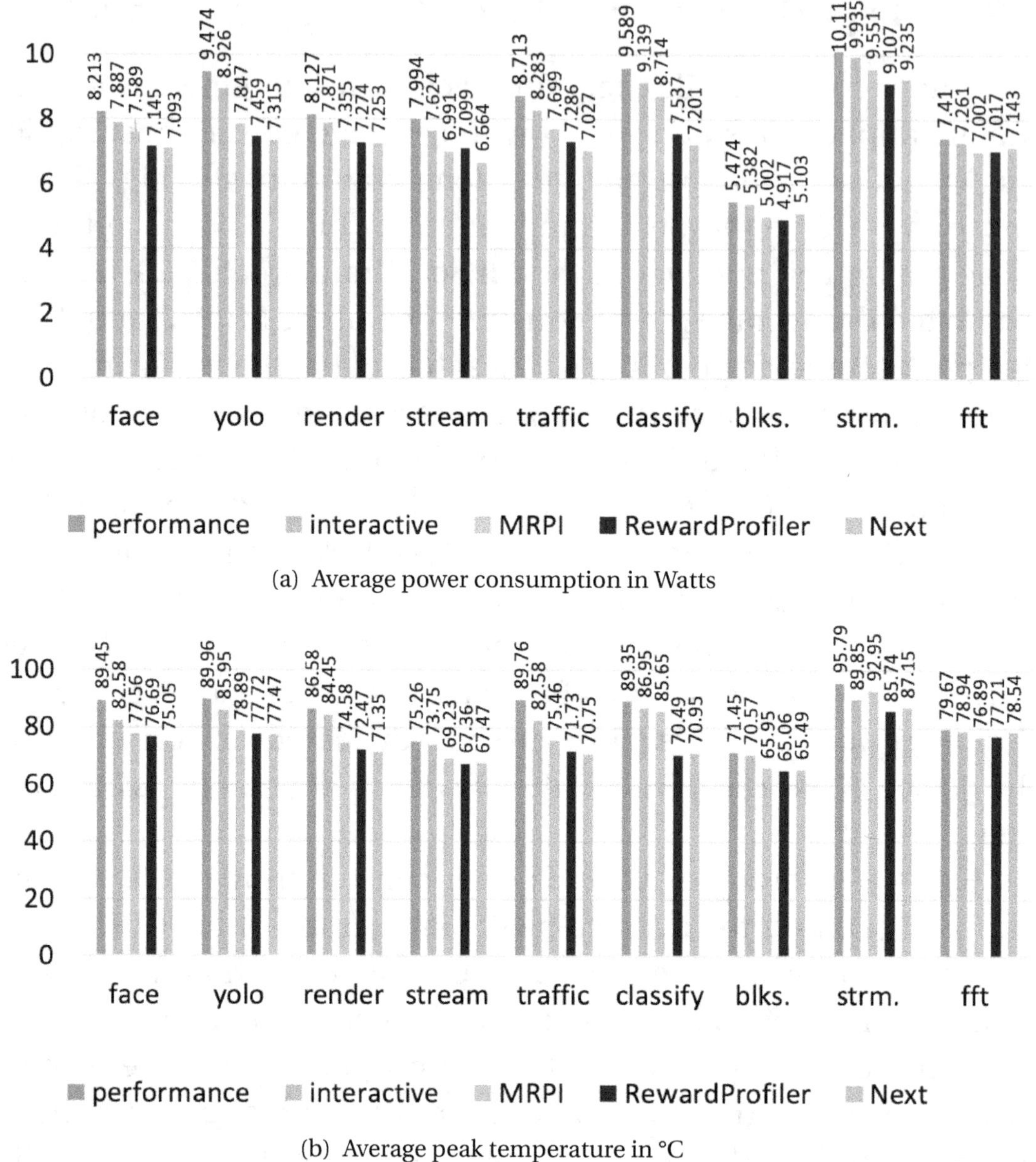

(a) Average power consumption in Watts

(b) Average peak temperature in °C

Figure 4.11: Average power consumption (Watts) and average peak temperature (°C) on Odroid XU4 (Exynos 5422 MPSoC) while executing different applications on different methodologies: performance, interactive, MRPI, RewardProfiler & Next

4.8   Discussion

Delayed RL approaches such as Q-Learning the agent must explore the dynamic system (dynamic environment) long enough to find the optimal outcome [John, 1994]. Although delayed RL approaches are good to optimize power consumption and temperature of the system in an application agnostic manner, however, often times given the number of actions (actions to perform DVFS on CPU, GPU) if the agent is not allowed to explore long enough in the dynamic environment then the agent will result in sub-optimal power consumption. The execution time of blks., strms. and fft applications were not long enough for the Next agent to explore the environment long enough to find the optimal power consumption and optimal peak temperature, and henceforth, for such applications the Next could be outperformed. Therefore, for applications with shorter execution time it could be a better approach to profile such applications specifically to observe the optimal operating frequency level of the CPU and GPU to achieve close to optimal power consumption.

Moreover, Next approach doesn't consider DVFS on RAM along side CPU and GPU, which has even higher opportunity to optimize power consumption and temperature of the device. This calls for an approach that is capable of performing DVFS on CPU, GPU and RAM together to cater the performance requirement of the executing application while consuming less power and thermal behaviour on the device.

4.9   Summary

In this chapter, we have proposed a power and thermal efficiency agent for mobile MPSoC platforms based on reinforcement learning, which maximizes performance while reducing power consumption and temperature of the mobile applications depending on the user's interaction with the display/UI and the desired QoS. Experimental evaluation on real hardware platforms shows the efficacy of the proposed approach along with its improvement over the state-of-the-art power and thermal management scheme.

In the next chapter, to explore DVFS on CPU, GPU and RAM together to optimize power consumption and thermal behaviour while catering for performance requirements of executing applications, we propose a novel methodology to achieve the same while also performing study on different processing elements (CPU, GPU, RAM) to observe their effect on different applications.

Chapter 5

Performing DVFS on CPU, GPU and RAM

In the Chapter 4, we presented a methodology, which caters for Quality of Service while being power and thermal efficient by performing DVFS on CPU and GPU in a mobile MPSoC. However, most popular smartphones come equipped with MPSoC that allows DVFS) on CPU, GPU and RAM (memory). We have noticed that based on some types of programs, especially memory intensive ones, DVFS on RAM could affect a significant portion of the total power consumption. Therefore, in this chapter, we propose a novel approach to perform DVFS on CPU, GPU and RAM in a mobile MPSoC, which caters for the performance requirement of the executing application while consuming low power.

5.1 Prologue to Third Contributory Chapter

This contributory chapter is based on the following articles along with my personal contribution to these articles.

5.1.1 Article Details

1. **Somdip Dey**, Sangeet Saha, Xiaohang Wang, Amit Kumar Singh and Klaus McDonald-Maier, "RewardProfiler: A Reward Based

Design Space Profiler on DVFS Enabled MPSoCs", 5th IEEE International Conference on Edge Computing and Scalable Cloud (IEEE EdgeCom), 2019.

2. **Somdip Dey**, Samuel Isuwa, Suman Saha, Amit Kumar Singh, and Klaus McDonald-Maier. "CPU- GPU-Memory DVFS for Power-Efficient Mobile MPSoC" in Future Internet.

Personal Contribution In The Articles: Conceptualization, methodology, and experimental software design was done by Somdip Dey. Validation of the research outcome was performed by Somdip Dey and Amit Singh while formal analysis was done by Somdip Dey. Investigation, resources gathering and data curation was performed by Somdip Dey along with the initial draft paper writing. Paper was reviewed by Somdip Dey, Amit Singh, Samuel Isuwa, Sangeet Saha, Xiaohang Wang and Klaus McDonald-Maier. Visualization of data was also done by Somdip Dey.

5.1.2 Media coverage

Given the popularity of the proposed methodology in this article, it is covered by media (news) outlets as follows.

* *"Effect of Different Frequency Scaling Levels on Memory in Regard to Total Power Consumption in Mobile MPSoC"*, Semiconductor Engineering. Article link

5.2 Introduction & Motivation

In Chapter 1, Sec. 1.1, we have already noticed that DVFS on RAM (denoted as memory only) could play a significant role in the overall reduction in power consumption (see Fig. 1.1 in Sec. 1.1). There has been a series of published studies to perform DVFS on CPU or

GPU or memory separately or combination of two of these components [Pathania et al., 2014, Isuwa et al., 2019, Dey et al., 2019a, Hsieh et al., 2015, Dey et al., 2020], however, to the best of our knowledge there hasn't been any study to perform DVFS on CPU, GPU and memory together in order to optimize performance and power consumption of executing applications in mobile MPSoC. Moreover, it is quite attractive to employ methods such as Reinforcement Learning (RL) to perform CPU/GPU/Memory DVFS since such methods could be application agnostic. However, for dynamic applications where the CPU, GPU and Memory usage vary dynamically, if RL methods are not allowed to explore the system long enough then the achieved power consumption could be sub-optimal [John, 1994]. We utilized the Next method (denoted as *Next (CPU-GPU)*) in Chapter 4 to perform CPU-GPU DVFS and extended the method to perform CPU-GPU-Memory DVFS (denoted as *Next_Mod (CPU-GPU-RAM)*) to compare the power consumption with our proposed method, denoted as *CGM-DVFS*, to perform CPU-GPU-Memory DVFS. Fig. 5.1 shows the average power consumption in Watts on the Odroid XU4 development platform [odr, b], employing Exynos 5422 MPSoC [exy, a], while executing different benchmark applications on different approaches. The benchmark applications are object detection using YOLO (*yolo*) [Redmon et al., 2016], blackscholes from PARSEC [Bienia, 2011b] and fft from Splash-2 [Woo et al., 1995b]. From Fig 5.1, it is evident that application agnostic approaches to perform DVFS on CPU-GPU-Memory might not lead to close to optimal power consumption and henceforth, makes DVFS on CPU, GPU & Memory in mobile MPSoCs more challenging.

5.2.1 Contributions

In this chapter, we study the effect of DVFS on memory towards the total power consumption in the mobile MPSoC for different types of applications and we also propose a novel approach, called *CGM-DVFS* (**CPU-GPU-Memory DVFS**), to perform DVFS on CPU (big and LITTLE), GPU and memory in mobile MPSoC to cater for the performance

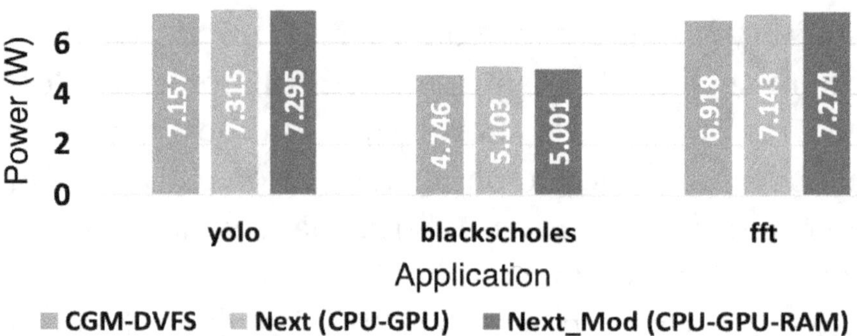

Figure 5.1: Average power consumption (Watts) while executing different benchmark applications on different approaches

requirement of the executing application while consuming the least power. To this extent the concrete contribution of this chapter are as follows.

1. Study the effect of DVFS on memory towards the total power consumption and performance of executing applications in a mobile MPSoC.

2. Propose a novel approach - CGM-DVFS - to perform DVFS on CPU-GPU-Memory in the mobile MPSoC to cater for performance requirements of executing applications while consuming least power.

3. Experimental evaluation of CGM-DVFS on a real hardware platform, Odroid XU4, and comparative study between CGM-DVFS and state-of-the-art approaches to optimize power consumption.

4. Performed a comparative study and analysis between CGM-DVFS and state-of-the-art delayed Reinforcement Learning approaches to show CGM-DVFS is better suited to achieve close ot optimal power consumption.

The rest of the chapter is organized as follows. In Sec. 5.3, we show the effect of DVFS on memory using different applications. Sec. 5.4

defines the problem formulation along with the hardware and software infrastructure used. In Sec. 5.5, we explain the proposed method, CGM-DVFS and in Sec. 5.6, we show the efficacy of CGM-DVFS via experimental evaluation. Finally, Sec. 5.7 discusses the future scope of this research and Sec. 5.8 summarizes the chapter.

5.3 Motivational Case Study: Effect of DVFS on memory

To observe the effect of DVFS on memory towards the total power consumption and performance of different types of executing applications in the mobile MPSoC, we choose benchmark applications from PARSEC [Bienia, 2011b], Whetstone [web, , Longbottom, 2005] and Splash-2 [Woo et al., 1995b] benchmark suits as well as RSA encryption [Rivest et al., 1983] and streaming Youtube videos in Chromium browser. Given the fact that streaming video on Youtube is one of the most popular application/workload on a mobile device [mos,], we chose this workload along with other benchmark applications. Due to the popularity of RSA encryption for key exchange [Thakkar, 2020] in most of the secured applications, we have chosen to perform RSA for 512, 1024, 2048 and 4096 bits encryption and observe the effect of DVFS on memory. Based on the parallelization, size of working set and data usage of the different types of benchmark applications from PARSEC and Splash-2, the applications (workload) were segregated into three types [Dey et al., 2019c]: Compute Intensive (denoted as Compute), Memory Intensive (denoted as Memory) & Mixed Workload (denoted as Mixed), where the workload is both compute and memory intensive. Table 5.1 shows the abbreviations of the different types of benchmark applications for our study on the effect of DVFS on memory. Note: Given the compute and memory intensive nature of RSA encryption and Youtube video streaming based on Chapter 3 [Dey et al., 2019c], both the applications are also considered to be Mixed workload.

Table 5.1: Abbreviation of different types of benchmark applications

Benchmark Applications

Type	Name (execution option)	Abbreviation
Compute	Whetstone	wht.
Compute	blackscholes (native)	blks.
Memory	x264 (simlarge)	x264
Memory	dedup (simlarge)	ded.
Memory	canneal (simlarge)	cann.
Mixed	FFT (simlarge)	fft
Mixed	facesim (simlarge)	fsim.
Mixed	streamcluster (native)	strm.
Mixed	Youtube in Chromium browser	ytub.
Mixed	RSA	rsa

In Odroid XU4, there are nine available operating frequencies for memory and we chose the highest (825 MHz), the middle (413 MHz) and the lowest (138 MHz) operating frequency levels to observe the effect of DVFS on power consumption and performance (execution time) of the executing benchmark applications mentioned in Table 5.1. We executed the benchmark applications five times on the aforementioned three operating frequencies of the memory and observed the average power consumption and performance (execution time), which are shown in Table 5.2. We also observed the power consumption for the aforementioned three operating frequencies of the memory while the system was idle (only executing background processes of the OS), which is also denoted as idle, running on Linux performance governor. This serves as a baseline to evaluate the effect of DVFS on memory in an idle Odroid XU4 system running on performance governor. From Table 5.2 we can notice that DVFS on memory can improve the power saving by 26.571% based on the type of application being executed.

In order to understand the tradeoff of power saving by performing DVFS on memory we need to observe other metrics such as Instruction per Cycle (IPC) and CPU utilization, which can be adversely affected by the memory. IPC is a performance metric used to evaluate the efficiency of a computer processor by measuring the average number of

Table 5.2: Power consumption (P. max) of different benchmark applications (App) while executing the App on maximum operating frequency of the memory. *P. middle* (%) and *P. min* (%) are the improvement in power saving while executing the App on the middle operating frequency and minimum operating frequency respectively. *Perf. middle* (%) and *Perf. min* (%) are the loss in performance for executing the App on the middle operating frequency and minimum operating frequency respectively.

App	P. max (W)	P. middle (%)	P. min (%)	Perf. middle (%)	Perf. min (%)
idle	3.313	5.192	5.886	-	-
wht.	3.556	4.415	5.202	-2.121	-3.638
blks.	5.474	5.298	9.81	-2.483	-7.823
x264	8.748	13.649	20.085	-6.486	-16.993
ded.	7.893	11.136	18.282	-7.674	-14.598
cann.	7.919	10.317	16.782	-7.847	-12.773
fft	7.41	4.575	14.008	-2.939	-15.834
fsim.	5.378	4.574	9.967	-3.475	-7.558
strm.	10.11	1.952	**26.571**	-2.116	**-29.374**
ytub.	7.014	1.725	7.214	-	-
rsa	6.119	1.994	4.935	-1.032	-1.894

instructions executed by the CPU for each clock cycle [Patterson and Hennessy, 2013]. A higher IPC indicates a more efficient processor, as it can execute more instructions in a given time period. The IPC is determined by the CPU architecture, the instruction set, and the software being executed. CPU utilization represents the percentage of time the CPU spends actively executing tasks as opposed to being idle [Eranian, 2008]. It indicates how much of the CPU's capacity is being used during a specific time period. A high CPU utilization value can indicate that the CPU is working at or near its capacity, while a low value indicates that the CPU has more available capacity to handle additional tasks [Ravindran et al., 2001]. Memory reads can significantly affect IPC because they often introduce latency due to the time it takes to access data from memory. When a CPU needs to fetch data from memory, it may have to wait for several clock cycles until the data is retrieved, effectively stalling the pipeline and reducing the overall IPC during that period. Similarly, CPU utilization value can also be affected by memory reads due to the time it takes to access data from memory, which can lead to waiting periods (stalls) in the CPU pipeline. As performing DVFS on memory affects the read/write operations on the memory, thus, it is important for us to observe the effect on IPC and CPU utilization while performing DVFS on memory.

Table 5.3: IPC and CPU utilization (referred to as CPU Utilized) for three different types of executing applications - strm. (mixed workload), blks. (compute intensive) & x264 (memory intensive) while running on the highest operating frequency (denoted as *Max*), the middle operating frequency (denoted as *Middle*) & the lowest operating frequency (denoted as *Min*) of memory

strm.	Max	Middle	Min
IPC	0.64	0.52	0.23
CPU Utilized	1.000	1.000	1.000

blks.	Max	Middle	Min
IPC	1.21	1.11	0.77
CPU Utilized	0.730	0.765	0.882

x264	Max	Middle	Min
IPC	1.75	1.6	1.06
CPU Utilized	1.002	1.003	1.005

The "perf" tool in Linux is a powerful utility that provides various performance counters and insights into the functioning of the CPU and other hardware components [Eranian, 2008]. It allows users to monitor and analyze performance metrics such as IPC and CPU utilization [Weaver, 2013]. Since, *strm.* application achieved the most power saving because of DVFS on memory, as shown in Table 5.2, the IPC and CPU utilization of the application were recorded while being executed on the highest, the middle and the lowest frequency of the memory to understand the effect of memory DVFS on the performance of executing such applications. The IPC and CPU utilization for blks. and x264 applications were also recorded, so, that we can observe the IPC and

CPU utilization for different types of application to get a holistic understanding of how these metrics could be affected by memory DVFS for different applications. Keep in mind, IPC and CPU utilization for the different types of application were observed while running on Linux performance governor.

Table 5.3 shows the different IPC and CPU utilization (referred to as CPU Utilized) values for three different types of executing applications - strm. (mixed workload), blks. (compute intensive) & x264 (memory intensive) while running on the highest operating frequency (denoted as *Max*), the middle operating frequency (denoted as *Middle*) & the lowest operating frequency (denoted as *Min*) of memory. From Table 5.3 we can observe that while executing a mixed workload such as strm. the IPC value dropped drastically by performing DVFS on memory, however, CPU utilization didn't change. The drop in IPC value for strm. application running on the lowest operating frequency of the memory coincides with the loss in performance as shown in Table 5.2. Another interesting observation from Table 5.3 is that while executing compute intensive workload such as blks. at different operating frequency of the memory, CPU utilization value went up while the IPC value went down on lower operating frequency of memory. The same observation is also made while running a memory intensive workload like x264. These observations show that as the operating frequency of the memory are scaled on performance governor CPUs compensate for memory running at lower frequency.

Anyhow, from Table 5.2 it is quite evident that there is a scope of saving more power consumption by performing DVFS on memory, and hence, this calls for an approach that is capable of performing DVFS on CPU, GPU and memory to cater for performance requirement of the executing application while consuming the least power.

5.4   System model and problem formulation

In this section, we explore the specific system model being used for the research and define the problem formulation, which forms the foundation of the proposed method.

5.4.1 Hardware & Software Infrastructure

We chose Odroid XU4 [odr, b] development board, as mentioned in Chapter 4, Sec. 4.7.1, to implement our CPU-GPU-Memory DVFS. This MPSoC also supports DVFS enabled 2 GB RAM, which has the following nine frequency scaling levels: 825, 728, 633, 543, 413, 275, 206, 165 and 138 MHz respectively. Exynos 5422 MPSoC also has 5 temperature sensors, 4 of which are located on 4 big CPUs and 1 on the GPU.

The Odroid XU4 was running on UbuntuMate version 14.04 (Linux Odroid Kernel: 3.10.105) and executing the performance governor. During the time of implementing and conducting our experiments the average ambient temperature of the room was 21°C.

5.4.2 Problem formulation

Given: Let us consider a system that has a set of applications, $S_{App} = \{App_1, App_2, ... App_i\}$, where App_i is the ith application and App_i consists of a set of tasks, $S_{task} = \{tsk_1, tsk_2, ... tsk_i\}$, where S_{task} always generates a fixed performance output Prf_i for the fixed DVFS configuration values R_i while executing App_i on the system. Here, R_i consists of the combination of the DVFS values for big CPUs ($DVFS_{b_i}$), LITTLE CPUs ($DVFS_{L_i}$), GPUs ($DVFS_{g_i}$) and memory ($DVFS_{m_i}$) such that $R_i = < DVFS_{b_i}, DVFS_{L_i}, DVFS_{g_i}, DVFS_{m_i} >$ leads to a fixed performance output Prf_i. Now, if we consider $Prf_{desired}$ as the desired value of the performance output for the executing App_i.

Find: The desired DVFS configuration values ($R_{desired}$), which are the combination of the desired DVFS values for big CPUs ($DVFS_{b_{desired}}$), LITTLE CPUs ($DVFS_{L_{desired}}$), GPUs ($DVFS_{g_{desired}}$) and memory ($DVFS_{m_{desired}}$).

Subject to: Meeting the desired performance $Prf_{desired}$ while consuming the least power (P_{least}) during the execution of App_i on $R_{desired}$.

5.5 Proposed methodology: CGM-DVFS

In this section, we introduce our proposed approach, CGM-DVFS, in details.

5.5.1 Overview of CGM-DVFS

Fig. 5.2 illustrates the block-diagram of our proposed CGM-DVFS methodology. CGM-DVFS is not just an approach, but also an automated agent that sets the appropriate DVFS on CPU, GPU and memory to achieve the desired performance of the executing application while consuming least power. For each App_i in S_{App}, the profiling of App_i (this step is denoted as *Profiling*) is performed where for different combination of $DVFS_{b_i}$, $DVFS_{L_i}$, $DVFS_{g_i}$ and $DVFS_{m_i}$, the corresponding value of Prf_i, the corresponding peak temperature instance (T_i) and the corresponding power consumption (P_i) of the device are recorded and stored on disk storage memory. More on Profiling is provided in Sec. 5.5.2.1. From the set containing the profiled values of $S_{Prf} = \{Prf_1, Prf_2, ...Prf_i\}$, the desired performance $Prf_{desired}$ is searched based on the equation: $Prf_{desired} \in S_{Prf}$; where $Prf_i \geq Prf_{desired}$. Now, for all the possible values of Prf_i that are equal or greater than $Prf_{desired}$ from S_{Prf}, the agent searches for the value with the least power consumption such that $P_{least} = min(S_P)$; where $S_P = \{P_1, P_2, ...P_i\}$ ($P_1, P_2, ...P_i$ are the corresponding power consumption of $Prf_1, Prf_2, ...Prf_i$). The agent then fetches the associated $DVFS_{b_i}$, $DVFS_{L_i}$, $DVFS_{g_i}$ and $DVFS_{m_i}$ configuration (this step is denoted as *Fetch desired config*), and then the desired DVFS values of big CPUs ($DVFS_{b_{desired}}$), LITTLE CPUs ($DVFS_{L_{desired}}$), GPUs ($DVFS_{g_{desired}}$) and memory ($DVFS_{m_{desired}}$) are set to this configuration (this step is denoted as *Set desired DVFS*).

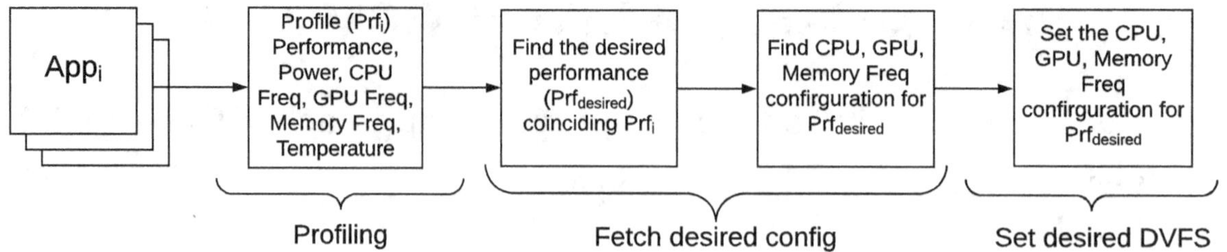

Figure 5.2: Block diagram illustrating CGM-DVFS Methodology

5.5.2 Steps in details

5.5.2.1 Profiling

In the profiling step, we utilize the concept of clustering performance for a range of DVFS as introduced in [Dey et al., 2019e], where it is proposed that for a group of DVFS values for the same processing element the performance outcome remains almost similar. For example, for App_i a set of consecutive DVFS values could lead to more or less the same performance output Prf_i and hence, instead of selecting each of these DVFS values during the design space exploration (Profiling) only one representative DVFS value from the set is selected and then profiled only for that value. In this way, the agent could reduce the number of configuration that it has to profile. Based on approximate computing we have clustered the different frequency scaling levels into major groups of varying numbers for different processing elements (CPU, GPU, memory).

For our experimental device, Odroid XU4, we chose the following DVFS configurations: 4 DVFS levels for big CPUs (2 GHz, 1.4 GHz, 0.8 GHz, 0.2 GHz); 4 DVFS levels for LITTLE CPUs (1.4 GHz, 1 GHz, 0.8 GHz, 0.2 GHz); 3 DVFS levels for GPUs (600 MHz, 420 MHz, 177 MHz) and 3 DVFS levels for memory (825 MHz, 413 MHz, 138 MHz). In [Dey et al., 2019e], the equation for the combined design point (CDP) is provided for a MPSoC, where DVFS capability is only considered in big CPUs, LITTLE CPUs and GPUs. Eq. 5.1 represents the equation governing CDP.

$$CDP = (\sum_{C=1}^{N} n_C \times f_C + \prod_{C=1}^{N} n_C \times f_C) \times f_{GPU},$$

$$where \ 1 \leq N \leq n_C$$

(5.1)

In Eq. 5.1, N is the number of clusters in the MPSoC, f_C is the number of frequency scaling levels for the whole cluster (we are only considering cluster wise DVFS capability), n_C is the number of cores in each cluster and f_{GPU} is the number of frequency scaling levels for the GPU, where we consider n_{GPU} is equal to 1 for Odroid XU4. In Eq. 5.1, the governing equation for CDP only works for DVFS enabled multi-core architecture, which means n_C and f_C is always more than 1. It could be inferred from the Eq. 5.1 that the number of clusters (N) present in the system is either less than or equal to the number of cores (n_C) present in each cluster. The reason to provide this constraint is because from design point of view it is more practical to have more number of cores on the die than the number of clusters due to die size constraint.

Since, in this chapter, we also consider DVFS in memory, the equation for CDP is modified to incorporate the operating frequency levels of memory as well and is represented in Eq. 5.2 based on Eq. 5.1. In Eq. 5.2, n_b and n_L represent the number of big CPUs and LITTLE CPUs respectively, whereas, f_b, f_L, f_{GPU}, f_{mem} represent the number of operating frequency levels for big CPUs, LITTLE CPUs, GPUs and memory respectively.

$$CDP = \{((n_b \times f_b) + (n_L \times f_L)) + (n_b \times f_b$$
$$\times n_L \times f_L)\} \times f_{GPU} \times f_{mem}$$

(5.2)

Since, in our chosen platform and methodology, DVFS in big and LITTLE CPUs happens cluster wise, the total number of reduced CDP for the aforementioned configuration, as per Eq. 5.2, is 216 ($\{\{((1 \times 4) + (1 \times 4)) + (1 \times 4 \times 1 \times 4)\} \times 3 \times 3$). The agent starts the profiling by selecting the maximum DVFS level for big, LITTLE CPUs, GPUs and memory, records the performance output, temperature and power consumption for that configuration and then selects the next lower DVFS level in the configuration to record the same. The agent uses a waterfall method where the DVFS levels are selected from high to low on big CPUs first, then on the LITTLE CPUs, then on the GPUs and then on the memory. From our empirical data we noticed that to profile accurately it is best to profile each of the reduced CDP every 100 milliseconds for 1 seconds and hence, the total number of profiling points become 2160 (216×10).

5.5.2.2   Fetch desired config & Set desired DVFS

Once all the 2160 profiling points are traversed and configurations are recorded, they are stored on the disk memory. These configurations will be used (as in Fetch desired config & Set desired DVFS) by the agent to find $Prf_{desired}$ for which the system consumes the least power (P_{least}) and set the DVFS values accordingly.

5.5.3   Justification of the design choices

In majority of commercial smartphones (mobile phones) utilizing MP-SoC, due to constraint in the display size, most consumers utilize one application at ay time period [Budiu, 2015]. Henceforth, we have considered profiling one application at a time to make the proposed method more commercially applicable. Moreover, in Chapter 4, Sec. 4.8 we already showed that for application agnostic approaches such as delayed Reinforcement Learning could lead to sub-optimal or worse power consumption than application specific profiling approaches such as CGM-DVFS. Additionally, since different DVFS configurations for dynamic applications (tasks) could lead to dynamic profiling output such as performance & power consumption, we invoke CGM-DVFS at random time period to update the profiling configurations and save them on the memory to perform *Fetch desired config & Set desired DVFS* steps.

5.6 Experimental results

5.6.1 Experimental applications

We chose the benchmark applications such as face, yolo, render, stream, traffic, classify, blks., strm. and fft as mentioned in Chapter 4, Sec. 4.7.3 to prove the efficacy of CGM-DVFS. In our experiments, we have chosen the desired FPS/performance ($Perf_{desried}$) to be 60 for *face, yolo, render, stream, traffic & classify* applications. We executed blks., strm. and fft 216 times (as per reduced CDP) such that each execution is performed on each configuration from the reduced CDP. The minimum execution time out of 216 executions of the respective benchmark application (228.18 secs for blks., 981.41 secs for strm. & 12.58 secs for fft) is chosen as the $Prf_{desried}$ for that application.

Since, we have chosen the minimum (best) execution time for the additional benchmark applications and given the fact that the media based benchmark applications such as face, yolo, render, stream, traffic and classify don't have a specific execution time since they are continuously executing, the power consumption here is equivalent to the energy consumption (energy = power × execution time) for executing the respective applications since the execution time is constant here.

5.6.2 Evaluation and Comparative study

We evaluated CGM-DVFS for each aforementioned experimental application fifteen times and we show the average power consumption of the MPSoC and the average peak temperature of the big CPUs. We chose to observe the peak temperature of big CPUs since they tend to be the hottest hot spot in the MPSoC [Iranfar et al., 2018]. We also evaluated the average power consumption of the MPSoC and the average peak temperature of big CPUs achieved by the performance governor (denoted as performance), interactive governor (denoted as interactive) and the state-of-the-art approaches as proposed in [Reddy et al., 2017], [Dey et al., 2019e] and Next, as described in Chapter 4, [Dey et al., 2020].

In [Reddy et al., 2017], the study performed thread-to-core mapping and DVFS on the cores to workloads that are classified based on a metric named Memory Reads Per Instruction (MRPI), and we denote this methodology as MRPI.

In [Dey et al., 2019e], the study performed DVFS on processing cores based on the desired reward, which is chosen to be reduced power consumption on the device in our case, and we denote this methodology as RewardProfiler. In Chapter 4 [Dey et al., 2020], we proposed *Next*, which performs DVFS on CPU and GPU based on the user interaction with the device using Q-Learning (Reinforcement Learning), where the reward function is Eq. 5.3, which is based on Eq. 5.4. We also denote this methodology as Next in our comparative study. In Eq. 5.3, the reward function tries to maximize the value of $PPDW$, which is a metric, *performance per degree watt*, incorporating performance (FPS_i), temperature (ΔT, where ΔT is the difference between the current temperature, T_i, and the ambient temperature, T_a) and power consumption (P_i) of the device. The agent in Next has the following states: big_CPU_{freq}, $LITTLE\_CPU_{freq}$, GPU_{freq}, $FPS_{current}$, $Target\_FPS$, $Power_{current}$, $Temperature_{big}$ and $Temperature_{device}$; where big_CPU_{freq} is the frequency of the big CPU, $LITTLE\_CPU_{freq}$ is the frequency of the LITTLE CPU, GPU_{freq} is the frequency of the GPU, $FPS_{current}$ is the current performance in terms of FPS, $Target\_FPS$ is the desired performance in terms of FPS, $Power_{current}$ is the current power consumption, and $Temperature_{big}$ and $Temperature_{device}$ are the temperature of the big CPU and the whole device consecutively. The actions performed by the Next agent are as follows: big frequency up, big frequency down, do not change big frequency, LITTLE frequency up, LITTLE frequency down, do not change LITTLE frequency, GPU frequency up, GPU frequency down & do not change GPU frequency. We modified Eq. 5.4 to incorporate performance of all types of applications, not just FPS based ones, and the modified equation for $PPDW$ is Eq. 5.5. Moreover, we also extended Next, as specified in Chapter 4, denoted as Next_Mod, to incorporate memory DVFS along with CPU and GPU such that we can draw a comparative study between Next and CGM-DVFS. In Next_Mod, the agent has a new state, RAM_{freq}, frequency of memory, and three more new actions: RAM frequency up, RAM frequency down, do not change RAM frequency. Both Next and Next_Mod are invoked every 100 ms. Exploration sessions for face, yolo, render, stream, traffic & classify applications for Next and Next_Mod were 5 minutes, whereas, blks., strm. and fft were executed for their execution lifespan for Next and Next_Mod to explore. [Reddy et al., 2017], [Dey et al., 2019e], [Dey et al., 2020] & Next_Mod were chosen for the comparative study because these methods perform DVFS on a combination of CPU, GPU, Memory or all.

$$max\ R(s_i, a_i) = max(PPDW_i),$$

$$\text{where} \qquad (5.3)$$

$$max(PPDW_i) = PPDW_{best} \geq PPDW_i > PPDW_{worst}$$

$$PPDW_i = \frac{FPS_i}{\Delta T \times P_i}, \text{where } \Delta T = T_i - T_a \qquad (5.4)$$

$$PPDW_i = \frac{Perf_i}{\Delta T \times P_i}, \text{where } \Delta T = T_i - T_a \qquad (5.5)$$

Fig. 5.3 shows the average power consumption of the device (see Fig. 5.3.(a)) and the average peak temperature of big CPUs (see Fig. 5.3.(b)) while executing the aforementioned benchmark applications using different DVFS methodologies: performance, interactive, MRPI, RewardProfiler, Next, Next_Mod & CGM-DVFS. Tables 5.4 and 5.5 show the improvement in power saving (%) and reduction of peak temperature (%) respectively of CGM-DVFS compared to performance, MRPI, RewardProfiler, interactive, Next & Next_Mod. Based on the tables CGM-DVFS is capable of saving 33.476% more power compared to performance governor, whereas, it is capable of saving 26.796% more power compared to the state-of-the-art approach, MRPI. On the other hand, CGM-DVFS is also capable of reducing the peak temperature of big CPUs by 25.567% compared to performance governor and by 21.238% compared to MRPI.

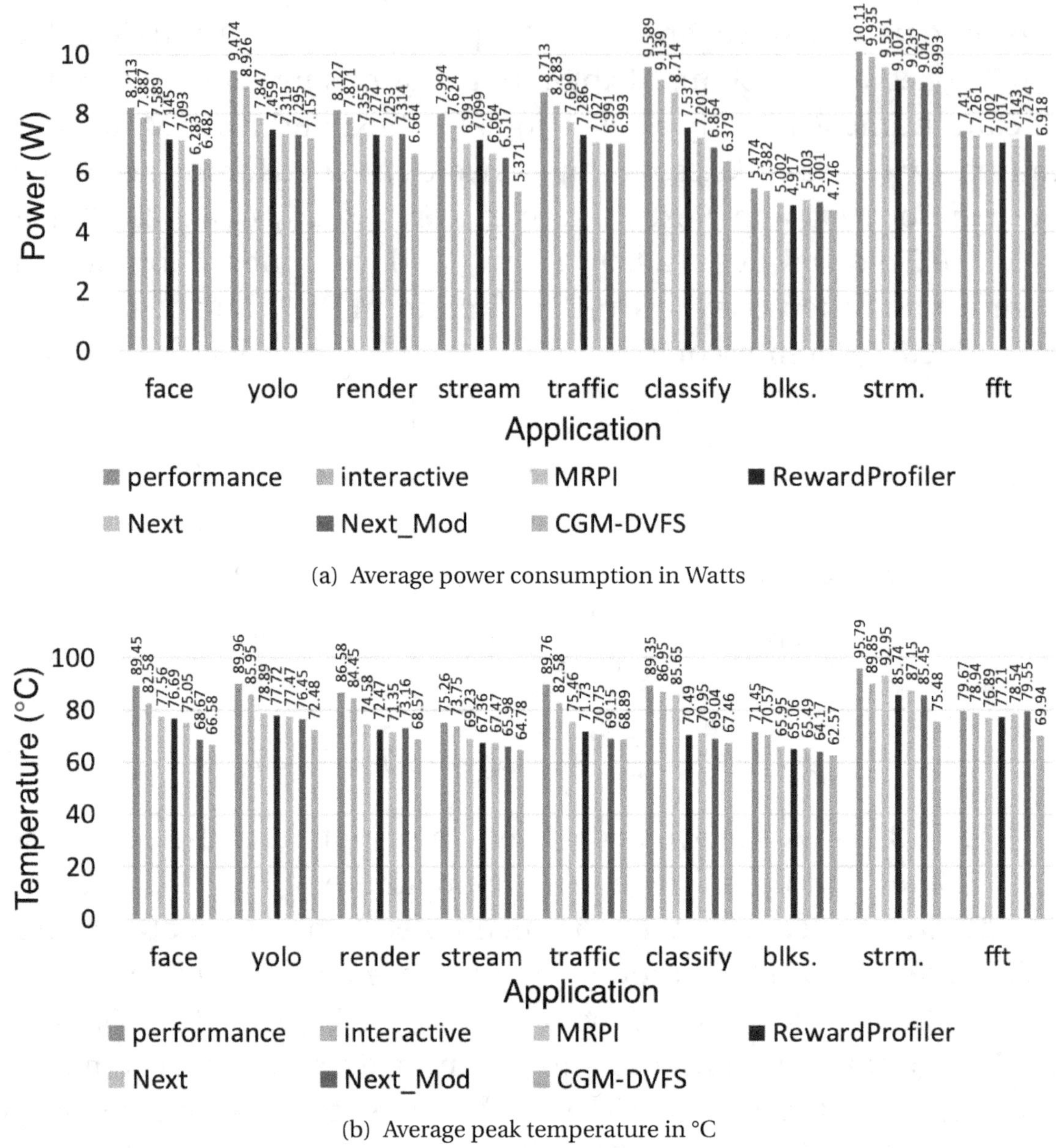

(a) Average power consumption in Watts

(b) Average peak temperature in °C

Figure 5.3: Average power consumption (Watts) and average peak temperature (°C) of Odroid XU4 while executing different applications on different methodologies: performance, interactive, MRPI, RewardProfiler, Next, Next_Mod & CGM-DVFS

Table 5.4: Improvement in power saving (%) of CGM-DVFS compared to performance (perf.), MRPI, RewardProfiler (RProfiler.), interactive (inter.), Next & Next_Mod (N_Mod.)

App	perf.	MRPI	RProfiler.	inter.	Next	N_Mod.
face	21.08	14.59	9.28	17.81	8.61	-3.17
yolo	24.46	8.79	4.049	19.82	2.16	1.89
render	18.00	9.40	8.39	15.34	8.12	8.89
stream	32.81	23.17	24.34	29.55	19.40	17.58
traffic	19.74	9.17	4.02	15.57	0.48	-0.03
classify	**33.48**	**26.80**	15.36	30.2	11.42	6.93
blks.	12.43	5.13	3.83	11.34	6.10	5.10
strm.	21.20	18.80	11.97	15.99	2.62	0.60
fft	12.21	9.04	9.42	11.40	3.15	4.89

Table 5.5: Reduction in peak temperature of big CPUs (%) of CGM-DVFS compared to performance (perf.), MRPI, RewardProfiler (RProfiler.), interactive (inter.), Next & Next_Mod (N_Mod.)

App	perf.	MRPI	RProfiler.	inter.	Next	N_Mod.
face	25.57	14.16	13.18	19.38	11.29	3.04
yolo	19.43	8.13	6.74	15.67	6.44	5.19
render	20.80	8.06	5.38	18.80	3.90	6.27
stream	13.93	6.428	3.83	12.16	3.99	1.82
traffic	23.25	8.71	3.96	16.58	2.63	0.38
classify	**24.50**	**21.24**	4.30	22.42	4.92	2.29
blks.	12.43	5.13	3.83	11.34	4.46	2.49
strm.	21.20	18.80	11.97	15.99	13.39	11.67
fft	12.21	9.04	9.42	11.40	10.95	12.08

From Table 5.4 & 5.5, as we can observe that for CGM-DVFS approach the most power saving and temperature reduction are achieved while executing *classify* and *strm.* applications compared to the performance governor, so, we wanted to explore the system behaviour further to investigate that. CGM-DVFS executed the classify application with the following maximum operating frequency settings: 1200 MHz on big CPU cluster, 1200 MHz on LITTLE CPU cluster and 728 MHz on memory. While executing strm. application CGM-DVFS ran the application with the following maximum operating frequency settings: 1500 MHz on big CPU cluster, 1200 MHz on LITTLE CPU cluster and 728 MHz on memory. On the other hand, performance governor executed both the classify and strm. applications at the max operating frequency of 2000 MHz on big CPU cluster, 1400 MHz on LITTLE CPU cluster and 825 MHz on memory. Since, CGM-DVFS executed the above applications at a significantly lower operating frequencies, especially for big CPU cluster, compared to the performance governor, the approach was able to achieve high power saving and temperature reduction comparatively.

The IPC and CPU utilization values were also recorded while executing classify and strm. applications on both CGM-DVFS and performance governor. From Table 5.6, we can observe that while executing the classify and strm. applications on the CGM-DVFS, the CPU utilization remained the same compared to performance governor, however, the IPC value increased comparatively, hinting that the CPU capacity was utilized more compared to the performance governor.

Overhead analysis: From our empirical data, we noticed that the average overhead to read the profiled data (2160 profiling points) in the *Fetch desired config* step is 29.507 milliseconds and the overhead to search for the desired DVFS configuration in this same step is 0.145 milliseconds.

Table 5.6: IPC and CPU utilization (denoted as CPU Utilized) while executing classify and strm. applications on performance governor and CGM-DVFS

classify	Performance	CGM-DVFS
IPC	1.79	1.88
CPU Utilized	1.002	1.002
strm.	**Performance**	**CGM-DVFS**
IPC	0.64	0.71
CPU Utilized	1.000	1.000

5.7 Discussion

From Fig. 5.3, Tables 5.4 and 5.5 it could be noticed that CGM-DVFS outperforms Q-Learning based Reinforcement Learning (RL) approach, Next, where DVFS is only performed on CPU and GPU. This was expected since CGM-DVFS performs DVFS on CPU, GPU and RAM in comparison to reduce the power consumption even more. However, when compared to Next_Mod, where DVFS is performed on CPU, GPU & RAM using Q-Learning, CGM-DVFS outperforms for yolo, render, stream, classify, blks., strm. and fft applications. Interestingly, Next_Mod seems to be producing sub-optimal (worse) results when compared to Next and CGM-DVFS, especially for render and fft applications. This is due to the fact that for delayed RL approaches such as Q-Learning the agent must explore the dynamic system (dynamic environment) long enough to find the optimal outcome [John, 1994]. As the number of actions and states increase in the environment, the time to explore for the RL agent also increases in order to reach the optimal output. Although delayed RL approaches are good to optimize power consumption and temperature of the system in an application agnostic manner, however, often times given the number of actions (actions to perform DVFS on CPU, GPU, RAM) if the agent is not allowed to explore long enough in the dynamic environment, then the agent will result in sub-optimal power consumption. Whereas, application specific profiling approaches such as CGM-DVFS will result in close to optimal power consumption since these approaches are specific to applications.

Given the advantages and disadvantages of both profiled application based DVFS approaches such as CGM-DVFS and application agnostic DVFS approaches such as RL based DVFS, it is desirable to use a combination of both the approaches to reach maximum power consumption and thermal behaviour reduction of the mobile MPSoC while catering for the performance requirement of the executing application.

On the other hand, in Chapters 3, 4 and 5, we have only explored the effect and approaches to perform DVFS such that performance, power and thermal behaviour could be optimized, however, DVFS on processing elements could also affect the security of the mobile MPSoC, especially security flaws arising due to temperature side-channel attack, which have not been addressed yet. This calls for mechanisms to perform DVFS to address this challenge as well.

5.8 Summary

In this chapter, we studied the effect of different frequency scaling level on RAM (memory) towards the total power consumption in the mobile MPSoC. We also proposed CGM-DVFS, an agent, to perform DVFS on big and LITTLE CPUs, GPUs and memory on the mobile MPSoC and experimental results prove the efficacy of CGM-DVFS in reducing power consumption and peak temperature while catering for performance requirement compared to the state-of-the-art approaches. Through experimental results we also show that application specific profiling approaches such as CGM-DVFS outperform and result in better optimal power consumption compared to delayed Reinforcement Learning approaches such as Q-Learning when the system (environment) is dynamic.

The primary focus in this chapter was to perform DVFS on CPU, GPU and RAM to optimize power consumption and henceforth, optimize thermal behaviour as well. However, performing DVFS on processing elements, especially in CPUs, could lead to temperature based side-channel attack in mobile MPSoCs. In the next chapter, we explore temperature side-channel attack that could be exploited because of performing DVFS on CPUs and also propose a mechanism to secure against such attack while optimizing the thermal behaviour of the device.

Chapter 6

DVFS & Temperature Side-Channel Attack

In the previous chapters (Chapter 3, 4 and 5), we observed the effect of DVFS on processing elements such as CPU & GPU, and memory unit such as RAM to optimize power consumption and thermal behaviour, however, DVFS on processing elements could also affect the security of the mobile MPSoC, especially security threats arising from temperature based side-channel attack. In this chapter, we explore such phenomenon and propose a novel approach, DATE: Defense Against TEmperature side-channel attacks, of reducing spatial and temporal thermal gradient, which makes the system more secure against temperature side-channel attacks while at the same time increases the reliability of the device in terms of lifespan.

6.1 Prologue to Fourth Contributory Chapter

This contributory chapter is based on the following articles along with my personal contribution to these articles.

6.1.1 Article Details

1. **Somdip Dey**, Sangeet Saha, Xiaohang Wang, Amit Kumar Singh and Klaus McDonald-Maier, "RewardProfiler: A Reward Based

Design Space Profiler on DVFS Enabled MPSoCs", 5th IEEE International Conference on Edge Computing and Scalable Cloud (IEEE EdgeCom), 2019.

2. **Somdip Dey**, Amit Kumar Singh, Xiaohang Wang and Klaus McDonald-Maier, "DeadPool: Performance Deadline Based FrequencyPooling and Thermal Management Agent in DVFS Enabled MPSoCs", 5th IEEE International Conference on Edge Computing and Scalable Cloud (IEEE EdgeCom), 2019.

3. **Somdip Dey**, Amit Kumar Singh and Klaus McDonald-Maier, "ThermalAttackNet: Are CNNs Making It Easy To Perform Temperature Side-Channel Attack In Mobile Edge Devices?", Future Internet 2021, 13, 146.

4. **Somdip Dey**, Amit Kumar Singh, Xiaohang Wang and Klaus McDonald-Maier, "DATE: Defense Against TEmperature Side-Channel Attacks in DVFS Enabled MPSoCs". (**Under revision**)

Personal Contribution In The Articles: Conceptualization, Somdip Dey; methodology, Somdip Dey; software, Somdip Dey; validation, Somdip Dey and Amit Singh; formal analysis, Somdip Dey; investigation, Somdip Dey; resources, Somdip Dey; data curation, Somdip Dey; writing–original draft preparation, Somdip Dey; writing–review and editing, Somdip Dey and Amit Singh and Xiaohang Wang and Sangeet Saha and Klaus McDonald-Maier; visualization, Somdip Dey; supervision, Somdip Dey; project administration, Somdip Dey.

6.2   Introduction & Motivation

In the study [Masti et al., 2015], thermal covert channels on multi-processors were exploited by observing the exponential rise and fall of CPU temperature while executing a CPU intensive application. In order to verify this behavior on embedded multi-processors we observed

138

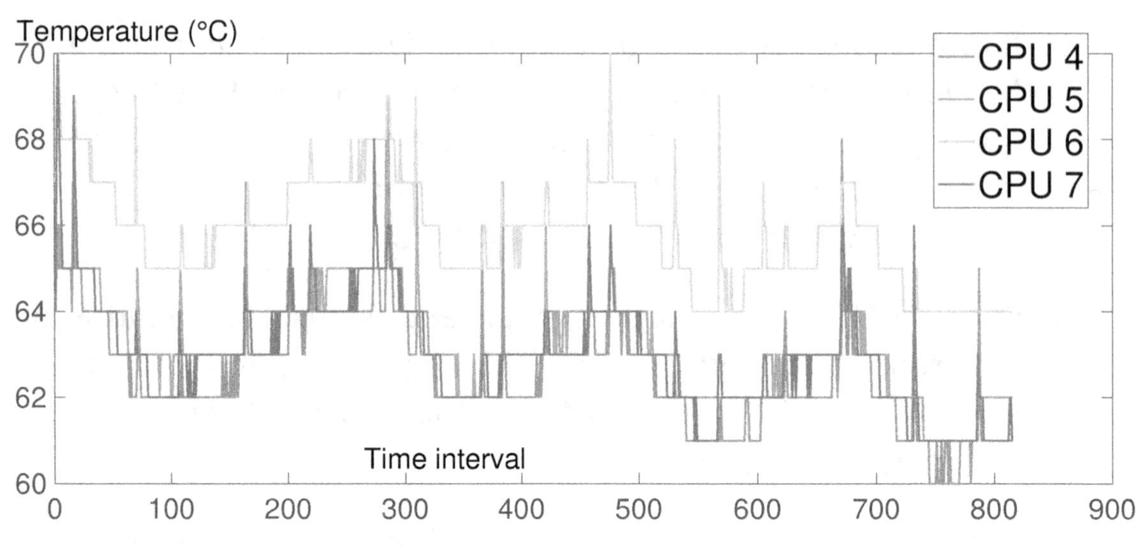

(a) Baseline temperature plot (°C vs Time interval)

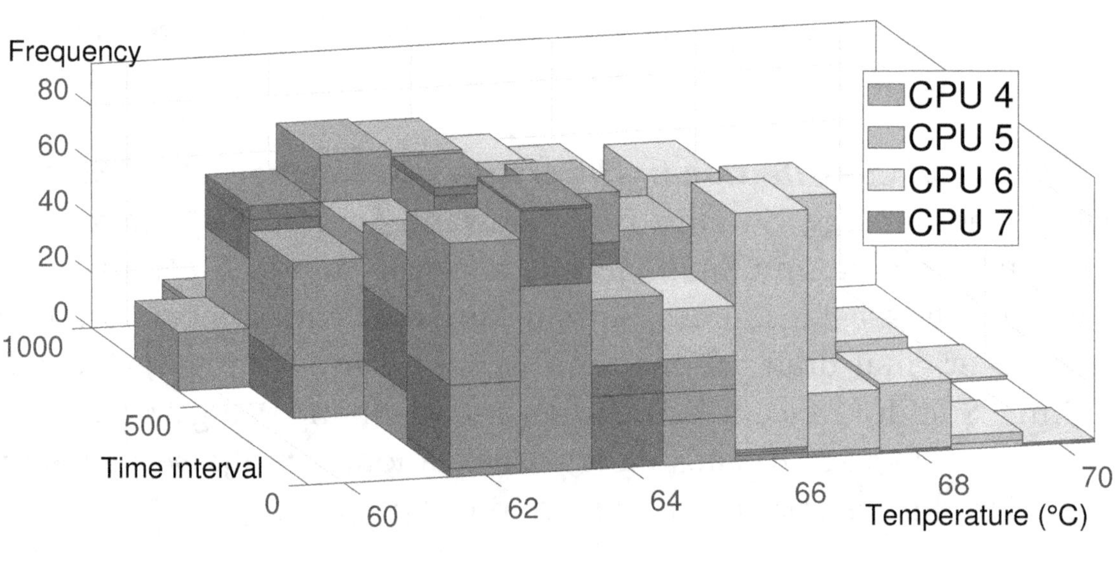

(b) Baseline temperature 3D plot

Figure 6.1: Temperature readings on 4 ARM A15 big CPU cores while idle

139

the temperature readings on 4 ARM Cortex A15 big CPU cores on the Exynos 5422 [exy, a] system-on-chip (SoC) while almost idle (the system was only executing background OS processes and the Linux governor was running *ondemand* power scheme), which we denote as *baseline temperature* of the CPU cores. In Fig. 6.1 we could notice *baseline temperature* of ARM Cortex A15 big CPUs in both 2D (Fig. 6.1.(a)) and 3D (Fig. 6.1.(b)) plots. In Fig. 6.1, the graph representing the *baseline temperature* readings for different ARM Cortex A15 big CPUs closely mimicked the oscillatory pattern that of simple harmonic motion [Serway and Jewett, 1998]. The reason to provide a visual representation of both 2D and 3D plots is to highlight the spatial as well as temporal thermal gradient because the 2D representation might not be able to provide a microscopic view of spatial thermal gradient over time. The X-axis of the 3D graph represents the temperature (°C), Y-axis of the graph represents time interval (millisecond) and the Z-axis represents the frequency (scaled to 0.1 MHz) of that particular temperature over time. Since the Odroid XU4 [odr, b] platform, which implements the Exynos 5422 MPSoC, only have temperature sensors on 4 ARM Cortex-A15 (big) CPU cores, we have only reported on their temperature behavior.

Based on [Masti et al., 2015] when we executed the Blackscholes benchmark from the PARSEC benchmark suits [Bienia, 2011a] with default Linux ondemand governor on the Exynos 5422 SoC, we could notice spikes in temperature at certain intervals along with a high frequency in thermal cycles (see Fig. 6.2). In Fig. 6.2, we noticed that the temporal and spatial thermal gradient on the CPU cores varies a lot during the execution period. When we compared the thermal behavior of the CPUs during the execution of Blackscholes and *baseline temperature* from our earlier observation, it became evident that heat dissipation from multiple processors could in fact lead to thermal covert channels and hence leading to temperature side-channel attacks.

Most of the relevant published works [Hutter and Schmidt, 2013, Masti et al., 2015, Bartolini et al., 2016, DeVogeleer et al., 2014, De Vo-

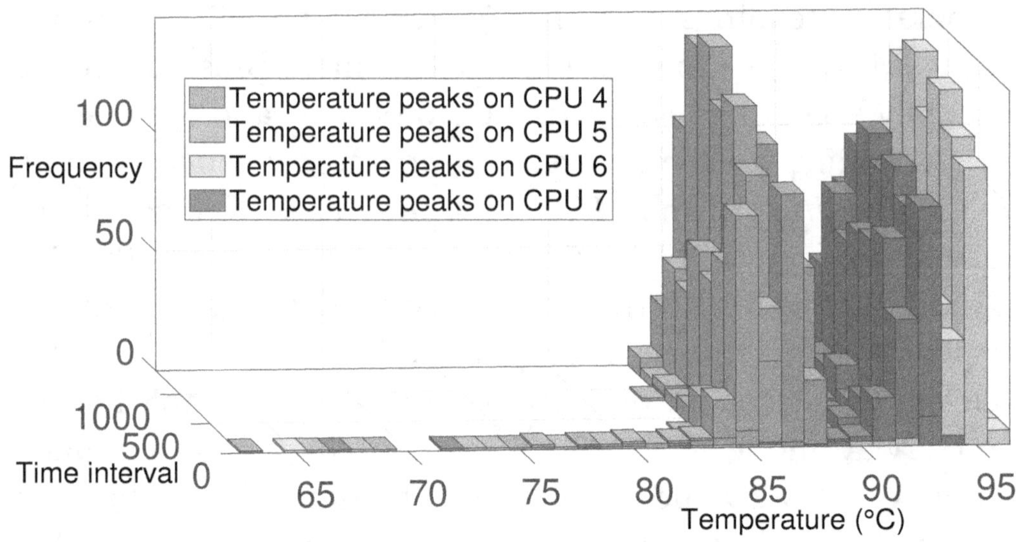

Figure 6.2: Temperature peaks on 4 ARM A15 big CPU cores while executing Blackscholes benchmark

geleer et al., , Gu et al., 2016, Long et al., 2018, Knechtel and Sinanoglu, 2017] in temperature side-channel attacks focus on various different element of pursuing such attack or protect from it. However, none of them has evaluated security against temperature side-channel attack as a cumulative entity. The main reason is that the definition of overall security of a device against temperature side-channel attacks is missing. Moreover, in [Demme et al., 2012], the scholars proposed a metric to measure information leakage in hardware systems called the side-channel vulnerability factor, which is based on commonalities in all side-channel attacks such as: the attacker always uses patterns in the victim system's behaviour to carry out an attack; patterns arising from the structure of programs used; typical user behavior, user inputs, and their interaction with the computing system. Although some of these factors are true in a temperature side-channel attack, the metric does not consider spatial and temporal thermal behaviour of the processing elements specifically, which are more relevant and of importance in such an attack. **Therefore**, in this chapter, we define a metric coined as *Thermal-Security-in-Multi-Processors* (*TSMP*), which indicates the cumulative security against such side-channel attacks.

The main objective of this chapter is to reduce the value of TSMP for any executing application/task in order to improve the security of the MPSoC from temperature based side-channel attacks. In order to overcome the pressing issue of temperature side-channel attacks, we propose a novel thermal management methodology on Dynamic Voltage Frequency Scaling (DVFS) [Aalsaud et al., 2016a, Reddy et al., 2017, Dey et al., 2019a, Dey et al., 2019c] enabled MPSoCs in an embedded device, and to the best of our knowledge it is the first documented methodology on securing against thermal side-channel attacks on DVFS. DVFS helps to reduce the energy consumption by executing the workload over extra time at a lower voltage and frequency, which could be accounted for reduced power consumption. We have coined our proposed methodology as $DATE$, Defense Against TEmperature side-channel attacks. Another important advantage of our proposed methodology is that due to the overall reduction of operating temperature the reliability of the device in terms of lifespan also increases. We have also performed temperature based side-channel attack on the latest Samsung Galaxy Note 9 [gal,] (utilizing Exynos 9810 MPSoC [exy, b]) phablet along side Odroid XU4 to show the efficacy of $DATE$ by using Covolutional Neural Network (CNN) [Chakradhar et al., 2010, Chen and Lin, 2014, He et al., 2016] based Deep Learning [LeCun et al., 2015] to analyze thermal behavior and predict which password is being used for cryptographic operation.

6.2.1 Contributions

In summary, this chapter makes the following concrete contributions.

1. A new metric to quantify the probability of the embedded device prone to temperature based side-channel attacks.

2. A novel thermal management scheme specific to executing application to secure against temperature side-channel attacks and improve reliability of the device in terms of lifespan.

3. Motivational case study with a real attack on real hardware platforms such as Galaxy Note 9 [gal,] and Odroid-XU4 [odr, b].

4. Implementation and validation of our proposed methodology on the real hardware platform (Odroid-XU4) using several benchmark applications.

The rest of the chapter is organized as follows. Sec. 6.3 describes the threat model based on temperature side-channel attack. Sec. 6.4 describes the problem definition and introduces some key terms useful to understand the proposed methodology along with the hardware/software infrastructure used in the research. In Sec. 6.5, we discuss the proposed methodology along with associated block diagram and algorithms. Sec. 6.7 explores the different experimentation and evaluation performed to prove the efficacy of our proposed methodology while discussing the future scope of this research (Sec. 6.8). Finally, Sec. 6.9 summarizes the chapter.

6.3   Threat Model

In this section, we explore the threat model in MPSoC enabled smartphone by leveraging temperature side-channel attack. Millions of smartphones are jail-broken around the world so that enhanced applications (apps) could be installed by the users. In 2013, more than 14 million iOS devices were jail-broken for the same purpose [jai,]. In 2014, Android Headlines reported that over 27.44% of Android users rooted their smartphones [Lucic, 2014], whereas, a more recent survey performed by Android Authority shows that 19.72% of Android users have their device rooted [Simons, 2022]. These surveys show that a lot of Android smartphone users, who have rooted their phone, could be potentially vulnerable to different types of attacks [Sinicki, 2022].

Injecting malicious code into popular apps on un-authorized app stores are common among hackers [Kumar, 2017, Yang, 2017, Carlon, 2017]. Any malicious person or a hacker could inject malicious code in

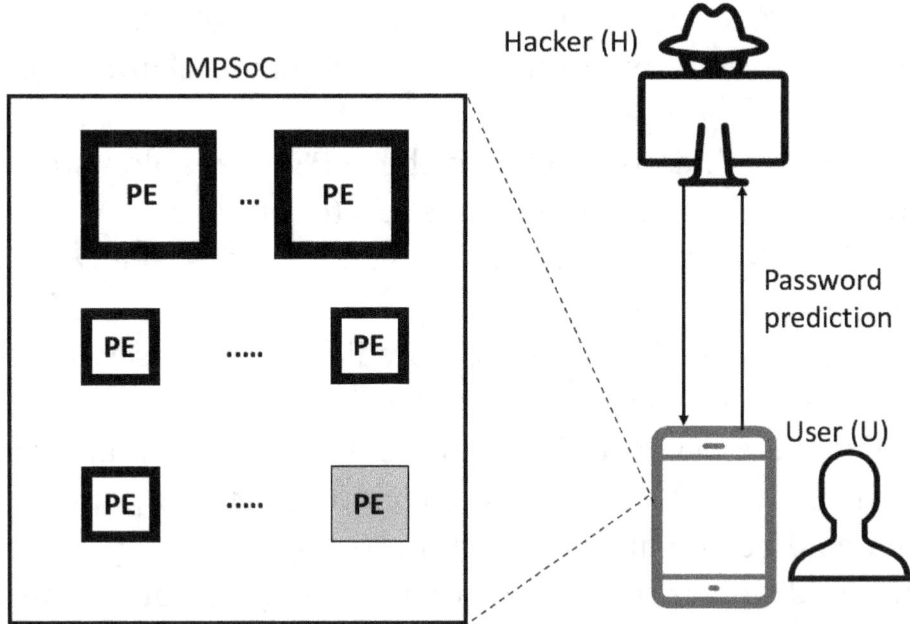

Figure 6.3: Diagrammatic representation of the threat model based on temperature side-channel attack, where PE represents the processing elements of the smartphone utilizing MPSoC, H represents the hacker & U represents the user of the smartphone utilizing MPSoC

smartphone apps and then allow unsuspecting smartphone users with rooted device to install and use such apps. Thus, allowing the hacker to utilize the injected malicious code in the app to snoop activities such as power consumption and thermal behaviour of the processing elements (PEs) such as CPUs.

Separately, it is also important to mention that modern Android devices comes with Google Autofill [goo, 2023], which is the default password manager on Android, and it's integrated with Google Chrome and other apps. Google Autofill helps the smartphone users store and manage their passwords on the device by securely storing them on-device/on-cloud by encrypting the passwords used by the user. However, encryption is a process that is executed on CPUs, thus, power consumption or thermal behaviour of the processing CPU could lead to information leakage about the password being used for encryption (as established in Sec. 2.6 of Chapter 2).

Below we can observe one possible threat model that hackers could leverage to perform temperature based side-channel attack on rooted smartphones.

Assumptions: Let's assume that in the MPSoC enabled smartphone there are n number of heterogeneous PEs (denoted as p) consisting of big & LITTLE CPU cores. There is a hacker, H, and a user, U, who owns the smartphone.

Objective: The objective of H is to predict which password is being used by U in his/her/them smartphone.

Threat: Fig. 6.3 shows the threat model in a diagrammatic representation. The hacker, H, can install malicious code in a popular mobile app that could be downloaded from non- Apple or Google authorized app stores and similar services. Upon installing the app by the user, U, this malicious code is embedded on to one of the LITTLE cores and it monitors the temperature of the CPU cores on the MPSoC, especially for banking or disk storage related apps (such as password manager). Most modern MPSoCs come equipped with temperature sensors on processing elements like CPU & GPU. For example, Exynos 5422 has individual temperature sensor on each of the big CPUs [exy, a]. These temperature sensors provide information on thermal activity of the respective component and helps with thermal management of the system. Here, embedding malicious code on the CPU means that the task associated with the malicious code is processed on one of the CPUs by attaching the task to it. The malicious code can then relay the thermal behaviour of the CPUs while executing different applications in incognito mode back to H after snooping. Sophisticated hackers might try to predict the password being used by analyzing the thermal behaviour of the CPUs. Often times Internet connectivity might be poor or not available on the smartphone and H can choose to train CNN models (online/offline) based on the thermal activity of the CPUs cores while executing banking apps on different passwords (more details in training CNN models for this purpose is in Sec. 6.6.1). Since, the malicious code snoops for thermal activity on the CPUs, thus, this approach of threat is considered as temperature side-channel attack. In such a threat model, the malicious app can detect the password being used by the user, U, of the smartphone and upon confirming the password it could be relayed back to the hacker such that the hacker can pursue more targeted attack on the user. In Fig. 6.3, the processing element highlighted in red is the affected CPU on which the malicious code is embedded. More details on predicting passwords in real smartphones are provided in Sec. 6.6.

Security: The goal is to secure the device from temperature based side-channel attack with respect to the aforementioned threat-model. The problem formulation based on temperature side-channel attack is provided in the next section.

6.4   System model and problem formulation

In this section, we explore the specific system model being used for the research and define the problem formulation, which forms the foundation of the proposed method.

6.4.1   Hardware & Software Infrastructure of Galaxy Note 9

Nowadays heterogeneous MPSoCs consist of different types of cores, either having the same or different instruction set architecture (ISA). Moreover, the number of cores of each type of ISA can vary based on MPSoCs and are usually clustered if the types of cores are similar. For this research, we have chosen an Asymmetric Multi-processors (AMPs) system-on-chip (AMPSoC), which has clustered cores on the system. We chose to execute a real attack on Galaxy Note9 [gal,], which is the latest mobile device from Samsung and utilizes the Exynos 9810 MP-SoC [exy, b]. This is the same MPSoC that we have mentioned in Chapter 4, Sec. 4.3.1.

Exynos 9810 has two CPU clusters, one for big CPU cores consisting of 4 Mongoose 3 CPU cores, and the other cluster for LITTLE CPU cores consisting of 4 Cortex A-55 CPU cores. The Mongoose 3 CPU cores allow cluster wise DVFS and has 18 frequency scaling levels ranging from 650 MHz to 2704 MHz (2704 MHz, 2652 MHz, 2496 MHz, 2314 MHz, 2106 MHz, 2002 MHz, 1924 MHz, 1794 MHz, 1690 MHz, 1586 MHz, 1469 MHz, 1261 MHz, 1170 MHz, 1066 MHz, 962 MHz, 858 MHz, 741 MHz, 650 MHz). Whereas, the LITTLE Cortex-A55 CPU cores has 10 frequency scaling levels ranging from 455 MHz to 1794 MHz (1794 MHz, 1690 MHz, 1456 MHz, 1248 MHz, 1053 MHz, 949 MHz, 832 MHz, 715 MHz, 598 MHz, and 455 MHz).

The Galaxy Note 9 was running on Android 9 (Pie) [and,] OS utilizing Linux kernel version 4.9.59, which has only one governor named *schedutil* based on Energy Aware Scheduling (EAS) [eas,]. The Galaxy Note 9 is only utilized for this case study to prove the threat of thermal side channel attack in real popular commercial device.

6.4.2 Hardware & Software Infrastructure of Odroid XU4

We chose Odroid XU4 [odr, b] development board, as mentioned in Chapter 4, Sec. 4.7.1, to execute the attack in order to verify the affect and scalability of thermal side-channel exploitation on a device other than Galaxy Note 9. We also used Odroid XU4 for the rest of the experimentation and validation because of more availability of software execution support since Galaxy Note 9 is vendor locked to only modify certain portions of the Android OS. Odroid XU4 employs the Samsung Exynos 5422 [exy, a] MPSoC. As mentioned earlier Exynos 5422 MPSoC contains clusters of big and LITTLE cores. This MPSoC provides DVFS feature per cluster, where the big core cluster has 19 frequency scaling levels, ranging from 200 MHz to 2000 MHz with each step of 100 MHz and the LITTLE cluster has 13 frequency scaling levels, ranging from 200 MHz to 1400 MHz, with each step of 100 MHz.

The Odroid XU4 was running on UbuntuMate version 14.04 (Linux Odroid Kernel: 3.10.105) and executing the performance governor.

6.4.3 Problem formulation

If we assume that there are n number of processing elements (p) in the MPSoC and P represent the set of all the processing elements then we get Eq. 6.1

$$P = \{p_1, p_2, ...p_n\} \tag{6.1}$$

Now, if we consider b_i be the *baseline temperature* for a processing element p_i, where baseline temperature is the temperature of the corresponding processing element i on the MPSoC while idle, and t_i be the maximum operating temperature of p_i while executing a task T, then we get the formula for Baseline Temperature Difference (BTD) for p_i for task T as Eq. 6.2.

$$BTD_{p_i} = |t_i - b_i| \tag{6.2}$$

If $S(BTD)$ be the set of all Baseline Temperature Difference for all processing elements for a particular task T in the system such that $S(BTD) = \{\, BTD_{p_1}, BTD_{p_2}, ...BTD_{p_n}, \}$, then from the Eq. 6.2 we can deduce the equation for *Baseline Maximum Thermal Deviation* (τ) as follows:

$$\forall p_i \in P : \tau = max(\, S(BTD)\,) \tag{6.3}$$

Let's assume that the temperature difference (d_i) between any two processing elements such as t_k and t_j be the average operating temperature of p_k and p_j, respectively, while executing a task T, then we get the following equation:

$$d_i = |t_j - t_k| \tag{6.4}$$

Now, for all the processing elements P we will achieve $\frac{n!}{2\,(n-2)!}$ combinations of temperature difference between any two processing elements in the system. If we consider *Spatial Processing Temperature Differences* ($SPTD$) be a set containing all the combinations ($\frac{n!}{2\,(n-2)!}$) of temperature differences between the processing elements while executing a task T then we could derive the formula for *Spatial Maximum Thermal Deviation* (ω) as follows:

$$\forall p_i \in P : \omega = max(\,SPTD\,) \tag{6.5}$$

For quantifying the security of a MPSoC against temperature side-channel attacks, we can derive an equation from the values of τ, ω and the frequency of thermal cycle during execution of task T (θ). The reason to choose these three variables (τ, ω & θ) is that from our experiments (described in Section 6.4.4) we observed that these three variables are directly correlated to thermal behavior of the processing elements. We define the security against temperature side-channel attacks as *Thermal-Security-in-Multi-Processors* ($TSMP$), shown in Eq. 6.6.

$$TSMP = \frac{1}{\tau + \omega + \theta} \,\bigg|\, 0 < TSMP < 1 \tag{6.6}$$

In Eq. 6.6 if the value is closer to 1 then it means that the device is more secure against temperature side-channel attacks, whereas, as value closer to 0 means that the device is more prone to security threats related to temperature side-channel. We also have to keep in mind that $(\tau + \omega + \theta)$ can never be ∞ or 0 in reality nor the value of τ, ω and θ could be decimal as per our platform. Now, from the Eq. 6.6 in order to improve the security of a device against temperature side-channel attacks our main objective is to keep the total value of $(\tau + \omega + \theta)$ as low as possible such that the value of $TSMP$ is as close to 1 as possible. Therefore, we could define our problem as follows.

Given: An application and a MPSoC platform with DVFS support.

Find: Maximum value of $TSMP$.

Subject to: Meeting performance requirement of each application within available MPSoC resources.

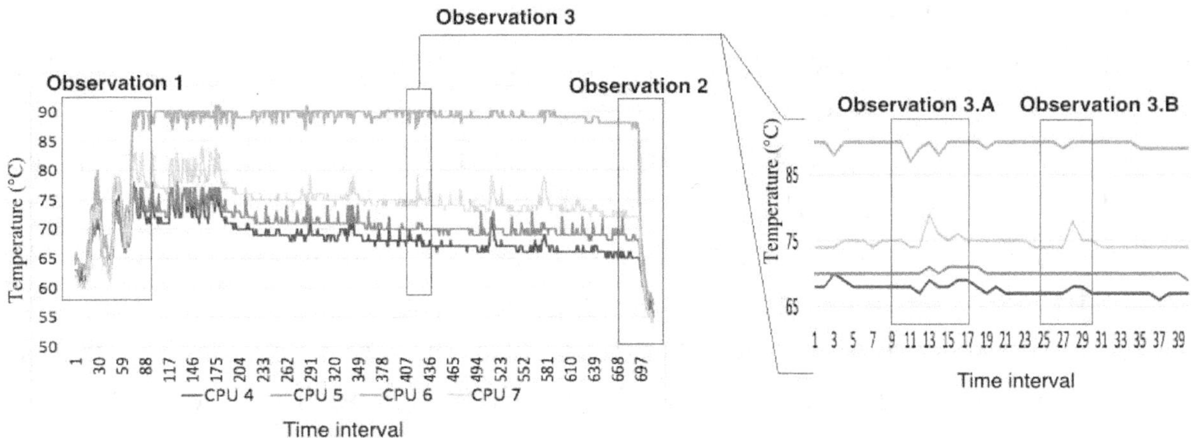

Figure 6.4: Observations of thermal behavior of four ARM Cortex A15 (big) CPUs on Odroid XU4 while performing RSA encryption and decryption

6.4.4   Importance of τ, ω and θ in TSMP metric

To understand the key factors that are related to establishing thermal side-channel attacks on a MPSoC such as Odroid XU4 [odr, b] , we performed RSA encryption and decryption several times on the platform and observed the thermal behavior of the four ARM A15 (big) CPU cores. On the Odroid XU4, the 8 CPU cores (big.LITTLE) are denoted as CPU 0, CPU 1 to CPU 7, where CPU 0 to CPU 3 are ARM A7 (LITTLE) cores and CPU 4 to CPU 7 are ARM A15 (big) cores. We are only performing the encryption and decryption on one of the big CPU cores (CPU 6) so that we could observe the thermal behavior on the other neighboring idle CPU cores (CPU 4, 5 and 7). Fig. 6.4 shows one such instance of the experiments performed where we are observing the thermal behavior 3 seconds before the RSA encryption and decryption is executed till 2 seconds after the execution completes. In Fig. 6.4 we have highlighted three important observations (see Observation 1, 2 and 3 in the figure), which were common in all the experiments performed. On the Y axis of Fig. 6.4 we could notice the temperature in degree centigrades of each of the A15 CPU cores, colour coded separately for individual CPU cores, and the X axis represents the time interval with 100 milliseconds gap between each interval. In Observation 1 we could notice that the temperature drastically increases on CPU 6 within 3 seconds and the most important thing to notice here is that not only the temperature of CPU 6 increases but at the same time temperature of all neighboring A15 CPU cores (CPU 4, 5 and 7) also increase. The reason for this phenomenon is due to heat dissipation and propagation in the lateral direction. In Observation 2 we can notice that once the encryption and decryption complete on CPU 6 the temperature plummets not only on that core but also on the neighboring cores. Although in this observation it could be noticed that temperature plummets over 2 seconds and not instantaneously. As stated by Masti et al. [Masti et al., 2015], thermal covert channels can be exploited by observing the exponential rise and fall of CPU temperature. Therefore, Observation 1 and Observation 2 proves the theory proposed in the study [Masti et al., 2015]. More importantly, *Baseline Maximum Thermal Deviation* (τ) and *Spatial Maximum Thermal Deviation* (ω) directly reflect the issues mentioned in Observation 1 and 2 of Fig. 6.4.

More interestingly, if we notice Observation 3 (3.A and 3.B) we can find that whenever there is a spike in temperature on CPU 6 there is also a spike in temperature on the neighboring CPUs due to heat propagation. Thus proving that when the temperature of one CPU core increases, due to heat propagation from that CPU core to the nearby CPU cores the thermal behavior of these adjacent cores are also affected. Therefore, potentially opening up a vulnerability if one such adjacent CPU core could be used to establish a temperature side-channel attack.

Since, τ and ω reflect the temporal as well as spatial thermal gradient difference of the CPU cores while they are executing a task (or set of tasks) and being idle, the aforementioned variables are very important in understanding the vulnerability of MPSoCs against temperature side-channel attack. Whereas, the frequency of thermal cycle during execution of a task (or set of tasks) (θ) directly reflects the phenomenon of Observation 3 (3.A and 3.B) and hence θ also plays an important role in deducing vulnerability related to temperature side-channel attack. Therefore, it is crucial to define the *Thermal-Security-in-Multi-Processors* (*TSMP*) metric incorporating τ, ω and θ.

6.5 Proposed Methodology: DATE

6.5.1 Overview of DATE

An overview of the proposed DATE methodology is illustrated in Fig. 6.5. It has some offline and online steps. During offline profiling computed results for various applications are used to identify the appropriate temperature (t_{App_i}) and frequency (f_{App_i}) such that a cumulative least value for ($\tau + \omega + \theta$) (see Eq. 6.6) is achieved. Since for each application we have to explore all the possible frequency values along with appropriate temperature and performance threshold such that TSMP is maximum for App_i, we do the profiling offline as part of the design space exploration. Once we have found out the best possible frequency and temperature which yields the least value for ($\tau + \omega + \theta$), we save the frequency and temperature values along with some other parameters. These values are later used during the online step where we set the frequency and temperature threshold of the system to these saved values. In DATE, we call the offline step as *Learning Module* whereas, the online step is called as *Decision Module*. Since, operating temperature of the device directly affects the reliability of such device in terms of lifespan, hence, DATE methodology affects the reliability of the device in a positive manner (more details in Sec. 6.7.3).

6.5.2 Learning Module

The complete algorithm explaining the working of *Learning Module* is provided in Algo. 11.

In the study [DeVogeleer et al., 2014] through experiments on real devices, it was noticed that on MPSoCs power and temperature follow a relationship of quadratic function. Moreover, in DVFS enabled MPSoCs dynamic power and frequency follow a quadratic relationship due

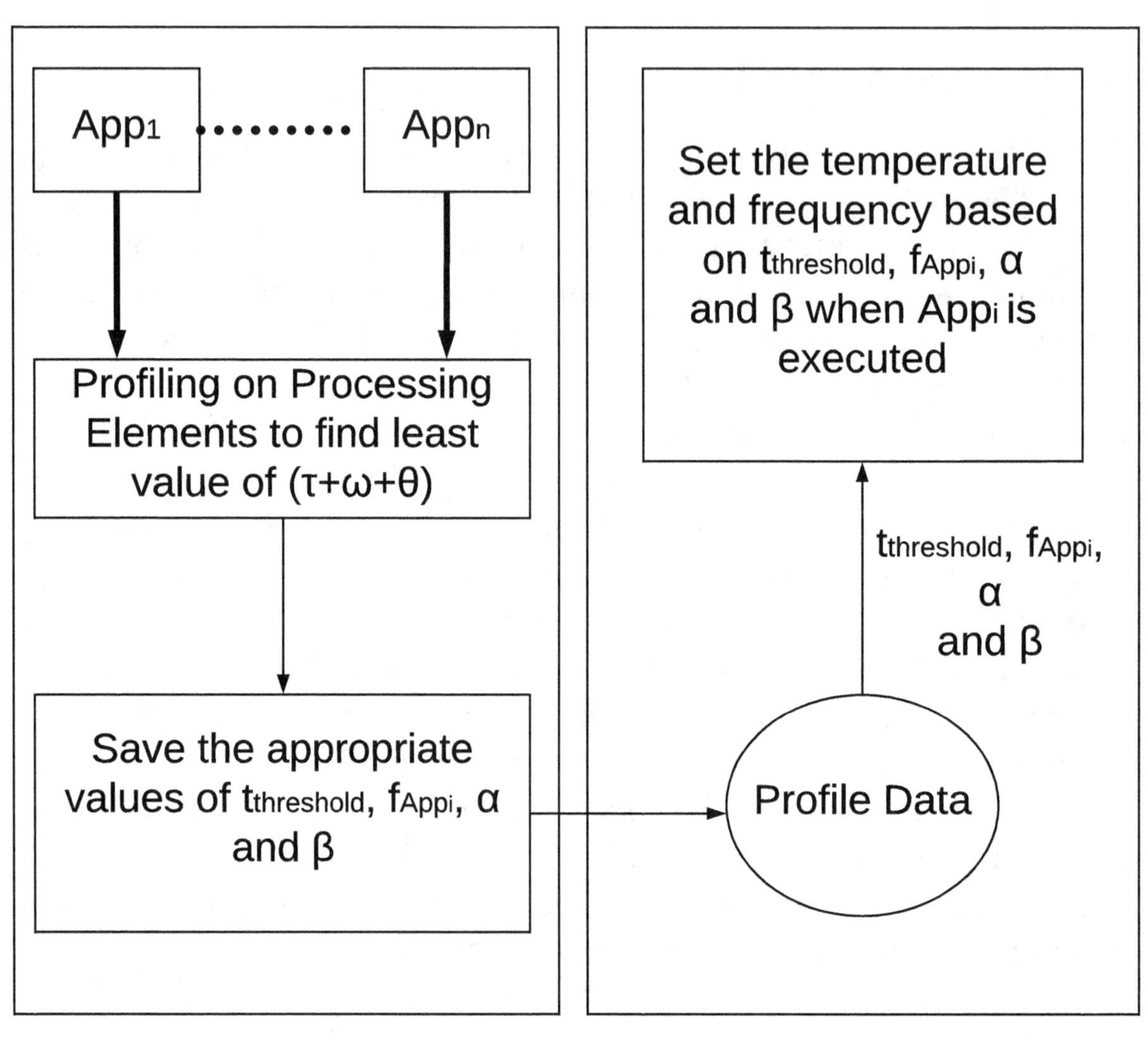

Figure 6.5: Proposed Methodology: DATE

to the power consumption ($P \propto V^2 f$) being directly affected by the operating frequency and voltage [Singh et al., 2020, Dey et al., 2020, Isuwa et al., 2019]. Here, quadratic relationship is mentioned in terms of algebraic equation/graph. However, to make our approach fast during run time (*Decision Module*) we assume that frequency and temperature follows a linear relationship represented by Eq. 6.7.

$$t_i = \alpha \times f_i + \beta \tag{6.7}$$

In Eq. 6.7, f_i is the operating frequency at time instance i, t_i is the operating temperature at the same time instance, α is the relationship variable and β is the intercept variable.

Now, we first set a performance deadline (for our case we choose execution time deadline for each application) and then start executing App_i and vary the frequency as well as the temperature threshold of the system to observe the performance. Here, the temperature threshold is the operating thermal cap, which can not be surpassed by the system during the execution of the application. If we consider $t_{available}$ is the set of all available operating temperature ($t_{available} = \{t_1, t_2, ... t_i\}$) of the system, which will be used as the thermal cap during the profiling, then for each instance of operating temperature ($t_{available_i}$) from $t_{available}$ we monitor the performance while setting the temperature threshold to $t_{available_i}$.

While monitoring performance the frequency of the PEs is reduced by one frequency scaling step (we start at the maximum frequency and this is denoted as *ReduceFrequencyByOneStep()* in Algo. 11) and returns the reduced frequency instance (f_i). We monitor the temperature of each PE (denoted as *MeasureTemperatureValue()* in Algo. 11) and returns the set of temperature values of all the PEs during the profiling. If the performance deadline for the application is met then the maximum value among the set of temperature is used as the temperature threshold. By this approach we leverage DVFS capability of the system and modify the frequency till the performance constraint is met and try to achieve least possible values for τ, ω and θ. After we have found the appropriate value of system's temperature threshold/cap (t_{App_i}) and frequency (f_{App_i}) we note the value of α and β (from Eq. 6.7). For App_i

the relationship variable and intercept are denoted by α_{App_i} and β_{App_i} respectively. For each profiled application we only save the values of maximum operating temperature threshold/cap ($t_{threshold_{App_i}}$) which should not be surpassed during the execution of App_i, operating frequency (f_{App_i}), α_{App_i}, β_{App_i} and baseline temperature (b_{App_i}) during the profiling period on the memory to be used in the *Decision Module*. Here, the baseline temperature (b_{App_i}) for the profiling application is the same baseline temperature, which is recorded before and after the application is executed such that $b_{App_i} = b_i$ in Eq. 6.2. In practice, we actually save the value of b_{App_i} for each processing element in the system as a set of baseline temperatures (B_{App_i}).

Algorithm 11: Learning Module Execution

Input:
1. $Perf_{max}$: performance deadline for an application instance App_i
2. B_i: a set of baseline temperature (b_i) for each processing element (PE)
Output: $< t_{threshold_{App_i}}, f_{App_i}, \alpha_{App_i}, \beta_{App_i}, B_{App_i} >$
Initialize: $\tau + \omega + \theta = \infty$;

foreach $t_{available_i}$ in $t_{available}$ *of the system* **do**
 $t_{threshold_{App_i}} = t_{available_i}$;
 %$Perf_{App_i}$ is the current performance of the application%
 while $Perf_{App_i} \leq Perf_{max}$ **do**
  f_i = ReduceFrequencyByOneStep(); (see Sec. 6.5.2)
  T_i = MeasureTemperatureValue();
  τ_i = CalculateTau(B_i); %see Eq. 6.3%
  ω_i = CalculateOmega(B_i); %see Eq. 6.5%
  θ_i = CalculateTheta(); %see Sec. 6.5.2%
  if $(\tau_i + \omega_i + \theta_i) < (\tau + \omega + \theta)$ **then**
   $\tau = \tau_i$, $\omega = \omega_i$, $\theta = \theta_i$;
   $t_{threshold_{App_i}} = max(T_i)$, $f_{App_i} = f_i$;
  end
 end
 $< \alpha_{App_i}, \beta_{App_i} >$ = CalculateAlphaBeta($t_{threshold_{App_i}}$, f_{App_i}); (Sec. 6.5.2)
end
return $< t_{threshold_{App_i}}, f_{App_i}, \alpha_{App_i}, \beta_{App_i}, B_{App_i} = B_i >$;

6.5.3 Decision Module

The algorithm for Decision Module is provided in Algo. 12. In the *Decision Module*, a software agent, which we call as *DATE* as well, first loads the baseline temperature (b_{App_i}) for the profiled application and compares the current temperature with baseline temperature during this time instance (b_{now}). The set of baseline temperatures for all PEs is B_{now}. Since baseline temperature can vary depending on the surrounding and other unforeseen circumstances, it is important DATE is aware of the difference between the baseline temperature when the application was profiled and the baseline temperature for the time period when the Decision Module of DATE acts and could be represented as $b_{diff} = b_{App_i} - b_{now}$. For set of PEs it is B_{diff}.

Now, if we assume that the value of α and β remains almost same (subject to some obvious deviation and we refer to it as error) then from Eq. 6.7 we can get the equation (see Eq. 6.8) that could define the relationship between two different operating temperature and their associated frequencies.

$$f_2 = \frac{(t_2 - t_1)}{\alpha} + f_1 \tag{6.8}$$

We can modify the Eq. 6.8 to reflect the governing equation (see Eq. 6.9) to decide the operating temperature threshold and associated frequency by DATE.

$$f_{desired} = \frac{(t_{desired\ threshold} - t_{threshold_{App_i}})}{\alpha} + f_{App_i} \tag{6.9}$$

If the value of b_{diff} is negative then DATE reduces the operating frequency by evaluating the new operating frequency value while considering that $b_{diff} = (t_{desired\ threshold} - t_{threshold_{App_i}})$ in Eq. 6.9. But if the value of b_{diff} is positive then Eq. 6.9 could be modified as follows:

$$f_{desired} = \frac{(t_{desired\ threshold} + b_{diff})}{\alpha} + f_{App_i} \tag{6.10}$$

If the value of calculated $f_{desired}$ is more than the available frequency of the CPU cores then DATE do not modify the operating frequency, thus, $f_{desried} = f_{App_i}$ but modifies the operating temperature threshold as $t_{desired\ threshold} = b_{diff} + t_{threshold_{App_i}}$. While executing the application, if the operating temperature of the CPU cores tries to go higher than the operating temperature threshold ($t_{desired\ threshold}$) then DATE drops the frequency ($f_{desired}$) to next frequency scaling level, which is again evaluated from the Eq. 6.8 by assuming that the operating temperature of the system needs to be reduced by 1° Centigrade. The governing equation to achieve this is as follows:

$$f_{desired} = f_{now} - \frac{1}{\alpha}$$

$$where,\ t_{desired} - t_{now} = -1$$

(6.11)

6.6 Case Study: Performing a real attack on Galaxy Note9 and Odroid XU4

We performed a real attack on the Galaxy Note 9 mobile device (as mentioned in Sec. 6.4.1), which is one of the top rated smart phones of 2018 and 2019 [top, a, top, b]. To prove the scalability and affect of the attack we also executed the same methodology on Odroid XU4 (as mentioned in Sec. 6.4.2). We executed a program sitting on one of the LITTLE cores on the device, while snooping the thermal behavior of the big core cluster during several encryption (AES-256 [Rijmen and Daemen, 2001]) operations of a text file with 4 of the most common passwords used by the users. The main motive of this attack is to evaluate the vulnerability of the latest smart-phone against thermal side-channel attack. More details on the device, experimental setup and evaluation of the attack is provided in the following subsections.

Algorithm 12: Decision Module Execution

Input:

$< t_{threshold_{App_i}}, f_{App_i}, \alpha_{App_i}, \beta_{App_i}, B_{App_i} > \& B_{now}$

$B_{diff} = $ CalculateBaselineDiff(B_{App_i}, B_{now}); (Sec. 6.5.3)

foreach *PE (P_i) in the set of PEs (P) on the system* **do**

    $b_{PE_{diff}} = $ GetBaselineDiff(B_{diff}, P_i); %Function to get the baseline difference ($b_{PE_{diff}}$) for P_i

    if $b_{PE_{diff}} > 0$ **then**

        $f_{desired} = $ CalculateDesiredFrequency$(b_{PE_{diff}})$; (using Eq. 6.10)

        SetFrequencyOfPE$(f_{desired})$; %Function to set the frequency of the PE with the value of $f_{desired}$%

        SetTempThres$(t_{threshold_{App_i}})$; %Function to set the maximum thermal cap of the PE as $t_{threshold_{App_i}}$%

    end

    else

        $f_{desired} = $ CalculateDesiredFrequency$(b_{PE_{diff}})$; (using Eq. 6.11)

        %$f_{PE_{max}}$ is the maximum frequency of the PE%

        if $f_{desired} > f_{PE_{max}}$ **then**

            $f_{desired} = f_{App_i}$; SetFrequencyOfPE$(f_{desired})$;

            $t_{desired\ threshold} = b_{PE_{diff}} + t_{threshold_{App_i}}$;

            (see Eq. 6.10 and Eq. 6.11)

            SetTempThres$(t_{desired\ threshold})$;

        end

        else

            SetFrequencyOfPE$(f_{desired})$;

            SetTempThres$(t_{threshold_{App_i}})$;

        end

    end

end

6.6.1   Dataset and CNN Model

To perform the attack we chose 4 of the 25 most common passwords of 2017 and 2018 [com, b, com, a] as surveyed by the Internet security firm SplashData. The 4 common passwords used by the user, which are chosen for our attack, are *123456, passw0rd, 111111* and *football.* We executed AES-256 [Rijmen and Daemen, 2001] encryption on a text file using the aforementioned passwords 500 times for each password. The reason to choose AES-256 is because of its popularity. The encryption operations were performed on the 4 Mongoose 3 big CPU cores (big

CPU cluster) while one of the LITTLE cores snoop the operating temperature data of the big CPU cluster. This is due to the fact that only one thermal sensor is present on the big CPU cluster of Galaxy Note 9 rather than individually placed on each big CPU core. After the temperature data for each password were collected, we transformed the data points into a graphical representation in order to be fed to a pre-trained CNN [Pan et al., 2010] for training and classification purposes. Since on the Odroid XU4 thermal sensors are individually placed on each big CPU cores, we chose to only record the thermal behavior of one of the big CPUs (CPU 7) for this experimental attack. It should be kept in mind that the length of the password that is being used for encryption does not matter with this approach (as mentioned in Sec. 6.3). When encryption is performed on the CPU, thermal behaviour of the CPU during the encryption process is observed, recorded and then transformed to graphical representation such that the dataset could be used to train the pre-trained CNN.

We chose ResNet50 CNN [He et al., 2016] as our network model, which could be used to train our graphical thermal data using *Transfer Learning* [Pan et al., 2010]. Since, CNN based Deep Learning usually requires a lot of training data in order to be used successfully for classification purposes, the network models are trained on large dataset such as ImageNet [Russakovsky et al., 2015], consisting of millions of images, and then the weights and parameters of the model are saved and used later to train for a specific target application. This way of training is called *transfer learning* and we have used ResNet 50, which is pre-trained on ImageNet. Since, ResNet50 is pre-trained on ImageNet and has the last fully connected layer to classify 1000 different classes/labels from the ImageNet, we had to modify the last fully connected layer to suit our target application.

Since, we have 4 passwords as the classes/labels to classify, we removed the last fully connected layer, which was pre-trained on ImageNet, to cater for only 4 labels instead. We have also added a new fully connected layer (called Dense in Fig. 6.6), dropout regularization

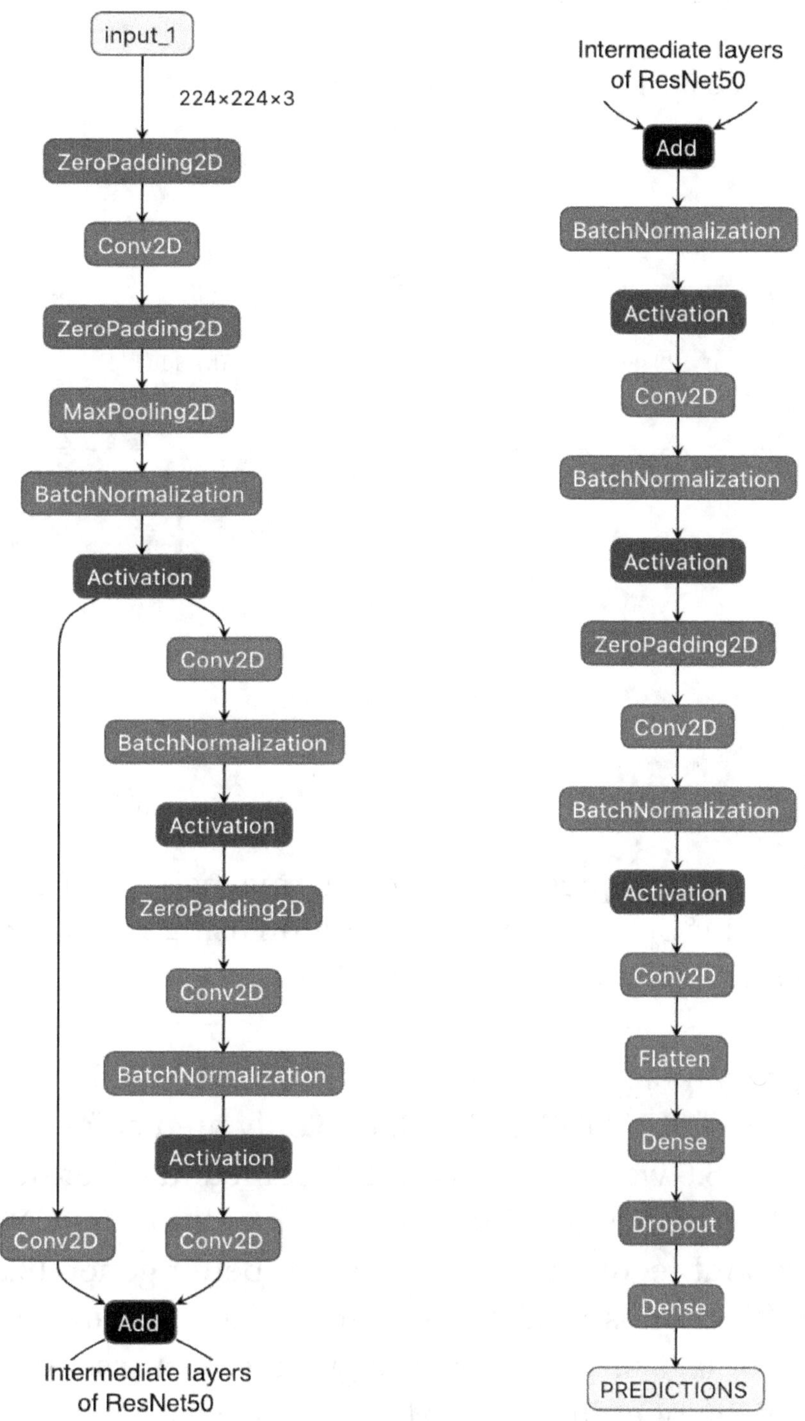

Figure 6.6: Architecture of ResNet50 CNN model with modified last fully connected layer used in password classification

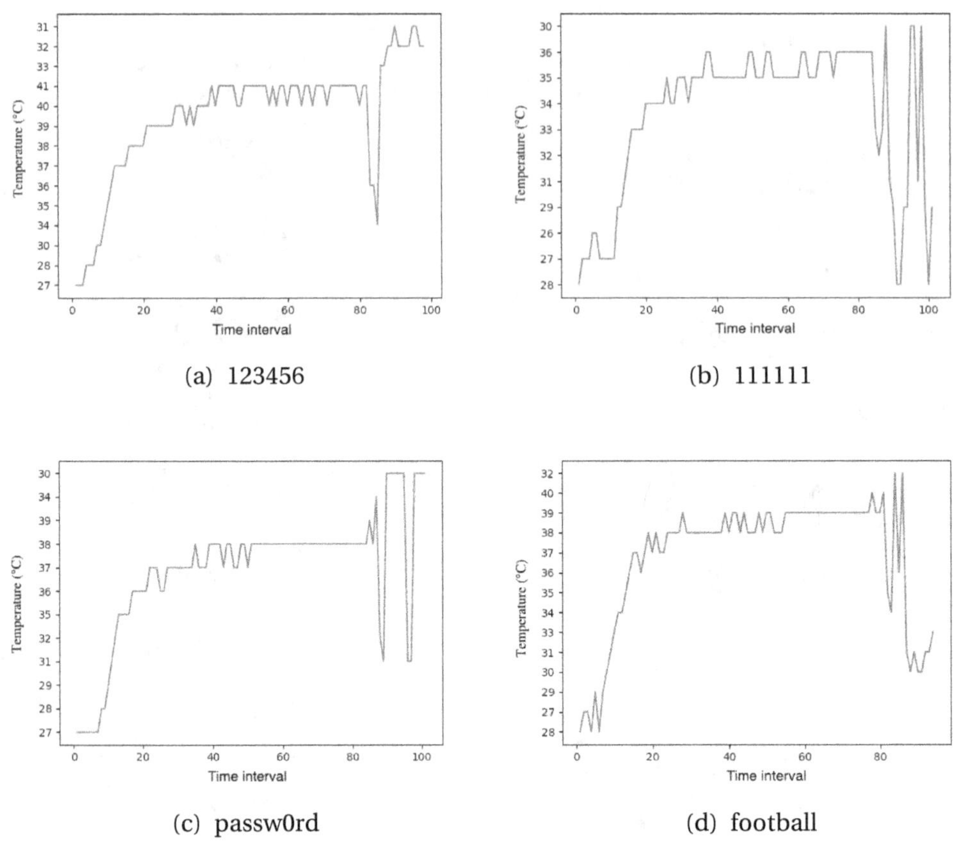

Figure 6.7: Graphical representation of thermal behavior (time interval vs temperature in °C) of encryption operation using the following passwords: *111111, 123456, passw0rd & football*

(called Dropout in Fig. 6.6) and a softmax function along with a classifier (called PREDICTIONS in Fig. 6.6) to only predict for 4 passwords (labels). In Fig. 6.6 we have shown the modified fully connected layer along with the custom classifier used in our ResNet50 CNN model. Here, the dropout regularization is used for better generalization and the softmax function is used for probability distribution for the 4 labels/classes. In Fig. 6.7, we show the graphical representation of the thermal behavior for each password label, which is fed to the ResNet50 CNN model for training and classification purpose.

From the 500 graphical data for each password label, we separated 100 graphical data for cross-validation testing purpose. Whereas 75%

of the remaining 400 graphical data for each password label were used
for training and rest of the 25% is used for validation during the training
period. Validation data is used to provide an unbiased evaluation of a
model fit on the training dataset while tuning hyperparameters of the
model.

It should also be kept in mind that CNNs are extremely good in automatically understanding features and patterns from the input image
and hence, we have used CNNs for the purpose so that the CNN model
could learn patterns associated with encryption process and thus, lead
to prediction of the respective password.

6.6.2   Predicting passwords

After training the ResNet50 model with the training and validation
dataset from Note 9, the total prediction accuracy achieved is 36.50%.
When we used 400 graphical data (100 data from each password label)
for cross-validation to evaluate the accuracy of the trained ResNet50
CNN in predicting the password being used for encryption operation,
the CNN could predict 146 instances correctly and achieving a prediction accuracy of 36.50%. Whereas, when we implemented DATE on the
system to improve the security against thermal side-channel on Note
9 and performed the same training methodology with the CNN, the
prediction accuracy achieved by the CNN model after the training is
26.75%. When we used the 400 graphical data for cross-validation the
CNN was only able to successfully predict 25.25 % (101 out of 400 data).
Hence, using DATE to secure the system against thermal side-channel
attack such as the one performed in this section, we are able to achieve
9.75% (for training process) and 11.25% (for cross-validation) increase
in security.

When we performed the same training on the thermal data collected from Odroid XU4, the CNN achieved a training prediction accuracy of 56.75% when DATE was not implemented on the system.
The CNN was also able to predict 52% of the 400 graphical data (208
out of 400) during the cross-validation. After we implemented DATE

on the Odroid XU4 the training prediction accuracy achieved by the CNN is 26.75% and was able to predict 29.5% of the 400 data (118 out of 400) during cross-validation. Therefore, using DATE we are able to achieve an increase in security against thermal side-channel by 30% during training period and an increase in security by 22.5% during cross-validation.

In order to determine whether our CNN is classifying the thermal data based on the features of the thermal peaks, we utilized Gradient-weighted Class Activation Mapping (Grad-CAM) [Selvaraju et al., 2017] to visualize in which areas of the graphical data the CNN was focusing on to predict which password is being used for encryption process. Grad-CAM methodology uses the gradient of the target classes flowing into the last convolutional layer to produce a coarse localization map highlighting the important regions in the image (graphical data) for predicting the class label. Fig. 6.8 shows the thermal graphical data generated while encrypting the plain text using 111111 as password (Fig. 6.8.(a)) and the subsequent localization mapping created from the last convolutional layer (Fig. 6.8.(b)) and then portraying the region of interest as thermal map on the original image (Fig. 6.8.(c)). Fig. 6.9, 6.10 and 6.11 consequently show the Grad-CAM generated for thermal behavior of the big CPU for individual password's (123456, football and passw0rd) encryption process. From the Grad-cam representation it is evident that our CNN is actually looking at certain thermal peaks to determine which password might have been used for encryption and hence, predict the label accordingly.

6.7 Experimental and Evaluation Results

6.7.1 Hardware & Software Setup for Experiments

Odroid XU4 could be utilized to run on both Android and Linux operating systems, and hence, we chose to perform most of our experiments on Odroid XU4 running on Linux OS. Further, since Linux is more versatile OS than Android and provides the ability to execute several es-

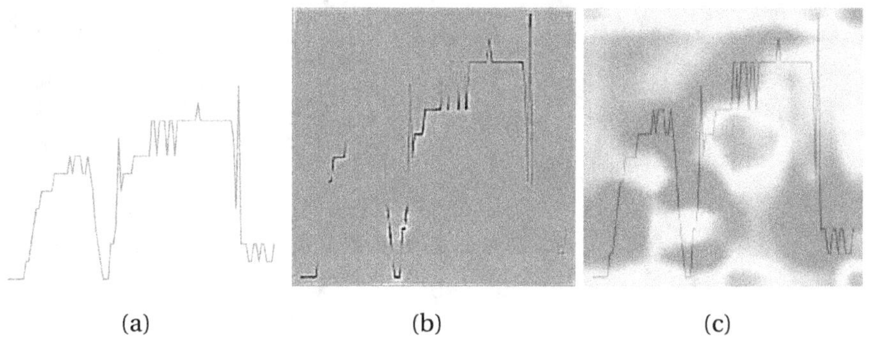

(a)   (b)   (c)

Figure 6.8: Focus area of ResNet50 network on a representative graph of password: 111111

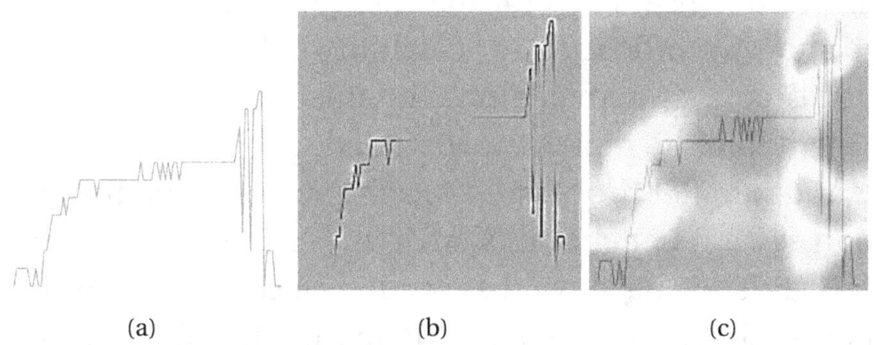

(a)   (b)   (c)

Figure 6.9: Focus area of ResNet50 network on a representative graph of password: 123456

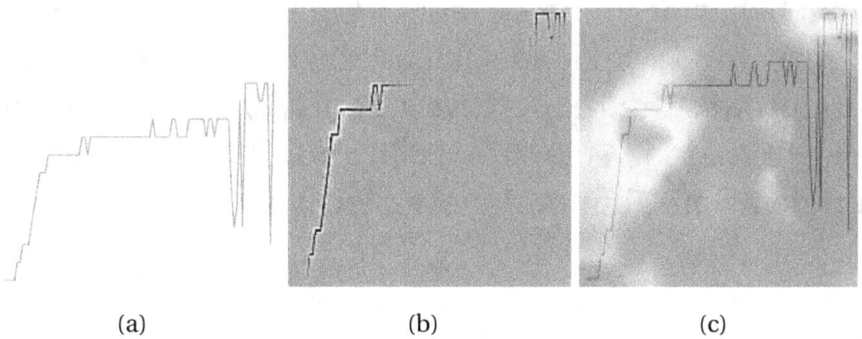

(a)   (b)   (c)

Figure 6.10: Focus area of ResNet50 network on a representative graph of password: Football

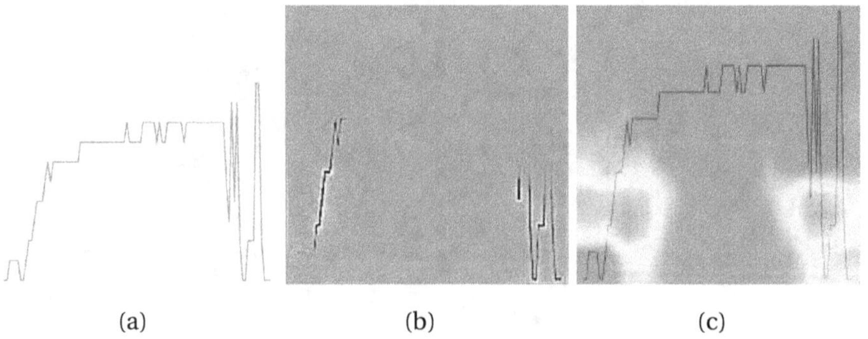

Figure 6.11: Focus area of ResNet50 network on a representative graph of password: passw0rd

tablished benhcmark suits such as PARSEC [Bienia, 2011a] unlike Android, we chose to use Linux for the experimentations provided in this section to show the efficacy and scalability of DATE.

For multi-core systems, multi-threaded applications are heavily used in recent times to represent workloads as they could leverage concurrency and parallel processing. Examples of such applications are available in several benchmarks such as PARSEC [Bienia, 2011a]. For our experiments we have tried several applications from the PARSEC benchmark such as Streamcluster, Blackscholes, Facesim etc. but to evaluate the effectiveness of our $DATE$ mechanism we chose Blackscholes and Streamclsuter with $native$ option because it closely represented a real-world mixed (compute and memory intensive) workload application and the execution period was long enough to observe the thermal behavior in the system. We also evaluated our approach for other real-world workload such as playing a Youtube video on the Chromium browser and RSA [Rivest et al., 1978] encryption and decryption algorithm for 512, 1024, 2048 and 4096 bits. We have run all our experiments on UbuntuMate version 14.04 (Linux Odroid Kernel: 3.10.105).

	Base. T.	Blackscholes				Streamcluster				RSA				Youtube			
		OnDemand	Performance	MRPI	DATE	OnDemand	Performance	MRPI	DATE	OnDemand	Performance	MRPI	DATE	OnDemand	Performance	MRPI	DATE
CPU 4	61	76	78	76	68	95	95	90	90	83	86	84	74	91	90	91	84
CPU 5	64	75	75	76	65	88	92	93	86	78	75	84	82	87	86	86	80
CPU 6	68	84	85	84	72	96	95	96	90	86	86	77	82	96	90	95	90
CPU 7	62	82	82	72	67	95	95	95	92	89	81	80	77	95	94	95	88
Base. T. Diff CPU 4		15	17	15	7	34	34	29	29	22	25	23	13	30	29	30	23
CPU 5		11	11	12	1	24	28	29	22	14	11	20	18	23	24	22	16
CPU 6		16	17	16	4	28	27	28	22	18	18	9	14	28	22	27	22
CPU 7		20	20	10	5	33	33	33	30	27	19	18	15	33	32	33	26
τ		20	20	16	7	34	34	33	30	27	25	23	18	33	32	33	26

Figure 6.12: Table showing maximum operating temperature of ARM A15 (big) CPUs for different applications along with *baseline temperature* and values of *Baseline Maximum Thermal Deviation* (τ) for corresponding CPUs

6.7.2 Experimental Results

In Fig. 6.12, 6.13 and 6.14 we can see step by step evaluation of Baseline Maximum Thermal Deviation (τ), Spatial Maximum Thermal Deviation (ω) and frequency of thermal cycle (θ) during execution of the application for different applications using DATE. In Fig. 6.12 Base T. represents the baseline temperature for different ARM Cortex A15 CPUs.

Table 6.1 shows TSMP values for different applications when various resource management methodologies are employed. We evaluated DATE against ondemand and performance governor of Linux and the state-of-the-art methodology proposed in [Reddy et al., 2017]. In [Reddy et al., 2017], the researchers have proposed a workload management system, which classifies workloads of the executing applications based on Memory Reads Per Instruction (MRPI) metric and manages DVFS levels of cores based on it.

RSA encryption and decryption was performed for 512, 1024, 2048, 4096 bits for 10 secs for each types. Based on the TSMP values in Table 6.1 DATE is 4.30% more secure for RSA encryption and decryption than the Linux Performance Governor. Whereas, DATE is 139.24% more secure for Streamcluster benchmark against temperature based side-channel attacks than the Linux Performance Governor. DATE is also 35.46% more secure than MRPI [Reddy et al., 2017] for the Streamcluster benchmark.

Fig. 6.15 graphically shows the temperature peaks achieved for the Blackscholes application using DATE, which closely resonates with

	Blackscholes				Streamcluster				RSA				Youtube			
	OnDemand	*Performance*	*MRPI*	*DATE*	*OnDemand*	*Performance*	*MRPI*	*DATE*	*OnDemand*	*Performance*	*MRPI*	*DATE*	*OnDemand*	*Performance*	*MRPI*	*DATE*
CPU 4	60	62	62	61	62	64	64	65	64	56	62	60	69	59	63	59
CPU 5	61	63	63	61	63	65	67	64	65	57	65	61	66	60	63	60
CPU 6	64	65	65	64	66	67	65	69	68	59	65	67	70	63	65	65
CPU 7	61	62	62	62	62	64	64	67	64	56	64	63	67	59	62	63
ω	21	20	19	8	33	31	31	25	25	30	22	21	28	35	33	25

Figure 6.13: Table showing least average operating temperature of ARM A15 (big) CPUs for different applications and values of *Spatial Maximum Thermal Deviation* (τ) for corresponding CPUs

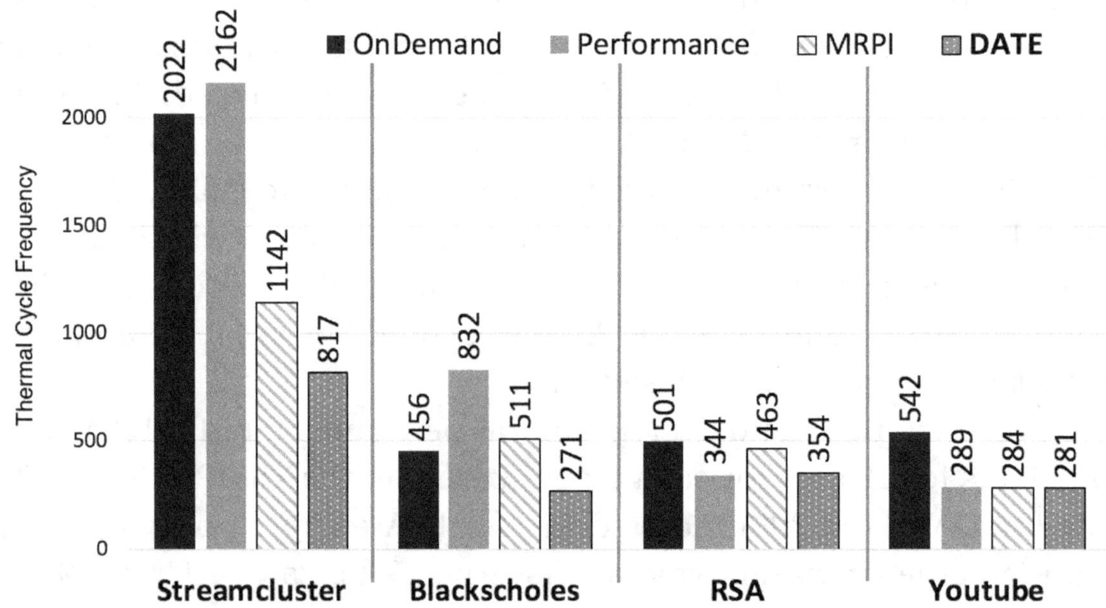

Figure 6.14: Frequency of thermal cycles for different benchmarking applications on different power and mapping schemes

Table 6.1: TSMP values for different methodologies

App	OnDemand	Performance	MRPI	DATE
Blackscholes	0.001968	0.001124	0.001792	0.003496
Streamcluster	0.000479	0.000450	0.000846	0.001146
RSA	0.001811	0.002439	0.001912	0.002544
Youtube	0.001661	0.002840	0.002906	0.003012

Table 6.2: Thermal cycle reduction comparison with DATE

App	OnDemand	Performance	MRPI
Blackscholes	40.57%	67.42%	46.96%
Streamcluster	59.59%	62.21%	28.45%
RSA	29.34%	-2.91%	23.54%
Youtube	48.15%	2.76%	1.06%

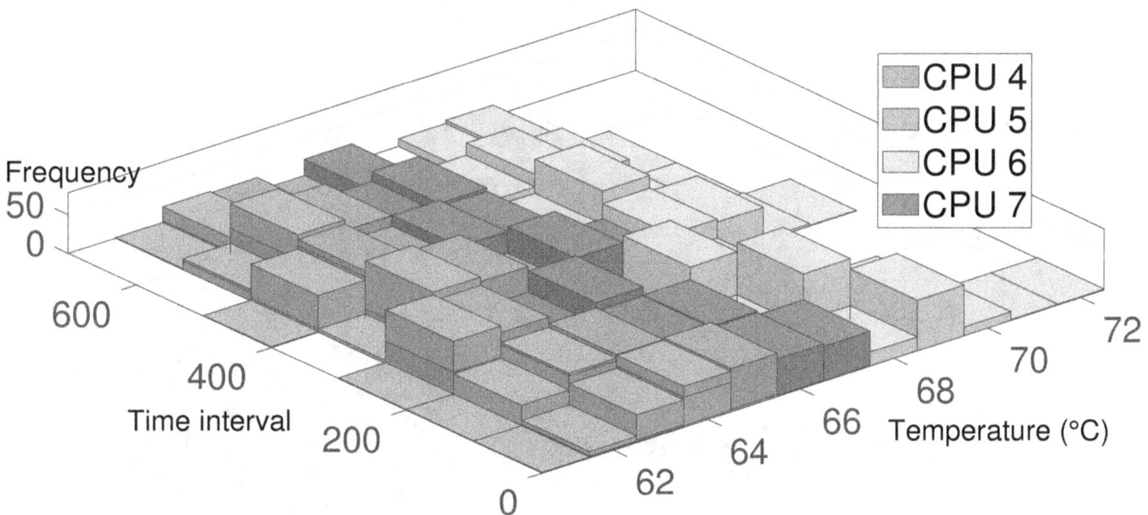

Figure 6.15: Temperature peaks of 4 ARM A15 big CPU cores while executing Blackscholes benchmark using DATE

baseline temperature (see Fig. 6.1). In Fig. 6.15, the 3D plot view is shown such that it is easier to get a holistic view of the spatial and temporal thermal behaviour of the big CPU cores (CPU 4, 5, 6 & 7). We have three axes in Fig. 6.15, where the X axis is labelled, "Temperature", represents the temperature of the respective big CPU cores (CPU 4, 5, 6 &

168

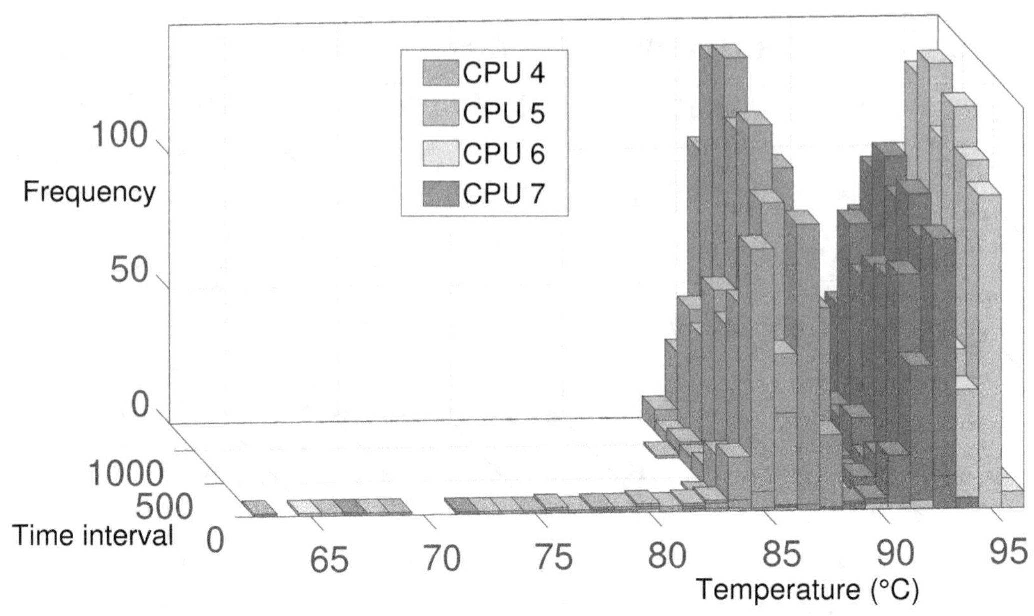

(a) Using Ondemand governor

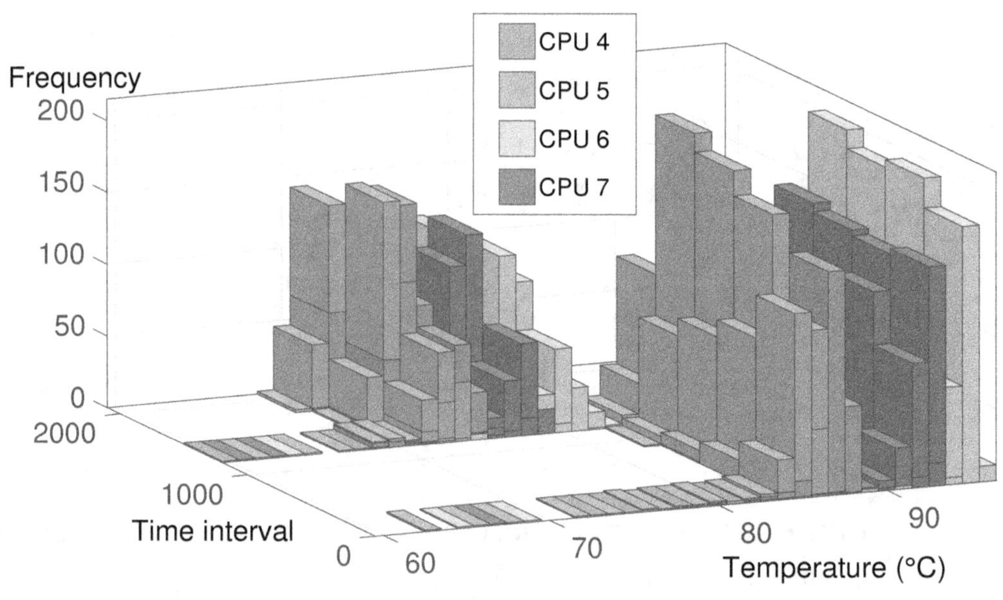

(b) Using Performance governor

Figure 6.16: Temperature peaks of 4 ARM A15 big CPU cores while executing Blackscholes benchmark using Linux's Ondemand and Performance governors

7) in °C; the Y axis is labelled, "Time interval", represents the execution time interval in milliseconds; and, the Z axis is labelled, "Frequency", represents the respective frequency of the big CPU cores scaled to 0.1 MHz). Fig. 6.16 is also represented with similar 3D plot view with similar axes.

In comparison to Fig. 6.15, Fig. 6.16 highlights the temperature peaks achieved for the Blackscholes application while executing on ondemand (refer to Fig. 6.16.(a)) and performance (refer to Fig. 6.16.(b)) governors of Linux. From the figures (Fig. 6.16 and Fig. 6.15) it is also very evident that DATE is able to achieve the reduction in spatial thermal gradient as well as temporal thermal gradient while the overall operating temperature of the CPUs is also reduced at the same time (also see the histogram comparison in Fig. 6.17).

Note: For data dependent applications over a network such as playing a video on Youtube in Chromium browser, it was still difficult to reduce the *Spatial Themal Deviation* due to data dependencies over the Internet or due to workload imbalance between the CPU cores.

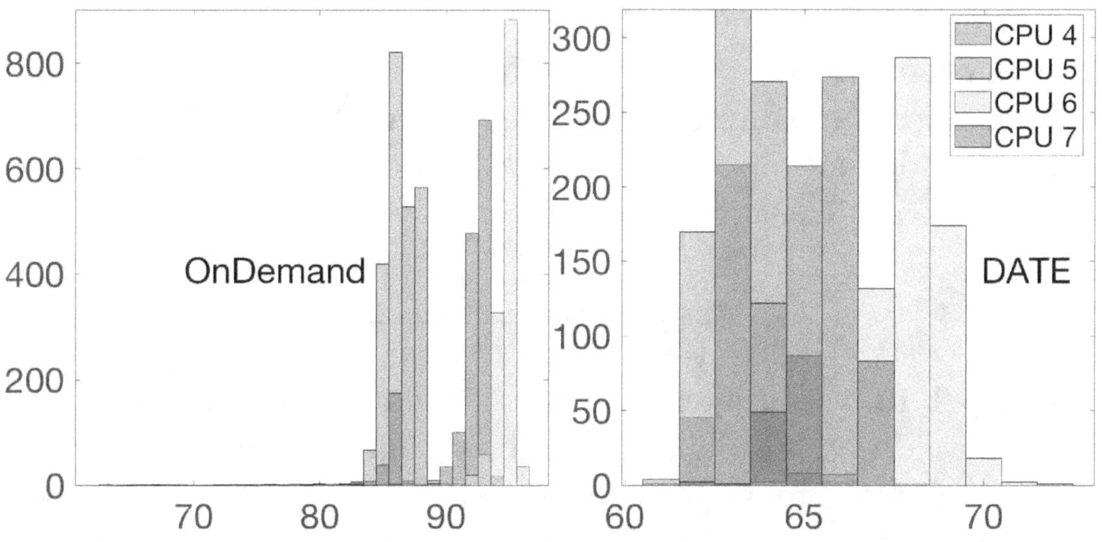

Figure 6.17: Histograms of temperature peaks of ARM big CPUs for Blackscholes using ondemand governor vs DATE (Frequency vs temperature (°C))

6.7.3   Effect on Device Reliability

Thermal gradient (spatial and temporal) and thermal cycling [Iranfar et al., 2018] play important role in the reliability of the system in terms of lifespan. The rate of temperature changes on the system affects the lifespan of the device over time due to degradation in the structural integrity and chemical property. More importantly, thermal cycle reduces the whole systems MTTF (Mean-time-to-failure) as the amplitude and/or frequency of thermal cycles increase. The number of the thermal cycles ($N_{TC}(i)$) that can result in the occurrence of failure due to the ith thermal cycle can be deduced from the modified Coffin-Manson equation (see Eq. 6.12) mentioned in [Xiang et al., 2010].

$$N_{TC}(i) = A_{TC}(\delta T_i - T_{th})^{-b} exp(\frac{E_{aTC}}{T_{max_i}}) \tag{6.12}$$

In Eq. 6.12, δT_i represents the maximum thermal amplitude change of the ith thermal cycle, T_{th} is the threshold temperature of the component/device at which inelastic deformation begins, A_{TC} is an empirically determined constant [Xiang et al., 2010], b is the Coffin-Manson exponent constant, E_{aTC} is the activation energy and T_{max_i} is the maximum temperature in the ith thermal cycle. Therefore, from Eq. 6.12 we can deduce the MTTF ($MTTF_{TC}$) [Coskun et al., 2008] related to thermal cycle (N_{TC}) as follows:

$$MTTF_{TC} = \frac{N_{TC}\sum_{i=0}^{n} t_i}{n} \tag{6.13}$$

In Eq. 6.13, t_i is the temperature of the component/device at i^{th} thermal cycle, and n is the total number (frequency) of thermal cycle. Since, we focused most of the experiments on the Odroid XU4 MP-SoC, and if we assume that the number of the thermal cycles (N_{TC}) that can result in the occurrence of failure due to the ith thermal cycle is same for the same device platform, then we can easily evaluate the $MTTF_{TC}$ for each executing application on individual thermal management methodologies. Now, if we take the example of Blackscholes application being executed on the MPSoC using Linux's ondemand governor and assume that t_i is the baseline maximum thermal deviation i.e. $t_i = \tau$ since baseline temperature is the same during all the experiments performed during the time of experimentation, then from Fig. 6.12 and Fig. 6.14 we could notice that t_i (τ) is 20 and n (frequency of thermal cycle) is 456. Hence, putting the value of t_i and n in Eq. 6.13, we get the value of $MTTF_{TC}$ as $\frac{N_{TC} \times 9140}{456}$. Now, if we consider the DATE methodology, where Blackscholes is executed on the Odroid XU4 using DATE, t_i is 7 (see Fig. 6.12) and n is 271 (see Fig. 6.14), then we get the value of $MTTF_{TC}$ as $\frac{N_{TC} \times 1904}{271}$. Therefore, comparing the $MTTF_{TC}$ of executing Blackscholes using the Linux's ondemand governor and the DATE, the DATE methodology is 2.85 (approx.) ($\simeq \frac{N_{TC} \times 9140}{456} / \frac{N_{TC} \times 1904}{271}$) times more reliable and improve the lifespan of the device over time.

6.8 Discussion

For applications with data dependencies over the Internet such as Youtube or applications with workload imbalance between the CPU cores, a possible solution to reduce the Spatial Themal Deviation is to add noise using software/algorithmic implementation to the temperature variance such that it becomes very difficult to understand the pattern of execution or data being processed on the CPU cores. Here, noise could be regarded as another random execution of secondary tasks in order to keep the CPU temperature high so that temperature dissipated due to execution of the current task could be masked. The main challenge in using such a solution is that to predict when to add the noise in order to mask thermal dissipation of the currently executing task properly.

6.9 Summary

In this chapter, we examined the affect of DVFS related to temperature side-channel attack on CPUs on a MPSoC. We also proposed a universal metric, TSMP, to quantify security of embedded devices against temperature side-channel attacks and introduced a novel approach, DATE, to secure DVFS enabled MPSoCs against the same. To prove the feasibility of such an attack we also performed a real thermal side channel attack on Samsung Note 9 mobile device and Odroid XU4 development board utilizing convolutional neural network based machine learning approach. Experimental studies were evaluated on the Exynos 5422 MPSoC in the Odroid XU4 and comparative study with the state-of-the-art proves the efficacy of DATE in securing the device from thermal side-channel attack. Moreover, from experimental evaluation we also proved that DATE is not just effective against temperature side-channel attacks but is also effective to enhance reliability in terms of the lifespan of the device.

Chapter 7

Conclusion

We conclude this book by providing a summary of our achievements and impacts as a result of this research work. We also outline some of the potential future directions for building on this work.

7.1 Achievements and impact

Low power mobile computing systems such as smartphones and wearables have become an integral part of our daily lives and are being used to achieve a plethora of tasks: playing mobile games, watching TV shows, managing food, managing our active and social lives. These devices employ heterogeneous multi-processor System-on-a-Chip (MPSoC), which comes equipped with different types of multiple processing elements such as CPU, GPU to cater for the performance and power consumption requirements of the executing applications on these platforms. Given the fact that these smartphones and wearables utilizing MPSoC are battery operated most of the times, thus, have limited power supply, the key challenges include catering for performance while reducing the power consumption. Moreover, the reliability in terms of lifespan of these devices are also affected by the peak thermal behaviour on the device, and henceforth, it is also crucial to reduce thermal behaviour of such devices s well. Another important challenge to address in these devices are security vulnerability and protection against side-channel attacks, especially temperature side-channel attack. One of the main approaches to resolve these aforementioned challenges is Dynamic Voltage and Frequency Scaling (DVFS).

In this book, we have examined the effect of DVFS on different processing elements on the MPSoC. We have also contributed several novel methodologies to perform DVFS on a combination of CPU, GPU and RAM to cater for the performance requirement of the executing applications while reducing the power consumption and peak temperature and improving security against temperature side-channel attack on the MPSoC. A brief account of the major contributions of the book is as follows.

In Chapter 3, we explored a novel approach, SoCodeCNN, to convert program source code into machine understandable image using computer vision methodology. Using this approach program source code of different types of applications could be classified into three categories: computer intensive, memory intensive and mixed workload (both compute and memory intensive), by Convolutional Neural Networks without the need for skilled human's intervention and henceforth, appropriate DVFS could be performed on the CPU of the mobile MPSoC to reduce the power consumption of the device. Experimental results also show that using SoCodeCNN we could classify the benchmarks from PARSEC, Splash-2, and MiBench in a completely automated manner and with high prediction accuracy. We also demonstrated the application of using SoCodeCNN perform DVFS on CPUs in a real hardware platform utilizing mobile MPSoC to optimize power consumption.

In Chapter 4, we introduced a power and thermal efficiency agent, Next, for mobile MPSoCs based on reinforcement learning (RL), which maximizes performance while reducing power consumption and temperature of the mobile applications depending on the user's interaction with the display/UI and the desired Quality of Service (QoS). Here, we also introduced a metric, Performance Per Degree Watt (PPDW), which incorporates the performance of the executing application, power consumption and peak temperature of the device. The proposed RL agent performs DVFS on CPU and GPU based on the PPDW metric to reduce power consumption and temperature of the device. Experimental evaluation on real hardware platforms shows the efficacy of the proposed approach, Next, along with its improvement over the state-of-the-art power and thermal management scheme.

In Chapter 5, we explored the affects of DVFS on RAM (memory) in the mobile MPSoC. Here, we also introduced a heuristic approach, CGM-DVFS, to perform DVFS on CPU, GPU and RAM. This mechanism is application specific rather than application agnostic and with experimental evaluation we have also showed that it is better suited to perform DVFS on CPU, GPU and RAM based on profiling of the application due to the challenges of optimizing power while performing DVFS on CPU, GPU and RAM together. Experimental results prove the efficacy of CGM-DVFS in reducing power consumption and peak temperature while catering for performance requirement compared to the state-of-the-art approaches. Through experimental results we have also shown that application specific profiling approaches such as CGM-DVFS outperform and result in closer to optimal power consumption compared to delayed Reinforcement Learning approaches such as Q-Learning when the system (environment) is dynamic.

In Chapter 6, we explored the effects of DVFS towards the vulnerabilities against temperature (thermal) side-channel attack in the mobile MPSoC. Here, we also proposed a universal metric, TSMP, to quantify security of embedded devices utilizing MPSoC against temperature side-channel attacks. We introduced a novel approach, DATE, to secure DVFS enabled MPSoCs against this type of attack. We also performed a real temperature side channel attack on real mobile devices utilizing machine learning approach to realize the feasibility of such an attack in commercial products. Experimental studies evaluated on the real hardware platform and comparative study with the state-of-the-art proves the efficacy of DATE in securing the device from thermal side-channel attack. Moreover, from experimental evaluation we also proved that DATE is not just effective against temperature side-channel attacks but is also effective to enhance reliability in terms of the lifespan of the device.

7.2 Extensions and future work

We believe this work opens up more questions and avenues to explore than it closes off. There is much more potential to perform DVFS in mobile MPSoCs to optimize power and thermal behaviour of the device while securing it from temperature based side-channel attack. This section highlights some of the potential future research directions to extend or augment the work presented in this book.

7.2.1 Automated program/application classification to perform bespoke DVFS on CPU, GPU and RAM

In Chapter 3, we have already explored an approach using SoCodeCNN to automatically classify programs / applications into three categories: compute intensive, memory intensive and mixed workload. We also introduced an automated power management agent, APM, that performs DVFS on CPU based on the program classification. However, in this chapter we have only shown one method of automatically classifying programs and then performing DVFS only on CPU. As we have already established that DVFS on GPU and RAM alongside CPU could contribute to overall power saving and thermal behaviour reduction, this paves the way for researchers to adopt the automated program classification approach of SoCodeCNN and then develop more holistic DVFS mechanisms for CPU, GPU & RAM.

On the other hand, it should also be kept in mind that even within the different classification of programs, not all applications would be needing the same CPU, GPU or RAM utilization. For example, some compute intensive workload could be dependent on more GPU rather than CPU and vice-versa. However, given the current state of the technology it is not possible to get an informed idea of the type of the application without the use of hardware performance counters in mobile computing systems. That said, given the fact that commercial mobile devices avoid including additional hardware performance counters due to space constraint on the MPSoC, it is much more desirable to introduce approaches that is capable of doing classification of application in a bespoke manner where appropriate DVFS on CPU, GPU and RAM could be performed based on needs to optimize power and thermal behaviour.

7.2.2   Prioritizing QoE alongside QoS

In Chapter 4, we observed that user's interaction with interactive mobile computing systems such as smartphones that could lead to different FPS during different interaction sessions and thus, perform DVFS on CPU & GPU accordingly. However, this work mostly focuses on generated FPS during interaction sessions and henceforth, focuses on QoS. That said, we need to keep in mind that when it comes to interactive mobile computing systems such as smartphones, Quality of Experience (QoE) [Isuwa et al., 2022] plays an important role as well. QoE, compared to QoS, is a more user-centric concept that encompasses the overall satisfaction and perception of a service's quality by its end users. QoE focuses on subjective factors and aims to measure the user experience from a holistic perspective. This includes not only the technical aspects of a service, such as FPS, but also factors such as content quality, and device brightness, as well as the user's individual preferences and expectations. Most smartphone users expect a certain level of QoE while interacting with their smartphones, however, the work proposed in Chapter 4 does not prioritize that. Moving forward this paves the way for researchers to design DVFS based approaches that are capable of achieving both QoE and QoS requirements.

7.2.3 Reducing exploration time of application agnostic RL approaches

In Chapter 4 and 5, we observed that an RL agent based approach to perform DVFS on CPU, GPU and RAM would require enough exploration time in a dynamic system (environment) to achieve the optimal power consumption and thermal behaviour. However, this might not be possible for all types of applications, especially the ones with shorter executing period. Right now, recurrent neural network (RNN) [Mandic and Chambers, 2001] [Sherstinsky, 2020] such as long short-term memory (LSTM), exhibits good performance in temporal dynamic behavior, and this approach could be utilized in combination with RL agent to optimize the power consumption and thermal behaviour of the device in an application agnostic manner without requiring a lot of exploration.

7.2.4 Deep Learning and Reinforcement Learning to secure against temperature side-channel attack

In Chapter 6, we explored a way to exploit vulnerability of MPSoCs against temperature side-channel attack using Deep Learning (DL). Currently, in this chapter, DL with CNN architecture (visual convolutional neural network) is utilized, however, it might be better use time-series based neural networks such as recurrent neural networks (RNNs), long short-term memory neural networks (LSTMs), attention-based models [Ekambaram et al., 2020], etc., without the need of data of the thermal behaviour of PEs to be converted to visual graphical representation to train the neural network. With the development of time-series based neural network architecture, the approach could also reduce the latency associated with the generation of visual graphical representation of the thermal data to be used for training/prediction.

In this chapter, though ResNet50 based DL model is utilized to exploit vulnerability of MPSoCs against temperature side-channel attack, this also paves the way to propose more advanced DL and RL approaches to secure against such attack as well. Given the fact that RL agents can maximize rewards and reach optimal solutions in an application antagonistic manner, in future, we could observe proposal of such approaches using the TSMP metric to secure against temperature side-channel attack in the mobile MPSoC.

Bibliography

[top, a] The 10 best smartphones of 2018. `https://www.zdnet.com/article/10-best-smartphones/`. Accessed: 2018-01-31.

[com, a] The 25 most popular passwords of 2018 will make you feel like a security genius. Accessed: 2018-01-31.

[com, b] The 25 worst passwords of 2017. Accessed: 2018-01-31.

[and,] Android 9 pie. `https://www.android.com/versions/pie-9-0/`. Accessed: 2018-01-31.

[arm,] Arm big.little technology. `http://www.arm.com/`. Accessed: 2018-07-23.

[top, b] The best smartphone of 2019: 15 top mobile phones tested and ranked. `https://www.techradar.com/uk/news/best-phone/2`. Accessed: 2018-01-31.

[eas,] Energy aware scheduling (eas). `https://developer.arm.com/open-source/energy-aware-scheduling`. Accessed: 2018-01-31.

[eop,] Eoptomizer lite - note 9 mobile app. `https://github.com/somdipdey/EOptomizer-Lite-Note-9`. Accessed: 2018-01-27.

[exy, a] Exynos 5 octa (5422). `https://www.samsung.com/exynos`. Accessed: 2018-07-23.

[exy, b] Exynos 9 series (9810). `https://www.samsung.com/semiconductor/minisite/exynos/products/mobileprocessor/exynos-9-series-9810`. Accessed: 2019-01-27.

[exy, c] Exynos 9825 mpsoc. `https://www.samsung.com/semiconductor/minisite/exynos/products/mobileprocessor/exynos-9825/`. Accessed: 2020-06-26.

[exy, d] Exynos 990 mpsoc. `https://www.samsung.com/semiconductor/minisite/exynos/products/mobileprocessor/exynos-990/`. Accessed: 2020-06-26.

[flu,] Flutter - build apps for any screen. `https://flutter.dev/`. Accessed: 2018-01-27.

[gal,] Galaxy note9. `https://www.samsung.com/global/galaxy/galaxy-note9/`. Accessed: 2018-01-27.

[del,] Global mobile consumer survey: Us edition. `https://www2.deloitte.com/us/en/pages/technology-media-and-telecommunications/articles/global-mobile-consumer-survey-us-edition.html`.

[goo,] Google play. `https://play.google.com/store`.

[med,] How much time do we spend on social media? `https://mediakix.com/blog/how-much-time-is-spent-on-social-media-lifetime/`.

[jai,] The latest jailbreak statistics are jaw-dropping. `https://www.businessinsider.com/jailbreak-statistics-2013-3`. Accessed: 2021-06-26.

[odr, a] Odroid smartpower2. `https://www.odroid.co.uk/odroid-smart-power-2`. Accessed: 2018-07-23.

[odr, b] Odroid-xu4. `https://goo.gl/KmHZRG`. Accessed: 2018-07-23.

[ope,] The open standard for parallel programming of heterogeneous systems. `https://www.khronos.org/opencl/`. Accessed: 2018-07-23.

[web,] Roy Longbottom's PC Benchmark Collection. `http://www.roylongbottom.org.uk`. [Online; accessed 10-Oct-2018].

[res,] Screen time stats 2019: Here's how much you use your phone during the workday. `https://blog.rescuetime.com/screen-time-stats-2018/`.

[mos,] These were the 10 most-downloaded apps of the decade.

[eMa,] Top 5 stats to know about us mobile usage. `https://www.emarketer.com/corporate/coverage/be-prepared-mobile`.

[goo, 2023] (2023). Google autofill. `https://support.google.com/accounts/answer/6197437?hl=en&co=GENIE.Platform%3DAndroid`.

[Aalsaud et al., 2016a] Aalsaud, A., Shafik, R., Rafiev, A., Xia, F., Yang, S., and Yakovlev, A. (2016a). Power–aware performance adaptation of concurrent applications in heterogeneous many-core systems. In *Proceedings of the 2016 International Symposium on Low Power Electronics and Design*, pages 368–373. ACM.

[Aalsaud et al., 2016b] Aalsaud, A., Shafik, R., Rafiev, A., Xia, F., Yang, S., and Yakovlev, A. (2016b). Power-aware performance adaptation of concurrent applications in heterogeneous many-core systems. In *Intl. Symp. on Low Power Electronics and Design*, pages 368–373. ACM.

[Ahissar et al., 2009] Ahissar, M., Nahum, M., Nelken, I., and Hochstein, S. (2009). Reverse hierarchies and sensory learning. *Philosophical Transactions of the Royal Society of London B: Biological Sciences*, 364(1515):285–299.

[Allamanis et al., 2018] Allamanis, M., Barr, E. T., Devanbu, P., and Sutton, C. (2018). A survey of machine learning for big code and naturalness. *ACM Computing Surveys (CSUR)*, 51(4):81.

[Ambrose et al., 2015] Ambrose, J. A., Ragel, R. G., Jayasinghe, D., Li, T., and Parameswaran, S. (2015). Side channel attacks in embedded systems: A tale of hostilities and deterrence. In *Quality Electronic Design (ISQED), 2015 16th International Symposium on*, pages 452–459. IEEE.

[Angioletti et al., 2019] Angioletti, D., Bertani, F., Bolchini, C., Cerizzi, F., and Miele, A. (2019). A runtime resource management policy for opencl workloads on heterogeneous multicores. In *2019 Design, Automation & Test in Europe Conference & Exhibition (DATE)*, pages 1385–1390. IEEE.

[Ashouri et al., 2018] Ashouri, A. H., Killian, W., Cavazos, J., Palermo, G., and Silvano, C. (2018). A survey on compiler autotuning using machine learning. *arXiv preprint arXiv:1801.04405*.

[Bartolini et al., 2016] Bartolini, D. B., Miedl, P., and Thiele, L. (2016). On the capacity of thermal covert channels in multicores. In *Proceedings of the Eleventh European Conference on Computer Systems*, pages 1–16.

[Basireddy, 2019] Basireddy, K. R. (2019). *Runtime energy management of concurrent applications for multi-core platforms*. PhD thesis, University of Southampton.

[Basireddy et al., 2019] Basireddy, K. R., Singh, A. K., Al-Hashimi, B. M., and Merrett, Geoff V., I. (2019). Adamd: Adaptive mapping and dvfs for energy-efficient heterogeneous multi-cores. *IEEE Transactions on Computer-Aided Design of Integrated Circuits and Systems*, page 12.

[Basireddy et al., 2018] Basireddy, K. R., Wachter, E. W., Al-Hashimi, B. M., and Merrett, G. V. (2018). Workload-aware runtime energy management for HPC systems. In *Intl. Conf. on High Performance Computing & Simulation*, page 8.

[Benoit and Robert, 2008] Benoit, A. and Robert, Y. (2008). Mapping pipeline skeletons onto heterogeneous platforms. *Journal of Parallel and Distributed Computing*, 68(6):790–808.

[B'far, 2004] B'far, R. (2004). *Mobile computing principles: designing and developing mobile applications with UML and XML*. Cambridge University Press.

[Bhat et al., 2017a] Bhat, G., Gumussoy, S., and Ogras, U. Y. (2017a). Power-temperature stability and safety analysis for multiprocessor systems. *ACM Transactions on Embedded Computing Systems (TECS)*, 16(5s):145.

[Bhat et al., 2019] Bhat, G., Gumussoy, S., and Ogras, U. Y. (2019). Power and thermal analysis of commercial mobile platforms: Experiments and case studies. In *2019 Design, Automation & Test in Europe Conference & Exhibition (DATE)*, pages 144–149. IEEE.

[Bhat et al., 2018] Bhat, G., Mandal, S. K., Gupta, U., and Ogras, U. Y. (2018). Online learning for adaptive optimization of heterogeneous socs. In *Proceedings of the International Conference on Computer-Aided Design*, pages 1–6.

[Bhat et al., 2017b] Bhat, G., Singla, G., Unver, A. K., and Ogras, U. Y. (2017b). Algorithmic optimization of thermal and power management for heterogeneous mobile platforms. *IEEE Transactions on Very Large Scale Integration (VLSI) Systems*, 26(3):544–557.

[Bienia, 2011a] Bienia, C. (2011a). *Benchmarking Modern Multiprocessors*. PhD thesis, Princeton University.

[Bienia, 2011b] Bienia, C. (2011b). *Benchmarking Modern Multiprocessors*. PhD thesis, Princeton University.

[Bienia et al., 2008] Bienia, C., Kumar, S., and Li, K. (2008). Parsec vs. splash-2: A quantitative comparison of two multithreaded benchmark suites on chip-multiprocessors. In *Workload Characterization,*

2008. IISWC 2008. IEEE International Symposium on, pages 47–56. IEEE.

[Bouvier et al., 2021] Bouvier, M., Valentian, A., and Sicard, G. (2021). Scalable pitch-constrained neural processing unit for 3d integration with event-based imagers. In *2021 58th ACM/IEEE Design Automation Conference (DAC)*, pages 385–390. IEEE.

[Budiu, 2015] Budiu, R. (2015). Multitasking on mobile devices. In *White Paper of Nielsen Norman Group logoNielsen Norman Group*. NNGroup.

[Carlon, 2017] Carlon, K. (2017). First android malware with code injection has arrived. `https://www.androidauthority.com/first-android-malware-code-injection-778969/`.

[Chakradhar et al., 2010] Chakradhar, S., Sankaradas, M., Jakkula, V., and Cadambi, S. (2010). A dynamically configurable coprocessor for convolutional neural networks. In *ACM SIGARCH Computer Architecture News*, volume 38, pages 247–257. ACM.

[Chantem et al., 2010] Chantem, T., Hu, X. S., and Dick, R. P. (2010). Temperature-aware scheduling and assignment for hard real-time applications on mpsocs. *IEEE Transactions on Very Large Scale Integration (VLSI) Systems*, 19(10):1884–1897.

[Chen and Lin, 2014] Chen, X.-W. and Lin, X. (2014). Big data deep learning: challenges and perspectives. *IEEE access*, 2:514–525.

[Cochran et al., 2011] Cochran, R., Hankendi, C., Coskun, A. K., and Reda, S. (2011). Pack & cap: adaptive DVFS and thread packing under power caps. In *Proc. of the IEEE/ACM Intl. symposium on microarchitecture*, pages 175–185.

[Coskun et al., 2008] Coskun, A. K., Rosing, T. S., and Gross, K. C. (2008). Temperature management in multiprocessor socs using online learning. In *2008 45th ACM/IEEE Design Automation Conference*, pages 890–893. IEEE.

[Coskun et al., 2007] Coskun, A. K., Rosing, T. S., and Whisnant, K. (2007). Temperature aware task scheduling in mpsocs. In *Design, Automation & Test in Europe Conference & Exhibition, 2007. DATE'07*, pages 1–6. IEEE.

[Cruz et al., 2019] Cruz, L., Abreu, R., and Lo, D. (2019). To the attention of mobile software developers: guess what, test your app! *Empirical Software Engineering*, 24(4):2438–2468.

[Cummins et al., 2017] Cummins, C., Petoumenos, P., Wang, Z., and Leather, H. (2017). End-to-end deep learning of optimization heuristics. In *Parallel Architectures and Compilation Techniques (PACT), 2017 26th International Conference on*, pages 219–232. IEEE.

[Dallow, 2009] Dallow, P. (2009). Th e visual complex: Mapping some interdisciplinary dimensions of visual literacy. In *Visual literacy*, pages 99–112. Routledge.

[De Haas, 2007] De Haas, J. (2007). Side channel attacks and counter-measures for embedded systems. *Black Hat, Las Vegas, NV, USA*, page 82.

[De Vogeleer et al.,] De Vogeleer, K., Jouvelot, P., and Memmi, G. The impact of surface area on the radiative thermal behavior of embedded systems.

[Demme et al., 2012] Demme, J., Martin, R., Waksman, A., and Sethumadhavan, S. (2012). Side-channel vulnerability factor: A metric for measuring information leakage. In *2012 39th Annual International Symposium on Computer Architecture (ISCA)*, pages 106–117. IEEE.

[DeVogeleer et al., 2014] DeVogeleer, K., Memmi, G., Jouvelot, P., and Coelho, F. (2014). Modeling the temperature bias of power consumption for nanometer-scale cpus in application processors. In *Embedded Computer Systems: Architectures, Modeling, and Simulation (SAMOS XIV), 2014 International Conference on*, pages 172–180. IEEE.

[Dey et al., 2020] Dey, S. et al. (2020). User interaction aware reinforcement learning for power and thermal efficiency of cpu-gpu mobile mpsocs. In *2020 DATE*. IEEE.

[Dey et al., 2019a] Dey, S., Guajardo, E. Z., Basireddy, K. R., Wang, X., Singh, A. K., and McDonald-Maier, K. (2019a). Edgecoolingmode: An agent based thermal management mechanism for dvfs enabled heterogeneous mpsocs. In *2019 32nd International Conference on VLSI Design and 2019 18th International Conference on Embedded Systems (VLSID)*, pages 19–24. IEEE.

[Dey et al., 2019b] Dey, S., Singh, A. K., and McDonald-Maier, K. (2019b). P-edgecoolingmode: An agent based performance aware thermal management unit for dvfs enabled heterogeneous mpsocs. *IET Computers & Digital Techniques*.

[Dey et al., 2019c] Dey, S., Singh, A. K., Prasad, D. K., and Mcdonald-Maier, K. D. (2019c). Socodecnn: Program source code for visual cnn classification using computer vision methodology. *IEEE Access*, 7:157158–157172.

[Dey et al., 2019d] Dey, S., Singh, A. K., Saha, S., Wang, X., and McDonald-Maier, K. D. (2019d). Rewardprofiler: A reward based design space profiler on dvfs enabled mpsocs. In *2019 6th IEEE International Conference on Cyber Security and Cloud Computing (CSCloud)/2019 5th IEEE International Conference on Edge Computing and Scalable Cloud (EdgeCom)*, pages 210–220. IEEE.

[Dey et al., 2019e] Dey, S., Singh, A. K., Saha, S., Wang, X., and McDonald-Maier, K. D. (2019e). Rewardprofiler: A reward based design space profiler on dvfs enabled mpsocs. In *2018 6th IEEE International Conference on Cyber Security and Cloud Computing (CSCloud)/2018 5th IEEE International Conference on Edge Computing and Scalable Cloud (EdgeCom)*. IEEE.

[Dey et al., 2019f] Dey, S., Singh, A. K., Wang, X., and McDonald-Maier, K. D. (2019f). Deadpool: Performance deadline based frequency pooling and thermal management agent in dvfs enabled mpsocs.

[Dillon and Spelke, 2017] Dillon, M. R. and Spelke, E. S. (2017). Young children's use of surface and object information in drawings of everyday scenes. *Child development*, 88(5):1701–1715.

[Donyanavard et al., 2016] Donyanavard, B., Mück, T., Sarma, S., and Dutt, N. (2016). SPARTA: runtime task allocation for energy efficient heterogeneous many-cores. In *Proc. of the Intl. Conf. on Hardware/Software Codesign and System Synthesis*, page 27. ACM.

[Ekambaram et al., 2020] Ekambaram, V., Manglik, K., Mukherjee, S., Sajja, S. S. K., Dwivedi, S., and Raykar, V. (2020). Attention based multi-modal new product sales time-series forecasting. In *Proceedings of the 26th ACM SIGKDD international conference on knowledge discovery & data mining*, pages 3110–3118.

[Eranian, 2008] Eranian, S. (2008). What can performance counters do for memory subsystem analysis? In *Proceedings of the 2008 ACM SIGPLAN workshop on Memory systems performance and correctness: held in conjunction with the Thirteenth International Conference on Architectural Support for Programming Languages and Operating Systems (ASPLOS'08)*, pages 26–30.

[Field et al., 2014] Field, H., Anderson, G., and Eder, K. (2014). Eacof: A framework for providing energy transparency to enable energy-aware software development. In *Proceedings of the 29th Annual ACM Symposium on Applied Computing*, pages 1194–1199. ACM.

[Georgiou et al., 2017] Georgiou, K., Kerrison, S., Chamski, Z., and Eder, K. (2017). Energy transparency for deeply embedded programs. *ACM Transactions on Architecture and Code Optimization (TACO)*, 14(1):8.

[Ghosh et al., 2019] Ghosh, S., Das, N., and Nasipuri, M. (2019). Reshaping inputs for convolutional neural network: Some common and uncommon methods. *Pattern Recognition*, 93:79–94.

[Goodfellow et al., 2016] Goodfellow, I., Bengio, Y., Courville, A., and Bengio, Y. (2016). *Deep learning*, volume 1. MIT press Cambridge.

[Goraczko et al., 2008] Goraczko, M., Liu, J., Lymberopoulos, D., Matic, S., Priyantha, B., and Zhao, F. (2008). Energy-optimal software partitioning in heterogeneous multiprocessor embedded systems. In *Proc. of the Design Automation Conference*, pages 191–196. ACM.

[Gordon-Ross et al., 2004] Gordon-Ross, A., Vahid, F., and Dutt, N. (2004). Automatic tuning of two-level caches to embedded applications. In *Proceedings of the conference on Design, automation and test in Europe-Volume 1*, page 10208. IEEE Computer Society.

[Gu et al., 2016] Gu, P., Stow, D., Barnes, R., Kursun, E., and Xie, Y. (2016). Thermal-aware 3d design for side-channel information leakage. In *Computer Design (ICCD), 2016 IEEE 34th International Conference on*, pages 520–527. IEEE.

[Gupta et al., 2017] Gupta, U., Patil, C. A., Bhat, G., Mishra, P., and Ogras, U. Y. (2017). Dypo: Dynamic pareto-optimal configuration selection for heterogeneous mpsocs. *ACM Transactions on Embedded Computing Systems (TECS)*, 16(5s):123.

[Guthaus et al., 2001] Guthaus, M. R., Ringenberg, J. S., Ernst, D., Austin, T. M., Mudge, T., and Brown, R. B. (2001). Mibench: A free, commercially representative embedded benchmark suite. In *Workload Characterization, 2001. WWC-4. 2001 IEEE International Workshop on*, pages 3–14. IEEE.

[Hanumaiah and Vrudhula, 2012] Hanumaiah, V. and Vrudhula, S. (2012). Energy-efficient operation of multicore processors by dvfs, task migration, and active cooling. *IEEE Transactions on Computers*, 63(2):349–360.

[He et al., 2016] He, K., Zhang, X., Ren, S., and Sun, J. (2016). Deep residual learning for image recognition. In *Proceedings of the IEEE conference on computer vision and pattern recognition*, pages 770–778.

[Hölzenspies et al., 2008] Hölzenspies, P. K., Hurink, J. L., Kuper, J., and Smit, G. J. (2008). Run-time spatial mapping of streaming applications to a heterogeneous multi-processor system-on-chip (MPSoC). In *Design, Automation and Test in Europe*, pages 212–217. ACM.

[Howard et al., 2017] Howard, A. G. et al. (2017). Mobilenets: Efficient convolutional neural networks for mobile vision applications. *arXiv preprint arXiv:1704.04861*.

[Hsieh et al., 2015] Hsieh, C.-Y., Park, J.-G., Dutt, N., and Lim, S.-S. (2015). Memory-aware cooperative cpu-gpu dvfs governor for mobile games. In *2015 13th IEEE Symposium on Embedded Systems For Real-time Multimedia (ESTIMedia)*, pages 1–8. IEEE.

[Hutter and Schmidt, 2013] Hutter, M. and Schmidt, J.-M. (2013). The temperature side channel and heating fault attacks. In *International Conference on Smart Card Research and Advanced Applications*, pages 219–235. Springer.

[Iranfar et al., 2018] Iranfar, A., Kamal, M., Afzali-Kusha, A., Pedram, M., and Atienza, D. (2018). Thespot: Thermal stress-aware power and temperature management for multiprocessor systems-on-chip. *IEEE Transactions on Computer-Aided Design of Integrated Circuits and Systems*, 37(8).

[Isuwa et al., 2022] Isuwa, S., Dey, S., Ortega, A. P., Singh, A. K., Al-Hashimi, B. M., and Merrett, G. V. (2022). Quarem: maximising qoe through adaptive resource management in mobile mpsoc platforms. *ACM Transactions on Embedded Computing Systems (TECS)*, 21(4):1–29.

[Isuwa et al., 2019] Isuwa, S., Dey, S., Singh, A. K., and McDonald-Maier, K. (2019). Teem: Online thermal-and energy-efficiency management on cpu-gpu mpsocs. In *2019 Design, Automation & Test in Europe Conference & Exhibition (DATE)*, pages 438–443. IEEE.

[Jan et al., 2003] Jan, M. R., Anantha, C., Borivoje, N., et al. (2003). Digital integrated circuits: a design perspective. *Pearson.*

[JANČOVÁ, 2010] JANČOVÁ, L. (2010). Translation and the role of the mother tongue in elt.

[Jerraya and Wolf, 2004] Jerraya, A. and Wolf, W. (2004). *Multiprocessor systems-on-chips.* Elsevier.

[Jiang et al., 2004] Jiang, L., Liu, D.-Y., and Yang, B. (2004). Smart home research. In *Proceedings of 2004 International Conference on Machine Learning and Cybernetics (IEEE Cat. No. 04EX826)*, volume 2, pages 659–663. IEEE.

[Johansson et al., 2016] Johansson, M. O., Midholt, M., Moliner, O. T. N., and Hunt, A. L. (2016). Adaptive touch panel synchronization. US Patent 9,354,744.

[John, 1994] John, G. H. (1994). When the best move isn't optimal: Q-learning with exploration. In *AAAI*, page 1464. Citeseer.

[Kalafatić et al.,] Kalafatić, Z. et al. Traffic sign detection and recognition. `https://shorturl.at/stDO6`.

[Khriji et al., 2022] Khriji, S., Chéour, R., and Kanoun, O. (2022). Dynamic voltage and frequency scaling and duty-cycling for ultra low-power wireless sensor nodes. *Electronics*, 11(24):4071.

[Kim et al., 2014] Kim, M. et al. (2014). Utilization-aware load balancing for the energy efficient operation of the big. little processor. In *2014 Design, Automation & Test in Europe Conference & Exhibition (DATE)*. IEEE.

[Knechtel and Sinanoglu, 2017] Knechtel, J. and Sinanoglu, O. (2017). On mitigation of side-channel attacks in 3d ics: Decorrelating thermal patterns from power and activity. In *Design Automation Conference (DAC), 2017 54th ACM/EDAC/IEEE*, pages 1–6. IEEE.

[Ko et al., 2015] Ko, Y., Burgstaller, B., and Scholz, B. (2015). Laminarir: compile-time queues for structured streams. In *ACM SIGPLAN Notices*, volume 50, pages 121–130. ACM.

[Koc, 2009] Koc, C. K. (2009). About cryptographic engineering. In *Cryptographic engineering*, pages 1–4. Springer.

[Kocher et al., 1999] Kocher, P., Jaffe, J., and Jun, B. (1999). Differential power analysis. In *Annual international cryptology conference*, pages 388–397. Springer.

[Kocher, 1996] Kocher, P. C. (1996). Timing attacks on implementations of diffie-hellman, rsa, dss, and other systems. In *Annual International Cryptology Conference*, pages 104–113. Springer.

[Konečný et al., 2016] Konečný, J., McMahan, H. B., Yu, F. X., Richtárik, P., Suresh, A. T., and Bacon, D. (2016). Federated learning: Strategies for improving communication efficiency. *arXiv preprint arXiv:1610.05492*.

[Kong et al., 2008] Kong, J., Aciicmez, O., Seifert, J.-P., and Zhou, H. (2008). Deconstructing new cache designs for thwarting software cache-based side channel attacks. In *Proceedings of the 2nd ACM workshop on Computer security architectures*, pages 25–34.

[Krajka, 2004] Krajka, J. (2004). Your mother tongue does matter! translation in the classroom and on the web. *Teaching English with Technology*, 4(4).

[Krizhevsky et al., 2012] Krizhevsky, A., Sutskever, I., and Hinton, G. E. (2012). Imagenet classification with deep convolutional neural networks. In *Advances in neural information processing systems*, pages 1097–1105.

[Krizhevsky et al., 2017] Krizhevsky, A., Sutskever, I., and Hinton, G. E. (2017). Imagenet classification with deep convolutional neural networks. *Communications of the ACM*, 60(6):84–90.

[Kumar, 2017] Kumar, M. (2017). First android-rooting trojan with code injection ability found on google play store. `https:// thehackernews.com/2017/06/android-rooting-malware.html`.

[Kumar et al., 2005] Kumar, R., Tullsen, D. M., Jouppi, N. P., and Ranganathan, P. (2005). Heterogeneous chip multiprocessors. *Computer*, 38(11):32–38.

[Kumar and Lee, 2014] Kumar, S. and Lee, S. R. (2014). Android based smart home system with control via bluetooth and internet connectivity. In *The 18th IEEE International Symposium on Consumer Electronics (ISCE 2014)*, pages 1–2. IEEE.

[Lattner, 2002] Lattner, C. A. (2002). *LLVM: An infrastructure for multistage optimization.* PhD thesis, University of Illinois at Urbana-Champaign.

[Leather et al., 2014] Leather, H., Bonilla, E., and O'boyle, M. (2014). Automatic feature generation for machine learning–based optimising compilation. *ACM Transactions on Architecture and Code Optimization (TACO)*, 11(1):14.

[LeCun et al., 2015] LeCun, Y., Bengio, Y., and Hinton, G. (2015). Deep learning. *nature*, 521(7553):436.

[Lin and Fei, 2010] Lin, H. and Fei, Y. (2010). Exploring custom instruction synthesis for application-specific instruction set processors with multiple design objectives. In *Low-Power Electronics and Design (ISLPED), 2010 ACM/IEEE International Symposium on*, pages 141–146. IEEE.

[Lin et al., 2016] Lin, T.-Y., Lee, M.-H., Chou, L., Peng, C., Hsu, J.-M., Chen, J.-M., Chen, J.-C., Chiou, A., Chiu, A., Lee, D., et al. (2016). Helio x20: The first tri-gear mobile soc with corepilot™ 3.0 technology. In *2016 IEEE Hot Chips 28 Symposium (HCS)*, pages 1–24. IEEE.

[Long et al., 2018] Long, Z., Wang, X., Jiang, Y., Cui, G., Zhang, L., and Mak, T. (2018). Improving the efficiency of thermal covert channels in multi-/many-core systems. In *2018 Design, Automation & Test in Europe Conference & Exhibition (DATE)*, pages 1459–1464. IEEE.

[Longbottom, 2005] Longbottom, R. (2005). Whetstone benchmark history and results.

[Lucic, 2014] Lucic, K. (2014). Over 27.44apps, are you one of them? https://www.androidheadlines.com/2014/11/50-users-root-phones-order-remove-built-apps-one.html.

[Lukowicz et al., 2004] Lukowicz, P., Kirstein, T., and Tröster, G. (2004). Wearable systems for health care applications. *Methods of information in medicine*, 43(03):232–238.

[Manaswi and Manaswi, 2018] Manaswi, N. K. and Manaswi, N. K. (2018). Cnn in keras. *Deep Learning with Applications Using Python: Chatbots and Face, Object, and Speech Recognition With TensorFlow and Keras*, pages 105–114.

[Mandal et al., 2019] Mandal, S. K., Bhat, G., Patil, C. A., Doppa, J. R., Pande, P. P., and Ogras, U. Y. (2019). Dynamic resource management of heterogeneous mobile platforms via imitation learning. *IEEE Transactions on Very Large Scale Integration (VLSI) Systems*.

[Mandic and Chambers, 2001] Mandic, D. and Chambers, J. (2001). *Recurrent neural networks for prediction: learning algorithms, architectures and stability*. Wiley.

[Marr, 1982] Marr, D. (1982). Vision: A computational investigation into the human representation and processing of visual information. mit press. *Cambridge, Massachusetts.*

[Martens and Meesters, 1998] Martens, J.-B. and Meesters, L. (1998). Image dissimilarity. *Signal processing*, 70(3):155–176.

[Masti et al., 2015] Masti, R. J., Rai, D., Ranganathan, A., Müller, C., Thiele, L., and Capkun, S. (2015). Thermal covert channels on multicore platforms. In *24th {USENIX} Security Symposium ({USENIX} Security 15)*, pages 865–880.

[Masure et al., 2020] Masure, L., Dumas, C., and Prouff, E. (2020). A comprehensive study of deep learning for side-channel analysis. *IACR Transactions on Cryptographic Hardware and Embedded Systems*, pages 348–375.

[Maurer et al., 2020] Maurer, F., Donyanavard, B., Rahmani, A. M., Dutt, N., and Herkersdorf, A. (2020). Emergent control of mpsoc operation by a hierarchical supervisor/reinforcement learning approach. In *2020 Design, Automation & Test in Europe Conference & Exhibition (DATE)*, pages 1562–1567. IEEE.

[Messaris, 1994] Messaris, P. (1994). *Visual" literacy": Image, mind, and reality.* Westview Press.

[Muthukaruppan et al., 2013] Muthukaruppan, T. S., Javaid, H., Mitra, T., and Parameswaran, S. (2013). Energy-aware synthesis of application specific mpsocs. In *Computer Design (ICCD), 2013 IEEE 31st International Conference on*, pages 62–69. IEEE.

[Namolaru et al., 2010] Namolaru, M., Cohen, A., Fursin, G., Zaks, A., and Freund, A. (2010). Practical aggregation of semantical program properties for machine learning based optimization. In *Proceedings of the 2010 international conference on Compilers, architectures and synthesis for embedded systems*, pages 197–206. ACM.

[Nilo et al., 2016] Nilo, B. D., Chan, D. M., Xiao, J. A., and Beaver, J. C. (2016). Devices and methods for processing touch inputs. US Patent App. 14/870,879.

[Pan and Yang, 2009] Pan, S. J. and Yang, Q. (2009). A survey on transfer learning. *IEEE Transactions on knowledge and data engineering*, 22(10):1345–1359.

[Pan et al., 2010] Pan, S. J., Yang, Q., et al. (2010). A survey on transfer learning. *IEEE Transactions on knowledge and data engineering*, 22(10):1345–1359.

[Pathania et al., 2015] Pathania, A., Irimiea, A. E., Prakash, A., and Mitra, T. (2015). Power-performance modelling of mobile gaming workloads on heterogeneous mpsocs. In *Proceedings of the 52nd Annual Design Automation Conference*, pages 1–6.

[Pathania et al., 2014] Pathania, A., Jiao, Q., Prakash, A., and Mitra, T. (2014). Integrated cpu-gpu power management for 3d mobile games. In *2014 51st ACM/EDAC/IEEE Design Automation Conference (DAC)*, pages 1–6. IEEE.

[Patterson et al., 2012] Patterson, C., Garside, J., Painkras, E., Temple, S., Plana, L. A., Navaridas, J., Sharp, T., and Furber, S. (2012). Scalable communications for a million-core neural processing architecture. *Journal of Parallel and Distributed Computing*, 72(11):1507–1520.

[Patterson and Ditzel, 1980] Patterson, D. A. and Ditzel, D. R. (1980). The case for the reduced instruction set computer. *ACM SIGARCH Computer Architecture News*, 8(6):25–33.

[Patterson and Hennessy, 2013] Patterson, D. A. and Hennessy, J. L. (2013). Computer organization and design mips edition: The.

[Patterson and Hennessy, 2016] Patterson, D. A. and Hennessy, J. L. (2016). *Computer organization and design ARM edition: the hardware software interface*. Morgan kaufmann.

[Peters et al., 2016] Peters, N., Füß, D., Park, S., and Chakraborty, S. (2016). Frame-based and thread-based power management for mobile games on hmp platforms. In *2016 IEEE 34th International Conference on Computer Design (ICCD)*, pages 169–176. IEEE.

[Petrucci et al., 2015] Petrucci, V., Loques, O., Mossé, D., Melhem, R., Gazala, N. A., and Gobriel, S. (2015). Energy-efficient thread assignment optimization for heterogeneous multicore systems. *ACM Transactions on Embedded Computing Systems*, 14(1):15.

[Pillai and Shin, 2001] Pillai, P. and Shin, K. G. (2001). Real-time dynamic voltage scaling for low-power embedded operating systems. In *ACM SIGOPS Operating Systems Review*, volume 35, pages 89–102. ACM.

[Prakash et al., 2016] Prakash, A., Amrouch, H., Shafique, M., Mitra, T., and Henkel, J. (2016). Improving mobile gaming performance through cooperative cpu-gpu thermal management. In *Proceedings of the 53rd Annual Design Automation Conference*, page 47. ACM.

[Prakash et al., 2015] Prakash, A., Wang, S., Irimiea, A. E., and Mitra, T. (2015). Energy-efficient execution of data-parallel applications on heterogeneous mobile platforms. In *2015 33rd IEEE International Conference on Computer Design (ICCD)*, pages 208–215. IEEE.

[Quan and Pimentel, 2013] Quan, W. and Pimentel, A. D. (2013). A scenario-based run-time task mapping algorithm for MPSoCs. In *Proc. of the Design Automation Conference*, page 131. ACM.

[Quan and Pimentel, 2015] Quan, W. and Pimentel, A. D. (2015). A hybrid task mapping algorithm for heterogeneous mpsocs. *ACM Transactions on Embedded Computing Systems (TECS)*, 14(1):14.

[Ravindran et al., 2001] Ravindran, B., Welch, L., and Shirazi, B. (2001). Resource management middleware for dynamic, dependable real-time systems. *Real-Time Systems*, 20:183–196.

[Reddy et al., 2018] Reddy, B. K., Merrett, G. V., Al-Hashimi, B. M., and Singh, A. K. (2018). Online concurrent workload classification for multi-core energy management. In *Design, Automation Test in Europe Conference Exhibition (DATE)*, pages 621–624.

[Reddy et al., 2017] Reddy, B. K., Singh, A., Biswas, D., Merrett, G., and Al-Hashimi, B. (2017). Inter-cluster thread-to-core mapping and dvfs on heterogeneous multi-cores. *IEEE Transactions on Multiscale Computing Systems*, pages 1–14.

[Redmon et al., 2016] Redmon, J. et al. (2016). You only look once: Unified, real-time object detection. In *Proceedings of the IEEE conference on computer vision and pattern recognition*, pages 779–788.

[Rijmen and Daemen, 2001] Rijmen, V. and Daemen, J. (2001). Advanced encryption standard. *Proceedings of Federal Information Processing Standards Publications, National Institute of Standards and Technology*, pages 19–22.

[Rivest et al., 1978] Rivest, R. L., Shamir, A., and Adleman, L. (1978). A method for obtaining digital signatures and public-key cryptosystems. *Communications of the ACM*, 21(2):120–126.

[Rivest et al., 1983] Rivest, R. L., Shamir, A., and Adleman, L. M. (1983). Cryptographic communications system and method. US Patent 4,405,829.

[Rupley et al., 2016] Rupley, J., Burgess, B., Grayson, B., and Zuraski, G. D. (2016). Samsung m3 processor. In *2016 IEEE Hot Chips 28 Symposium (HCS)*, pages 1–24. IEEE.

[Russakovsky et al., 2015] Russakovsky, O., Deng, J., Su, H., Krause, J., Satheesh, S., Ma, S., Huang, Z., Karpathy, A., Khosla, A., Bernstein, M., et al. (2015). Imagenet large scale visual recognition challenge. *International Journal of Computer Vision*, 115(3):211–252.

[Sahin and Coskun, 2015] Sahin, O. and Coskun, A. K. (2015). On the impacts of greedy thermal management in mobile devices. *IEEE Embedded Systems Letters*, 7(2):55–58.

[Sasaki et al., 2013] Sasaki, H., Imamura, S., and Inoue, K. (2013). Co-ordinated power-performance optimization in manycores. In *Proc.*

of the Intl. Conf. on Parallel architectures and compilation techniques, pages 51–61. IEEE.

[Satyanarayanan, 2010] Satyanarayanan, M. (2010). Mobile computing: the next decade. In *Proceedings of the 1st ACM workshop on mobile cloud computing & services: social networks and beyond*, pages 1–6.

[Schranzhofer et al., 2010] Schranzhofer, A., Chen, J.-J., and Thiele, L. (2010). Dynamic power-aware mapping of applications onto heterogeneous MPSoC platforms. *IEEE Transactions on Industrial Informatics*, 6(4):692–707.

[Selvaraju et al., 2017] Selvaraju, R. R., Cogswell, M., Das, A., Vedantam, R., Parikh, D., and Batra, D. (2017). Grad-cam: Visual explanations from deep networks via gradient-based localization. In *Proceedings of the IEEE International Conference on Computer Vision*, pages 618–626.

[Serway and Jewett, 1998] Serway, R. A. and Jewett, J. W. (1998). *Principles of physics*, volume 1. Saunders College Pub. Fort Worth, TX.

[Shafik et al., 2016] Shafik, R. A., Das, A. K., Maeda-Nunez, L. A., Yang, S., Merrett, G. V., and Al-Hashimi, B. (2016). Learning transfer-based adaptive energy minimization in embedded systems. *IEEE Transactions on Computer-Aided Design of Integrated Circuits and Systems*, 35(6):877–890.

[Sherstinsky, 2020] Sherstinsky, A. (2020). Fundamentals of recurrent neural network (rnn) and long short-term memory (lstm) network. *Physica D: Nonlinear Phenomena*, 404:132306.

[Shin et al., 2000] Shin, Y., Choi, K., and Sakurai, T. (2000). Power optimization of real-time embedded systems on variable speed processors. In *Proceedings of the 2000 IEEE/ACM international conference on Computer-aided design*, pages 365–368. IEEE Press.

[Shinskey and Jachens, 2014] Shinskey, J. L. and Jachens, L. J. (2014). Picturing objects in infancy. *Child development*, 85(5):1813–1820.

[Simons, 2022] Simons, H. (2022). We asked, you told us: Your android phone definitely isn't rooted. `https://www.androidauthority.com/android-phone-rooted-poll-results-3225345/`.

[Simonyan and Zisserman, 2014] Simonyan, K. and Zisserman, A. (2014). Very deep convolutional networks for large-scale image recognition. *arXiv preprint arXiv:1409.1556*.

[Singh et al., 2020] Singh, A. K., Dey, S., McDonald-Maier, K., Basireddy, K. R., Merrett, G. V., and Al-Hashimi, B. M. (2020). Dynamic energy and thermal management of multi-core mobile platforms: A survey. *IEEE Design & Test*, 37(5):25–33.

[Singh et al., 2017a] Singh, A. K., Leech, C., Reddy, B. K., Al-Hashimi, B. M., and Merrett, G. V. (2017a). Learning-based run-time power and energy management of multi/many-core systems: current and future trends. *Journal of Low Power Electronics*, 13(3):310–325.

[Singh et al., 2017b] Singh, A. K., Prakash, A., Basireddy, K. R., Merrett, G. V., and Al-Hashimi, B. M. (2017b). Energy-efficient run-time mapping and thread partitioning of concurrent opencl applications on cpu-gpu mpsocs. *ACM Transactions on Embedded Computing Systems (TECS)*, 16(5s):147.

[Singh et al., 2013] Singh, A. K., Shafique, M., Kumar, A., and Henkel, J. (2013). Mapping on multi/many-core systems: survey of current and emerging trends. In *Design automation conference (dac), 2013 50th acm/edac/ieee*, pages 1–10. IEEE.

[Singla et al., 2015] Singla, G., Kaur, G., Unver, A. K., and Ogras, U. Y. (2015). Predictive dynamic thermal and power management for heterogeneous mobile platforms. In *Proceedings of the 2015 Design, Automation & Test in Europe Conference & Exhibition*, pages 960–965. EDA Consortium.

[Singleton et al., 2005] Singleton, L. C., Poellabauer, C., and Schwan, K. (2005). Monitoring of cache miss rates for accurate dynamic voltage and frequency scaling. In *Electronic Imaging*, pages 121–125. Intl. Society for Optics and Photonics.

[Sinicki, 2022] Sinicki, A. (2022). Root android: Everything you need to know! https://www.androidauthority.com/root-android-277350/.

[Smit et al., 2005] Smit, L. T., Hurink, J. L., and Smit, G. J. (2005). Run-time mapping of applications to a heterogeneous soc. In *2005 International Symposium on System-on-Chip*, pages 78–81. IEEE.

[Soo, 2014] Soo, S. (2014). Object detection using haar-cascade classifier. *Institute of Computer Science, University of Tartu*, pages 1–12.

[Sozzo et al., 2016] Sozzo, E. D., Durelli, G. C., Trainiti, E., Miele, A., Santambrogio, M. D., and Bolchini, C. (2016). Workload-aware power optimization strategy for asymmetric multiprocessors. In *Design, Automation & Test in Europe Conference & Exhibition*, pages 531–534. IEEE.

[Stamoulis and Marculescu, 2016] Stamoulis, D. and Marculescu, D. (2016). Can we guarantee performance requirements under workload and process variations? In *Intl. Symp. on Low Power Electronics and Design*, pages 308–313. ACM.

[Sutton and Barto, 2018] Sutton, R. S. and Barto, A. G. (2018). *Reinforcement learning: An introduction.* MIT press.

[Szegedy et al., 2015] Szegedy, C., Liu, W., Jia, Y., Sermanet, P., Reed, S., Anguelov, D., Erhan, D., Vanhoucke, V., and Rabinovich, A. (2015). Going deeper with convolutions. In *Proceedings of the IEEE conference on computer vision and pattern recognition*, pages 1–9.

[Tan et al., 2018] Tan, C., Kulkarni, A., Venkataramani, V., Karunaratne, M., Mitra, T., and Peh, L.-S. (2018). Locus: Low-power customizable many-core architecture for wearables. *ACM Transactions on Embedded Computing Systems (TECS)*, 17(1):16.

[Taylor et al., 2017] Taylor, B., Marco, V. S., and Wang, Z. (2017). Adaptive optimization for opencl programs on embedded heterogeneous systems. In *ACM SIGPLAN Notices*, volume 52, pages 11–20. ACM.

[Thakkar, 2020] Thakkar, J. (2020). Types of encryption: 5 encryption algorithms and how to choose the right one.

[Thompson, 2001] Thompson, R. A. (2001). Development in the first years of life. *The future of children*, pages 21–33.

[Van Craeynest et al., 2012] Van Craeynest, K., Jaleel, A., Eeckhout, L., Narvaez, P., and Emer, J. (2012). Scheduling heterogeneous multi-cores through performance impact estimation (PIE). In *ACM SIGARCH Computer Architecture News*, volume 40, pages 213–224.

[van Elsloo, 2016] van Elsloo, T. (2016). Multi-objective optimization of secure embedded systems architectures.

[Wächter et al., 2019] Wächter, E. W., de Bellefroid, C., Basireddy, K. R., Singh, A. K., Al-Hashimi, B. M., and Merrett, G. (2019). Predictive thermal management for energy-efficient execution of concurrent applications on heterogeneous multicores. *IEEE Transactions on Very Large Scale Integration (VLSI) Systems*, 27(6):1404–1415.

[Wachter et al., 2017] Wachter, E. W., Merrett, G. V., Al-Hashimi, B. M., and Singh, A. K. (2017). Reliable mapping and partitioning of performance-constrained opencl applications on cpu-gpu mpsocs. In *Proceedings of the 15th IEEE/ACM Symposium on Embedded Systems for Real-Time Multimedia*, pages 78–83. ACM.

[Wang et al., 2013] Wang, H., Saboune, J., and El Saddik, A. (2013). Control your smart home with an autonomously mobile smartphone. In *2013 IEEE international conference on multimedia and expo workshops (ICMEW)*, pages 1–6. IEEE.

[Wang and Bovik, 2002] Wang, Z. and Bovik, A. C. (2002). A universal image quality index. *IEEE signal processing letters*, 9(3):81–84.

[Wang et al., 2004] Wang, Z., Bovik, A. C., Sheikh, H. R., and Simoncelli, E. P. (2004). Image quality assessment: from error visibility to structural similarity. *IEEE transactions on image processing*, 13(4):600–612.

[Wang and Lee, 2007] Wang, Z. and Lee, R. B. (2007). New cache designs for thwarting software cache-based side channel attacks. In *Proceedings of the 34th annual international symposium on Computer architecture*, pages 494–505.

[Wang and Lee, 2008] Wang, Z. and Lee, R. B. (2008). A novel cache architecture with enhanced performance and security. In *2008 41st IEEE/ACM International Symposium on Microarchitecture*, pages 83–93. IEEE.

[Watkins and Dayan, 1992] Watkins, C. J. and Dayan, P. (1992). Q-learning. *Machine learning*, 8(3-4):279–292.

[Weaver, 2013] Weaver, V. M. (2013). Linux perf_event features and overhead. In *The 2nd international workshop on performance analysis of workload optimized systems, FastPath*, volume 13, page 5.

[Weissel and Bellosa, 2002] Weissel, A. and Bellosa, F. (2002). Process cruise control: event-driven clock scaling for dynamic power management. In *Proc. of Intl. Conf. on Compilers, architecture, and synthesis for embedded systems*, pages 238–246. ACM.

[Wiriyathammabhum et al., 2017] Wiriyathammabhum, P., Summers-Stay, D., Fermüller, C., and Aloimonos, Y. (2017). Computer vision and natural language processing: recent approaches in multimedia and robotics. *ACM Computing Surveys (CSUR)*, 49(4):71.

[Wolf et al., 2008] Wolf, W., Jerraya, A. A., and Martin, G. (2008). Multiprocessor system-on-chip (mpsoc) technology. *IEEE Transactions on Computer-Aided Design of Integrated Circuits and Systems*, 27(10):1701–1713.

[Woo et al., 1995a] Woo, S. C., Ohara, M., Torrie, E., Singh, J. P., and Gupta, A. (1995a). The splash-2 programs: Characterization and methodological considerations. In *ACM SIGARCH computer architecture news*, volume 23, pages 24–36. ACM.

[Woo et al., 1995b] Woo, S. C., Ohara, M., Torrie, E., Singh, J. P., and Gupta, A. (1995b). The SPLASH-2 programs: Characterization and methodological considerations. In *ACM SIGARCH Computer Architecture News*, volume 23, pages 24–36.

[Xiang et al., 2010] Xiang, Y., Chantem, T., Dick, R. P., Hu, X. S., and Shang, L. (2010). System-level reliability modeling for mpsocs. In *Proceedings of the eighth IEEE/ACM/IFIP international conference on Hardware/software codesign and system synthesis*, pages 297–306. ACM.

[Yang, 2017] Yang, M. (2017). Android trojan that can inject code, root devices, removed from play store.

[Yu et al., 2020] Yu, Z., Machado, P., Zahid, A., Abdulghani, A. M., Dashtipour, K., Heidari, H., Imran, M. A., and Abbasi, Q. H. (2020). Energy and performance trade-off optimization in heterogeneous computing via reinforcement learning. *Electronics*, 9(11):1812.

[Zhang et al., 2018] Zhang, Q., Lin, M., Yang, L. T., Chen, Z., Khan, S. U., and Li, P. (2018). A double deep q-learning model for energy-efficient edge scheduling. *IEEE TSC*.

[Zhou et al., 2015] Zhou, J., Wei, T., Chen, M., Yan, J., Hu, X. S., and Ma, Y. (2015). Thermal-aware task scheduling for energy minimization in heterogeneous real-time mpsoc systems. *IEEE Transac-*

tions on Computer-Aided Design of Integrated Circuits and Systems, 35(8):1269–1282.

www.ingramcontent.com/pod-product-compliance
Lightning Source LLC
Chambersburg PA
CBHW060510120726
48002CB00011B/3105